Junctures
in Women's Leadership

⟨ Media and Journalism ⟩

JUNCTURES

Case Studies in Women's Leadership
Mary K. Trigg, Series Editor

The books in this series explore decisions women leaders make in a variety of fields. Using the case study method, the editors of each volume focus on strategies employed by the women profiled as they face important leadership challenges in business, various social movements, the arts, public health and health care, and other sectors. The goal of the series is to broaden our conceptions of what constitutes successful leadership in these changing times.

Junctures in Women's Leadership: Social Movements, edited by Mary K. Trigg and Alison R. Bernstein

Junctures in Women's Leadership: Business, edited by Lisa Hetfield and Dana M. Britton

Junctures in Women's Leadership: The Arts, by Judith K. Brodsky and Ferris Olin

Junctures in Women's Leadership: Higher Education, edited by Carmen Twillie Ambar, Carol T. Christ, and Michele Ozumba

Junctures in Women's Leadership: Health Care and Public Health, edited by Mary E. O'Dowd and Ruth Charbonneau

Junctures in Women's Leadership: Media and Journalism, edited by Linda Steiner

Junctures
in Women's Leadership

⟨ Media and Journalism ⟩

Edited by Linda Steiner

RUTGERS UNIVERSITY PRESS
NEW BRUNSWICK, CAMDEN, AND NEWARK, NEW JERSEY
LONDON AND OXFORD

Rutgers University Press is a department of Rutgers, The State University of New Jersey, one of the leading public research universities in the nation. By publishing worldwide, it furthers the University's mission of dedication to excellence in teaching, scholarship, research, and clinical care.

Library of Congress Cataloging-in-Publication Data

Names: Steiner, Linda, author.
Title: Junctures in women's leadership : media and journalism / edited by Linda Steiner.
Description: New Brunswick : Rutgers University Press, 2025. | Series: Junctures: case studies in women's leadership | Includes bibliographical references and index.
Identifiers: LCCN 2024049525 | ISBN 9781978834248 (paperback) | ISBN 9781978834255 (hardcover) | ISBN 9781978834262 (epub) | ISBN 9781978834279 (pdf)
Subjects: LCSH: Women in the mass media industry. | Women in journalism. | Leadership in women. | Women executives.
Classification: LCC P94.5.W65 J684 2025 | DDC 302.2308—dc23/eng/20250115
LC record available at https://lccn.loc.gov/2024049525

A British Cataloging-in-Publication record for this book is available from the British Library.

♾ The paper used in this publication meets the requirements of the American National Standard for Information Sciences—Permanence of Paper for Printed Library Materials, ANSI Z39.48-1992.

rutgersuniversitypress.org

Contents

Foreword to the Series

Junctures: Case Studies in Women's Leadership

Throughout history, women have been leaders in their societies and communities. Whether the leadership role was up front such as hereditary queens and clan mothers, as elected officials, or as business executives and founders of organizations, women have participated at the highest levels of decision-making. Yet, up through most of the twentieth century, we seldom associated the word *leader* with women. I might even argue that the noun *leader* is one of the most masculinized words in the English language. When we thought of leaders, our minds seldom conjured up a woman.

Fortunately, there has been a recent shift in our thinking, our images, and our imaginations. In the United States, credit may go to those women in the public eye like Gloria Steinem, Oprah Winfrey, Cecile Richards, and even Eleanor Roosevelt, who have blazed new trails in politics, media, and statecraft. Now leadership is beginning to look more gender neutral. That said, it's important to remember that, in many parts of the world, women leaders, including prominent feminists, have risen to power more rapidly than seems to be the case here. I think of Gro Bundtland in Norway, Helen Clarke in New Zealand, Michelle Bachelet in Chile, and others. These leaders certainly raise new and interesting questions about linking feminism with powerful political leadership. We in the United States also have Sheryl Sandberg to thank for using the word *feminist* in the same sentence as *leadership*.

Despite progress in the past few decades, women have not reached any kind of rough parity with men in terms of positional leadership—that is, the form of leadership that is appointed or elected and recognized as powerful and influential in coeducational public life. Women continue to be dramatically underrepresented in all major domains of leadership from politics to Fortune 500 companies, to labor unions, to academic administration, and even in fields where they are the majority like health care, teaching, or the arts. Scholars like Deborah Rhode and Nannerl O. Keohane note that, at the rate the United States is going, there will not be a "convergence toward parity" for an additional three centuries. Given the need for outstanding leadership at all levels and sectors of society, and given the huge waste of talent that exists when so many capable women are not encouraged to move into senior leadership positions, we cannot afford to wait for parity even three decades, let alone three centuries!

If we wish to accelerate the process of gender parity in producing leaders in the twenty-first century, what steps might we take and what role can academia play in helping to increase the pool and percentage of women leaders? Historically, women's colleges, according to pioneering research by Elizabeth Tidball and others, graduated disproportionate numbers of women leaders through the 1970s. More recently, business schools, which were largely male bastions, have educated a share of women leaders.

Today, in interdisciplinary fields such as women's and gender studies, examining the concept of "leadership" and teaching women students to be more effective leaders in a given profession or context is highly contested. For example, *Ms.* magazine noted that, in 2011, "only a handful of the more than 650 women's studies programs at colleges and universities provide practical and theoretical knowledge necessary for the next generation to make a significant impact on their communities and world" as leaders. Many feminists and women scholars have negative associations with traditional ideas of leadership, arguing that the concept is elitist, individualistic, hierarchical, and justifies putting work ahead of family and parenting. Moreover, traditional leadership studies often have failed to take account of structural and contextual frameworks of unequal power and privilege, especially around gender and race. And yet, approaching the study of leadership with a gender-sensitive lens is crucial if we are to make more progress toward a fairer and more just distribution of power and opportunity for women and men alike.

Which brings us to the genesis of this series, *Junctures in Women's Leadership*. The volumes in the series are designed to provide insights into the decision-making process undertaken by women leaders, both well-known and deserving to be better known. The case studies run the gamut from current affairs to past history. The Rutgers Institute for Women's Leadership (IWL) consortium, a group of nine separate units at the university including Douglass Residential College, the Department of Women's and Gender Studies, and the Center for American Women in Politics, is sponsoring this series as a way to provide new pedagogical tools for understanding leadership that has been exercised by women. Each volume consists of a dozen or so case studies of leaders in a specific field of endeavor. The focus is not on the woman leader per se, but rather on the context that surrounded her decision, the factors she considered in making the decision, and the aftermath of the decision. Also, even though the series is focused on decision-making by women leaders, it is not designed to demonstrate that all decisions were good ones or yielded the results expected.

The series does not promote the notion that there are biologically determined differences between women's and men's decision-making practices. There is no such thing as a "women's" approach to leadership. Nothing universally characterizes women's approaches to leadership as opposed to men's. Neither gender is genetically wired to be one kind of leader as opposed to another. That kind of biologically determined, reductionist thinking has no place in this series. Nor does the series suggest that women make decisions according to a single set of "women's values or issues," though there is some evidence to suggest that once women reach a critical mass of decision-makers, they tend to elevate issues of family and human welfare more than men. This evidence, collected by Rutgers University's Center for American Women and Politics, also suggests that women are more likely to seek compromise across rigid ideologies than are men in the same position.

Our series of case studies on women in leadership is not designed to prove that simply electing or appointing women to leadership positions will miraculously improve the standard of living outcomes for all people. Few of us believe that. On the other hand, it is important to examine some questions that are fundamental to understanding the values and practices of women leaders who, against the odds, have risen to shape the worlds in which we all live. The series employs the "case study" method because it provides a concrete, real-life example of a woman leader in action. We hope the case studies will prompt many questions, not the least of which is, What fresh perspectives and expanded insights do women bring to leadership decisions? And, more theoretical and controversial, Is there a feminist model of leadership?

In conclusion, the IWL is delighted to bring these studies to the attention of faculty, students, and leaders across a wide range of disciplines and professional fields. We believe it will contribute to accelerating the progress of women toward a more genuinely gender-equal power structure in which both men and women share the responsibility for forging a better and more just world for generations to come.

Alison R. Bernstein (1947–2016)
Director, Institute for Women's Leadership (IWL) Consortium
Professor of History and Women's and Gender Studies
Rutgers University—New Brunswick
April 2015

New Foreword to the Series

Junctures: Case Studies in Women's Leadership

Women's lived experiences are distinct from men's, and their lives interact with history in unique ways. By highlighting case studies of women leaders—past and present—in social movements, business, the arts, higher education, health care and public health, and media (the six volumes published so far), the *Junctures* series seeks to redress the underrepresentation of women in leadership positions and to suggest a different kind of future. The series illuminates barriers of class, race, and gender that women leaders in various contexts have faced (and continue to face). It also demonstrates the ways that social justice–based women's leadership has made a difference. The volumes collectively suggest that when women wield power and influence, they transform organizations, ideas, industries, institutions, culture, and leadership itself.[1] Moreover, the diversity of experience among women further enriches their perspectives; who sits around decision-making tables matters. As the editor of the media volume concludes, "Who can move into top news leadership affects how journalism is practiced and what news is documented."[2] That, in turn, influences the ways that all of us interpret and understand the world.

Women's leadership is often transformative. For example, women curators broaden art and museum collections to include more work by women and artists from diverse backgrounds. This is not insignificant. The arts volume makes a persuasive case for the necessity of women artists and arts professionals in leadership positions to advance gender and racial parity in the arts. "Women leaders make a difference," its editors conclude.[3] Similarly, the editors of the business volume determine that "from their [women leading change in business] experiences come unique business ideas and the passion to address women's needs and interests."[4] The coeditors of the health care and public health volume conclude that the leadership philosophy of many of the women profiled in their book originates from a shared vision: "Within individuals, particularly women, there is a power to create change; and acquiring a diversity of thought and elevating the voices of those heard less often promotes positive change."[5] There are unique social problems that disproportionately affect women, from pay inequities to reproductive health care. We need to train and encourage women to step up as leaders to be able to influence policies that uniquely affect the lives of girls and women, half of our population. Women's underrepresentation in leadership roles, and societal and cultural expectations of leaders as male, leave us all poorer. We need diversity of leadership and the perspectives and life experiences that women bring. Each volume, in its way, illustrates this.

The *Junctures* series aims to capture women's leadership in action and at pivotal junctures or moments of decision-making. Its goal is to broaden our conceptions of what constitutes successful leadership and to offer pedagogical tools to examine and interpret leadership that is not male-centric, as much of leadership scholarship tends to be. Although case studies as teaching tools have a long history, case studies focusing on women's leadership and applying a gender lens have been rare. This series, then, is an intervention. Our approach is intersectional: we consider gender, race, class, ethnicity, physical and social location, and how they influence access to, and the practice of, leadership. We move through time and historical context and consider multiple ways of leading. Authors and editors of each volume conducted interviews with some of the living subjects, which makes this compendium a unique contribution to academic scholarship on women's leadership. Collectively the volumes also contemplate the ways that gender conventions influenced how some women have practiced leadership, the pain and incentive of gender and/or racial discrimination and exclusion, and the challenge—and leadership impetus—some women leaders have felt as mothers, caregivers, and primary caretakers of home and children.

We use the format of the "case study" broadly. Each essay or case study is organized into a "Background" section, which describes the protagonist's rise to leadership and lays out a decision-making juncture or problem, and a "Resolution" section, which traces the ways the leader "resolved" the problem or juncture, as well as her legacy. The authors consider what prepared these particular women for leadership, highlight personal strategies and qualities, and investigate the ways that family, education, mentors, personal injustice, interaction with social movements, and pivotal moments in history shaped these protagonists' approaches and contributions as leaders in varied contexts. We have sought to cast a wide net and gather examples from the United States as well as around the world (the first three volumes include case studies from Kenya, Nicaragua, South Africa [two], the United Kingdom, and Laos). Necessarily, volume editors have had to make difficult decisions about whom to include and exclude. Our goal is to offer a rich abundance of diverse examples of women's leadership and the difference it makes, rather than a comprehensive theory about women's leadership. We seek to prompt questions as well as provide answers.

As the series has grown, we at the Institute for Women's Leadership have increasingly embraced the term feminist leadership studies to describe our work. Feminist leadership studies examines the connections between feminisms, leadership, and social justice. It strives to bring a feminist perspective to the study of leaders in order to bring new models of leadership into focus. It examines the fundamental concepts and dynamics of power and includes the ethos of accountability. It advocates for more diverse leadership, especially more women and people of color in decision-making positions who understand and practice feminist approaches. It challenges the notion that leadership is male/masculine. It is inclusive and considers strategies to make leadership more diverse. It strives to bring marginalized voices to the center of the conversation.[6] With these criteria in mind, it seems clear to me that while not every leader profiled in the series is necessarily a feminist leader, the founding vision of the series and the impetus that shapes each volume is a feminist one. If given the chance, women might indeed lead us to a different kind of future. Their leadership has the potential to forge gender and racial equity, to bring about innovative solutions, and to advance social justice. The Institute for Women's Leadership sends these stories out into the world to document and preserve them and to educate and inspire faculty, students, and leaders across a range of fields and disciplines. We hope these volumes will inform those who aspire to leadership and apprise those who practice it.

Mary K. Trigg
Faculty Director, Leadership Scholars Certificate Program,
Institute for Women's Leadership
Associate Professor, Department of Women's,
Gender, and Sexuality Studies
Rutgers University—New Brunswick
November 2024

Notes

1 Lisa Hetfield and Dana M. Britton, *Junctures in Women's Leadership: Business* (Rutgers University Press, 2016), xi.
2 Linda Steiner, *Junctures in Women's Leadership: Media and Journalism* (Rutgers University Press), this volume.
3 Judith Brodsky and Ferris Olin, *Junctures in Women's Leadership: The Arts* (Rutgers University Press, 2018), xv.
4 Hetfield and Britton, *Junctures: Business*, xiii.
5 Mary E. O'Dowd and Ruth Charbonneau, *Junctures in Women's Leadership: Health Care and Public Health* (Rutgers University Press, 2021), xxix.
6 "Guidelines for Feminist Leadership Studies," https://iwl.rutgers.edu/wp-content/uploads/2018/05/Guidelines_FeministLeadershipStudies52714.pdf. Three years of conversations between faculty and staff of the Rutgers Institute for Women's Leadership, Barnard College's Athena Center for Leadership, and Spelman College's Women's Research and Resource Center led to the creation of these guidelines.

Junctures
in Women's Leadership

⟨ Media and Journalism ⟩

A Brief History of Making It as a Media Leader

Linda Steiner

Going back to the colonial period, women's patchy history in U.S. media betrays a pattern of working for and under the men who controlled and dominated mainstream news outlets and media organizations. This is highly evident in leadership, especially if leadership is defined in conventional terms, at the uppermost rungs of a hierarchy. For this reason, a robust, useful understanding of women's leadership in journalism and media—what motivates and enables women to become leaders, what obstacles and constraints they have faced, the ways and extents to which gender has been an issue including as gender intersects with other identity dimensions—requires more flexible and generous definitions of journalism or news media, of leadership, and of news media leadership.

That full view likewise requires as much diversity as possible in terms of "medium" and type of leadership. This book needed to encompass as many news or public service media platforms as possible. The book therefore includes at least one chapter involving leadership in print, radio, television, film, and online and streamed digital media. It incorporates commercial, large-scale noncommercial, and small-scale alternative (social justice) media. One public relations leader is included, given the responsibility of public relations professionals to indirectly and directly inform the public and support journalists by providing information and interpretations, access to organizational leaders for interviews, and research that provides journalists with context to use for background.

The goal here was also maximum diversity along relevant dimensions of identity, including by race and ethnicity, religion, sexual orientation, and family background and marital status, as well as by the era and age or generation when the individuals sought and/or attained their leadership status, although younger women are slightly privileged, given the book's likely readers. Unsurprisingly, given the history of women's media work, the experiences of the women profiled here are all specifically gendered. But other dimensions mattered, too. Ida B. Wells and Oprah Winfrey, probably the two most famous women profiled in this volume, were doubly oppressed by gender and race. As Patricia Hill Collins notes, Wells's journalism exposing attacks on, and subordination of, Black people stands as an early example of intersectional analysis through race, gender, and class.[1]

Showing how the central themes intersect and crisscross, the chapters appear in order of birth year. The women leaders profiled here are Mary Ann Shadd Cary, publisher of the *Provincial Freeman* in Canada; Ida B. Wells, famously impactful for her *Memphis Free Speech* and her exposés about lynchings; Mary Margaret McBride, who pioneered the unscripted, unrehearsed radio show marketed directly to sponsors; Katharine Graham, *Washington Post* publisher during crucial times for the *Post* and journalism; Joan Ganz Cooney, who came up with the idea for a popular educational children's television show and directed the creation of what eventually became *Sesame Street*; Ann Barkelew, a public relations executive in the public and private sectors; Oprah Winfrey, best known for her nationally syndicated talk show, with its intimate, confessional style; Frances Stevens, founder and publisher of a much beloved lesbian magazine; Lisa Wilson, the first Black woman to head the Associated Press Sports Editors and proving a woman could devote herself to both journalism and family; S. Mitra Kalita, a senior executive at many major media organizations and who launched several companies of her own; and Iman Zawahry, a Muslim hijabi filmmaker.

Until recently, few women made it as editors in chief. Even fewer were publishers or owners of large news organizations. In the 2020s, news stories about Black women assuming leadership positions still refer to "firsts": Rashida Jones became the first Black chief executive of a cable news network when she was named

MSNBC president in 2021 (she stepped down on the eve of Donald Trump's return to the White House). When ABC News appointed Kimberly Godwin, who rose up through the CBS ranks (including as its executive director for development and diversity) as its president, she became the first Black woman to lead a major U.S. broadcast network.[2] A 2022 report commissioned by the Bill & Melinda Gates Foundation urged greater focus on recruiting and nurturing editors of color, given its blunt conclusion about the current situation: "The perception that women have almost caught up with men in news leadership and coverage strengthens further with every high-profile editorial appointment of a woman in journalism. Nonetheless, this perception is wrong. Women are significantly underrepresented in editorial leadership roles and news coverage and their voices remain muted in a global news industry still dominated by men."[3]

The United States *is* witnessing some progress, however. Twenty years ago, a survey of Fortune 500 companies in telecommunication, publishing, entertainment, and advertising found that women were about 15 percent of the executive officers; of 208 executive women, 68 had "clout titles."[4] In 2023, the Reuters Institute studied top editors of major online and offline news outlets in twelve countries. Women held 44 percent of the top editorial positions in the United States and were 50 percent of the recently appointed top editors.[5] Opportunity to lead is a matter of equity: people should be able to succeed on their merits. Who can serve as leaders also matters to society, including in terms of who will navigate and survive the media industry's increasing precarity and be able to investigate important questions. Top news leadership affects how journalism is practiced and what and whose news is disseminated.

The assumption that only top executives are leaders means that women are not always defined as leaders and perhaps do not even call themselves leaders. But, people with clout titles are not the only ones who matter or make important decisions. Media women demonstrate many ways to achieve and exercise leadership besides reaching the apex of the hierarchy, and the women profiled here have been creative and persistent in confronting and resolving critical junctures. Some invented or reinvented formats and genres for underserved or unappreciated audiences. Some advocated the cause of misrepresented communities, for example, by commissioning or producing more and more fair representations, or by hiring people to do this. Others bore the heavy burden of legal action or establishing professional organizations. They modeled courage and ethics. They demonstrated moral leadership. Michel Martin says that as the cohost of NPR's flagship news program, she doesn't hire or fire people. "But you're the brain trust of the show, the intellectual leadership of the show. And you're a part of the emotional leadership of the show, helping people to bring out the best in themselves."[6]

For that matter, women's leadership manifests as role models. In 2018, President Donald Trump gratuitously attacked the professionalism, not for the first time, of three Black journalists: Abby Phillip, then a CNN reporter; Yamiche Alcindor, then the White House correspondent of the *PBS NewsHour*; and April Ryan, then the White House correspondent for American Urban Radio Networks. They stood their ground, unflappable, principled, maintaining their focus on their larger purpose. Alcindor tweeted, "We press on. We focus on the privilege of asking questions for a living. We do the work."[7] Indeed, in January 2025, Alcindor was preparing to return to the White House, this time for NBC.

The attempt to achieve breadth here, however, sometimes leaves one profile standing in as a proxy for a long historical period or an entire platform. To fill out the account of the diverse ways in which women have led, the rest of this introduction offers additional examples of how women have led and continue to lead in media and journalism. Moreover, it contextualizes the key themes that emerge in the careers of historical and contemporary women leaders in media industries. These include the significance of family connections; using or amassing clout to produce impactful content specifically for or about women; inventing journalism/media forms that provide employment for women; protofeminist and feminist leadership; the significance of organizing, unionizing, and legal action; debates over the extent to which leadership is gendered; the importance of willingness to innovate and be entrepreneurial; and the centrality of passion and moral commitment.

Family Relationships in Publishing

That spouses, siblings, and children of journalists would come to appreciate journalism and learn professional skills is no surprise. Especially in the colonial era, when chronic labor shortages required everyone to help out, some women successfully assisted family members in their publishing and printing businesses. Elizabeth Timothy (d. 1757) began supporting herself and her seven children by publishing the *South-Carolina Gazette* after her husband died in 1738. Apparently, Benjamin Franklin regarded Elizabeth as a better business manager than her late husband.[8] Eight years later, her son Peter took over the Charleston newspaper; after Peter died, his wife Ann Timothy (c. 1727–1792) sustained it.

Likewise, Ann Smith Franklin (1696–1763) needed to provide for her children after her husband James Franklin died in 1735; she took over his print shop and revived and published the *Rhode Island Almanack*. Ann's two daughters helped her with the business while her son was apprenticing with his uncle, Benjamin Franklin. Once James Jr. returned to Rhode Island, mother and son worked together, including by launching the *Newport Mercury* in 1758. After her son died, Ann continued to publish the newspaper.[9] Clementina Bird Rind (c. 1740–1774) took over the *Virginia Gazette*, needing to support her five children after her husband died; as such, she was one of the relatively rare women to earn a profit as a writer.[10] And in 1842, after the death of the *Boston Transcript* editor, the paper's owner hired his sister Cornelia Walter (c. 1813–1898); she edited the paper until she married, five years later; among other things, she famously reported on Black citizens left homeless by a Philadelphia race riot.[11]

Often the main challenge for these women came when the men in their lives and/or in the government removed them. Sarah Updike Goddard (c. 1701–1770) and her daughter Mary Katherine Goddard (1738–1816) were instrumental in the publishing and printing business of William Goddard, their son and brother, respectively. The two women published the *Providence Gazette* from 1765 to 1768, while William established offices in Philadelphia and Baltimore.[12] When he began traveling throughout the colonies to set up a mail delivery system, Mary Katherine moved to Baltimore to run the *Maryland Journal*. She also published a popular almanac and ran a Baltimore bookselling and bookbinding business. In 1784, however, the siblings grew estranged; William resumed control of the paper. Moreover, Mary Katherine served as postmaster of Baltimore, doing so successfully for fourteen years. But, in 1789, just as the job was finally becoming profitable, the new federal postmaster general replaced her with a man on grounds that the job involved travel. This, he said, was beyond her as a woman.[13]

Eleanor Medill "Cissy" Patterson (1881–1948) was the granddaughter of Joseph Medill, owner of the *Chicago Tribune*.[14] In 1930, she became editor and publisher of the *Washington Herald*, which she later merged with the *Washington Times*. She apparently had good judgment with respect to layout and photography and produced reform-oriented investigative reporting.[15] Patterson not only courted women readers but also hired many women and allegedly treated them generously. Katharine Graham's story echoes Cissy Patterson in that each was bypassed when the patriarch gave the paper to the son-in-law.[16]

Quite recently the family connection emerged for Linda Johnson Rice (b. 1958), the daughter of John Johnson, who founded Johnson Publishing Company, the largest Black-owned magazine publisher in the United States, and Eunice Johnson, who directed the Ebony Fashion Fair. As a child, Linda took notes during business meetings and accompanied her mother to Paris fashion shows. Linda worked her way up the Johnson Publishing Company ladder after college in 1980 and started working on the syndicated television show *Ebony/Jet Showcase*. She became president and CEO in 2002. In 2016, the company was sold to Clear View Group, a private equity firm; Rice severed her ties in 2019 when the company declared bankruptcy.[17]

Journalism for, about, and by Women

Not surprisingly, women's magazines and women's pages provided leadership opportunities for women, even if men controlled these profitable, if essentially ghettoized, genres intended for women consumers. Notably, although some women could push upward and forward because they had few or no family obligations, many women leaders at women's magazines (but also other platforms) often needed to earn a living to support their families. Indeed, given the challenges of balancing career and family responsibilities, some needed to change jobs frequently and to juggle a host of paid jobs and unpaid tasks.

For example, when her husband died days after the birth of their fifth child, Sarah Josepha Hale (1788–1879) decided to supplement her hat-making income by writing. After writing poetry but also one of the first novels about slavery, she moved to Boston to launch and edit *Ladies' Magazine*. In the first (January 1828) issue, Hale urged "lovers" to give subscriptions to the "ladies" they loved.[18] When *Ladies' Magazine* was insufficiently profitable, Hale moved to Philadelphia to work with Louis Godey. *Godey's Lady's Book* launched in 1830 with Hale as editor. *Godey's* soon became the most widely read U.S. periodical. Hale's highly influential columns advocated women's education and abolition of slavery (but not women's suffrage).[19] She was said to have a keen sense of her readers' tastes even as she tried to advance women's interests.[20] Hale continued to work until 1877, by which time, however, the literary level of *Godey's* had fallen.[21]

In 1834, Ann Stephens (1810–1886) and her husband Edward Stephens founded a literary monthly. She edited the *Portland Magazine*; he published it. Then she became editor of the *Ladies' Companion* but left after four years, when George Rex Graham, the founder and first editor of *Graham's Lady's and Gentleman's Magazine*, offered her more money.[22] She became associate editor of *Peterson's Magazine* in 1842, when its publisher and founding editor offered her even more. She remained until 1853. In 1856 she launched *Mrs. Stephens' Illustrated New Monthly*, with her husband as publisher. She ultimately merged her monthly with *Peterson's Magazine*, which all along had been publishing her novels in serial form.

Through the twentieth century, the biggest women's magazines were typically edited by men. Between 1961 and 1994, John Mack Carter served as editor in chief of each of the Big Three women's magazines: *McCall's*, *Ladies' Home Journal*, and *Good Housekeeping*. Indeed, it was Carter's *Ladies Home Journal* office that two hundred members of the National Organization for Women, the Redstockings, and the New York Radical Feminists invaded in March 1970. For eleven hours, women debated Carter and Lenore Hershey, the only woman who was a senior *Journal* editor; protesters demanded (but did not win) an all-women advertising and editorial staff, free day care for employees, and an end to exploitative advertising.[23] In August 1970 the protesters got what *was* promised them: an eight-page section that they themselves wrote and edited. It included, instead of the objectionable "Can This Marriage Be Saved?" regular *LHJ* column, one titled "Should This Marriage Be Saved?"

So-called service magazines for women survive, now largely in women's hands. In contrast, newspaper women's pages lasted less than a century. Many women journalists despised them—often taking women's page jobs only because they were desperate and/or hoped they could graduate to something else. Nevertheless, during their golden age in the early twentieth century, women's pages or sections provided opportunities not only for women journalists, sometimes their only opportunity, but also for one woman to edit a section. Editors had come to understand what magazine publishers understood—advertisers wanted to reach women consumers. To attract that profitable constituency, general interest newspapers hired women to develop, write, and even edit the women's page. By 1894 the *New York World*'s daily edition included a page headlined "For and About Women."[24] It could have added "By Women" if by women it meant white middle-class women. And the Black press also had women's pages. The *Chicago Defender*'s publisher, for example, hired Rebecca Stiles Taylor in 1939 to develop the women's pages and increase the number of women readers.[25]

Post–World War II women's page editors and journalists redefined women's news to reflect women's changing roles, thereby, according to women's media historian Kimberly Voss, setting the scene for the Women's Liberation Movement.[26] As editor of the *Miami Herald*'s women's page, Marie Anderson (who graduated Phi Beta Kappa from Duke University in 1937 and two years later attended the Katharine Gibbs School to learn shorthand and typing) moved away from "the four Fs" (food, fashion, furnishings, and family). Without alienating women who wanted to remain in the domestic sphere, Anderson tilted toward a new F: feminism. Women's page editors' power was circumscribed. For example, Marjorie Paxson (once Anderson's assistant editor) led a staff of seven women at the *St. Petersburg Times* but could not make hiring, firing, or budget decisions.[27] On the other hand, after 1960, many women's section editors abandoned society coverage and began covering substantive issues omitted in the rest of the newspaper. For example, Vivian Castleberry (1922–2017) remade the highly conservative women's page of the *Dallas Times-Herald* into a serious lifestyle section.[28] (Eventually elected to the newspaper's editorial board, Castleberry notably returned to work after the births of each of her five children.) Voss calls the mix of hard and soft news in women's pages "quilted news": it included domestic abuse, workplace inequities, and reproductive rights, sexism, health, politics, and race.[29]

In the 1970s, under pressure from feminists, news organizations abandoned these special sections. Most of the women's page editors lost their jobs when the substitution became feature or style sections edited by men. Paxson was demoted at two newspapers after the women's section was abolished.[30] Seeing herself as a "casualty of the women's movement," Paxson not unreasonably blamed feminist activists for denigrating women's pages and ignoring how women's page editors had supported the women's movement.[31] Still, Paxson landed on her feet, first as assistant managing editor at a Gannett paper in Idaho, where she learned to prepare the newsroom budget, and later as publisher of two Gannett papers.

Indeed, after Gannett merged with GateHouse Media in 2019, thereby becoming the largest newspaper chain in the United States, Gannett pledged to foster a newsroom "culture of inclusion" for women, people of color, and other underrepresented groups, promising that its workforce would be as diverse as the country by 2025 and to hire more journalists to cover issues related to race and identity, social justice, and equality. In 2021, its *USA Today* became a "majority-female" newsroom.[32] In 2023, after two years at Chalkbeat, a national nonprofit focused on education, Avery Nichols returned to the Gannett-owned *Free Press*, where she had spent much of her career, but now as its first Black editor in chief.

Pamela McAllister Johnson partly credited the assistance of Gannett's organization and business structure when she was named the first Black woman publisher of a general circulation daily; she also learned corporate politics; refused to see being a woman, Black, and young as handicaps; and defined herself "as intelligent, as a firm and fair manager, as someone who could promote my staff, and as a visionary."[33] In 2005, after serving as publisher of the *Reno Gazette-Journal*, Johnson (1948–2015) became the first woman to preside over Gannett's Newspaper Division. Earlier, in a departure from its typical trend of moving people around, Gannett let her stay at the *Ithaca Journal* for thirteen years so as not to disrupt the lives of her children.[34] Dorothy Bland, who is Black, also spent much of her career at Gannett newspapers, including as president and publisher of the *Fort Collins Coloradoan*, 1994–2005. Bland attributed her upward mobility to her willingness to work in every department and even do undesirable work.[35] Dorothy Butler Gilliam also quotes several Hispanic and Asian women emphasizing the roles of good mentors and role models—sometimes also people of color and sometimes white men—as well as of ambition, skill, and opportunity in their rise to the top;[36] that is, leadership opportunities depended on a combination of mission-based policies and processes as well as people.

Inventing Forms and Genres

Women blazed trails by carving out new roles for themselves and other women, such as front-page stunt girls, "sob sisters" wielding purple pens, and advice and humor columnists. Newspapers ran in-house advertising for their women journalists who performed dramatic investigative stunts that were regarded as daring or dangerous for women (perhaps even for men). The most famous "stunt girl" was Elizabeth "Nellie Bly" Cochrane (1864–1922). Intrigued by her witty response to a *Pittsburgh Dispatch* editorial that claimed that women should stick to domestic tasks, the paper's managing editor hired her. She initially focused on women workers, but after factory owners complained to the *Dispatch* about her investigations, she was reassigned to women's pages. She quit and spent six months reporting on Mexico until she was essentially chased out of the country. Finally, the *New York World*, already known for "yellow journalism," hired her to feign insanity—cleverly and convincingly—so that she could investigate brutality and neglect at the "Women's Lunatic Asylum." Bly's ten-day stint ultimately spurred a large-scale government investigation and improvements in mental health care. Some of her later works were pure stunts. Still, Cochrane's detective work was a precursor to undercover investigative journalism,[37] and women like Bly and Winifred Sweet Black (1863–1936) arguably led to the popular "front page gals" of the 1920s, '30s, and '40s.[38]

Women pioneered other genres, too. Under the name Beatrice Fairfax, Marie Manning (1872–1945) wrote the first "advice to the lovelorn" column. Manning and two "Hen Coop" colleagues had created a women's page for the *New York Evening Journal*, and after three readers wrote seeking personal advice, Manning suggested another new department.[39] Her advice column was immediately popular. But Manning's pay and status remained low for nearly thirty years. She resigned and another woman took over the column. Then, after losing her money during the 1929 economic crash, Manning returned to the *Journal* and provided advice until her death.

Elizabeth Meriwether Gilmer (1870–1951) needed to support herself after her husband suffered severe mental illness. In 1896 her neighbor, Eliza P. Nicholson, owner of the New Orleans *Picayune*, hired Gilmer to write, under the pseudonym Dorothy Dix, a Sunday advice column for women; with that success, Gilmer soon became editor of the women's section and the *Picayune*'s assistant editor.[40] In 1901 Gilmer took a better-paying offer from William Randolph Hearst's *New York Journal*, where she wrote "Dorothy Dix Talks" and "sob-sister" stories. A study of so-called Middletown, USA (actually, a city in Indiana) described Dix as "perhaps the most potent single agency of diffusion from without shaping the habits of thought in Middletown in regard to marriage."[41]

Women essentially invented the tear-jerking feature story emphasizing human interest and sentimentality. The term "sob sister" was first applied to Gilmer, Black, and two other women who were covering a murder trial. Harry Thaw had killed a man who had sex with—and allegedly raped—a teenaged chorus girl and artist's model before she married Thaw. Historian Jean Lutes suggests that women and men covering this trial adopted similar "overwrought" language and melodramatic tropes, but the prominence of the women in the courtroom and the newspapers' promotional publicity about their "woman's angle" on the trial drew attention. The term "sob sister" was derogatory, implying manufactured tears[42] and something less than a "real" reporter.[43] Mary Margaret McBride, then writing for the *New York Evening Mail*, explained her opposition to being called a "sob sister": "The assumption that I was good for one type of story made me feel like a sort of second-class citizen."[44]

Such columns led directly to the contemporary variety of local and syndicated advice columns about personal relationships, fashion, ethics, and sex. Written by experts, hobbyists, people of color, and sexual minorities, such columns appear in print, online, and through podcasts. Advice givers developed distinct personal styles. The exceptions proving the rule were the Friedman sisters, identical twins who became fiercely competitive and estranged rivals with their advice columns that adopted a similarly confident, blunt, commonsense approach. Each became a leader, if the metric is impact on readers, including readers who were major celebrities and political leaders. Esther and Pauline Friedman had cowritten a gossip column for their college newspaper and majored in journalism and psychology. Esther "Eppie" Lederer (1918–2002) took over the "Ask Ann Landers" column in 1955, after the death of Ruth Crowley, the Chicago nurse who had started it, and continued to advise readers until 2002.[45]

Pauline Phillips (1918–2013), who chose her pseudonym Abigail Van Buren, began her well-known "Dear Abby" newspaper column in 1956. From 1963 to 1975, Phillips hosted a daily *Dear Abby* program on CBS Radio. Besides advice, Phillips also imparted information using experts and documented resources; she did not always claim to be the last word, although she sometimes disagreed with her correspondents' premises. Starting in 1987, her daughter Jeanne cowrote and then wholly wrote "Dear Abby." Even a highly unflattering biography of the two sisters (highlighting their tendency to feuds and self-promotion) notes that they were the world's most widely syndicated columnists; by the late 1980s, for the United States one or both had been named the most admired women (Gallup), the most important women (UPI), and the most influential women (UPI and *World Almanac*).[46]

The interest of advice seekers in anonymity is obvious. The use of pseudonyms by so many of these leading women stunt reporters, sob sisters, and advice columnists, however, is nonobvious and wholly understudied. Discussing Canadian women journalists in the 1880–1945 period, Marjory Louise Lang posits that pseudonyms preserved a psychologically necessary barrier "between the public personality a woman writer projected for her readers and her private identity."[47] Lang also suggests that some U.S. women chose "silly pseudonyms" (Fanny Fern, Jennie June) "to disarm with coyness those who might charge them with boldness for venturing to express themselves."[48] Perhaps choosing a pen name represented the power to create a second self and, literally, to write under multiple identities, perhaps profitably. The cases of advice columnists also show the flip side: pseudonyms allowed newspapers to retain the brand when replacing a writer who died or quit.

Karola Ruth Westheimer (1928–2024), fondly and widely known as Dr. Ruth, represents a highly dramatic story. Born in Germany and orphaned by the Holocaust, she was seriously wounded in action during the 1947–1949 Palestine war. She and her child immigrated in 1956 to the United States.[49] She worked as a maid while earning an MA and a PhD and then opened a sex therapy practice. Between 1980 and 1990, she had a taboo-breaking radio call-in show, *Sexually Speaking*, that soon ran on ninety stations.[50] In 1984, Westheimer began hosting several programs on the Lifetime TV network. On *Good Sex! With Dr. Ruth Westheimer*, renamed *The Dr. Ruth Show* when it was expanded in 1985 to an hour, she issued serious, candid, highly specific, pragmatic advice about sex and sexual practices in an enthusiastic, funny, respectful way. The *New York Times* said, "It's hard to explain how revolutionary her humor, candor and sexual explicitness seemed for the time. Nothing was off the table: when H.I.V./AIDS and homosexuality were barely acknowledged publicly, she was there with fact-based advice and encouragement."[51] Among other activities, she had two advice shows for teens, a sex talk show on Israeli television, wrote forty-five books plus a column distributed nationally and internationally, and hosted a series of *Playboy* instructional videos.

Just as the sex talk show is the child of Dr. Ruth, the newspaper humor column is nearly synonymous with its creator Erma Bombeck (1927–1996). Bombeck began her career in earnest in 1965 when, with three children at home, Bombeck finally convinced the local editor to let her work from home to write a humor column featuring suburban housewives. By 1978, her semiweekly "At Wit's End" column appeared in nine hundred newspapers in the United States and Canada.[52] She also wrote for *Good Housekeeping*, *Reader's Digest*, *Family Circle*, *Redbook*, *McCall's*, and *Teen* magazines.

Experiments in Feminist Organizations

Women were, of course, largely leaders of the nineteenth-century protofeminist and later feminist newspapers and magazines that advocated progressive/radical causes—voting rights, reproductive rights, professional rights, and sexual rights. These publications enabled women to take on business and decision-making roles, participate in the public sphere on their own terms, and dramatize still-emerging ideas about womanhood. These projects often represented the thinking and energy of one person. The novelist, utopian feminist, and progressive activist Charlotte Perkins Gilman (1860–1935) wrote all the content for every issue of her ad-free, self-subsidized monthly, *The Forerunner*: from 1909 to 1916, she wrote its essays, editorials, articles (often about women's rights and suffrage), book reviews, and fiction, including six serialized novels.

Men's assistance was not always rejected. Indeed, women media leaders have often (except for some radical feminist and/or lesbian cases) cooperated and partnered with men. *The Revolution*, arguably the most famous of the women's rights and suffrage papers, was coedited by the lively "strong-minded" Elizabeth Cady Stanton (1815–1902) and Parker Pillsbury, an ardent suffragist and active abolitionist (he edited the *National Anti-Slavery Standard* in 1866).[53] Family help was even better. In 1870, Lucy Stone (1818–1893) and her husband Henry Blackwell founded and then edited the *Woman's*

Journal, the official organ of the suffrage organization they founded to compete with Stanton's. Friends helped but essentially Stone and Blackwell saw to everything, including soliciting subscriptions and advertisements. Their daughter Alice Stone Blackwell (1857–1950) began editing in 1883 and was sole editor from 1909 until 1917. Between 1871 and 1888, Abigail Duniway (1834–1915) produced the *New Northwest*—"A Journal for the People, Devoted to the Interests of Humanity, Independent in Politics and Religion. Alive to all live Issues. Thoroughly Radical in Opposing and Exposing the Wrongs of the Masses"—with the help of her six children. In 1894, Josephine St. Pierre Ruffin (1842–1924), a member of the New England Woman's Press Association and founder of the Woman's Era Club, launched *Woman's Era*, by and for middle-class African American women. Ruffin was editor and publisher; her daughter, Florida, was the assistant editor; and her husband, a prosuffrage state legislator and the first African American municipal judge in Boston (and the United States), also helped.

Starting in the 1970s and continuing to this day, women involved in a host of kinds of feminist media have tried out distinctive ways of working: cooperative, nonhierarchical, and collective management; operating by consensus, rotating jobs, and eliminating titles—that is, they redefined the notion of leadership. They experimented with funding: some charged men more than women or rejected advertising. A special case, perhaps, is *Ms.*, whose three hundred thousand test copies sold out in 1972, in eight days.[54] The magazine's cofounders (including powerhouse star Gloria Steinem) pioneered a glossy feminist outlet with high production values that resonated with mainstream middle-class women (although it was criticized for insufficient support for radicals and lesbians). *Ms.* had a masthead listing staffers. But it rejected advertisements the editors deemed sexist or that required them to provide "complementary" (i.e., free and complimentary) content. It continues into the twenty-first century. But, otherwise, the feminists who launched such projects rarely sought to make a profit, and almost none do. This often means burnout and a short, if intense, lifespan.

Women writing for the Black press face even greater precarity, needing to carve out new areas of reporting and juggle multiple affiliations while also navigating the politics of Black respectability. A highly popular Black "lady writer" was Victoria Earle Matthews (1861–1907), who was born into slavery a month before the start of the Civil War. Despite having only a few years of education, she began freelancing for several New York papers. Soon she was writing for a variety of religious papers and especially for many Black papers around the country; she also served on the editorial board of the *Woman's Era*.[55]

Organizational/Union Leadership

Beginning in the 1880s, enough women were working in journalism for them to organize clubs that served various professional interests as well as social and networking purposes. Indeed, in this sense they paralleled the exclusively men's press organizations, which helped shore up a sense of professional prestige and status. When women journalists were banned from an 1868 press club's reception for Charles Dickens, Jane Cunningham Croly (1829–1901), then the editor of a fashion magazine, founded Sororis, which promoted professional opportunities for women, and then in 1890, its successor, the General Federation of Women's Clubs.[56] In 1889, she founded the Women's Press Club of New York City, serving as its president until her death in 1901. Under the byline Jennie June, Croly continued to write a widely popular syndicated column after having children.

The early women's press organizations promoted women's professional status and prestige and engaged in charity, philanthropy, and reform. Camaraderie was another important goal. In 1885, six women met at the *Boston Herald* office of Sallie Joy White (1847–1909) to organize the New England Woman's Press Association (NEWPA).[57] White had briefly written for the then-new *Woman's Journal*; but Mary Livermore, also a Stone ally, decided White could better serve the women's movement as a mainstream reporter. Another organizer was Marion A. McBride, a *Boston Post* reporter who had helped found the Illinois Woman's Press Association and the National Woman's Press Association. NEWPA stated its intentions: "Promoting acquaintance and good fellowship among newspaper women; elevating the work and the workers; and forwarding by concerted action through the Press such good objects in social, philanthropic and reformatory lines as may from time to time present themselves."[58] Membership required employment as "a vocation, and not an avocation, a breadwinning occupation, and not an amusement."[59] Eventually, interest waned; NEWPA ended in 1982. Nevertheless, one former president, Muriel Knight, a reporter for Boston's Black radio station and a Black community newspaper and who was the NEWPA's only Black officer, credited the NEWPA for working on behalf of parity.[60]

Similar patterns of rise and fall occurred in many other places, as well as at the national level. The Women's National Press Club (WNPC) formed in 1919 when women journalists—for whom social news was their bread and butter—learned they would not be allowed to attend the visit of the Prince of Wales to the National Press Club. Cora Rigby, the Washington bureau chief of the *Christian Science Monitor*, declared that a women's club was necessary to combat "the conspiracy of men to keep women off the newspapers or at least reduce their number, wages and importance."[61] The first WNPC president was Lily Lykes Shepard, the *New York Tribune*'s Washington woman. Shepard later joined the Defense Department's public relations division, first working for Oveta Culp Hobby, head of the Women's Army Corps.[62] The men's and women's clubs merged in 1985, adopting the former's "unmarked" name.

The women's journalism organizations that continue into the present and have kept "women" in their names have relatively flat designs. They are not leaderless; rather, they often spread tasks out among dozens of officers. This preference for collegiality over hierarchy is evident in the Journalism & Women Symposium (JAWS), which began in 1985 as a congenial annual meeting of women journalists and educators for mutual support, socializing, and professional development. JAWS continues to advocate professional empowerment of women in journalism and more inclusive coverage; it provides online skills training and an annual Conference and Mentoring Project (CAMP). It says, "We believe that by advancing women in journalism, we transform the world. We are a powerful network of women committed to supporting one another with the friendship, knowledge, tools and career advice we need to succeed at every stage of our careers. . . . We believe in paying it forward."[63]

Although many women were among the founders, in 1975, of the National Association of Black Journalists, its first eight presidents were men; but since 1991, about half the presidents have been women. Similarly, women were among the founders of the National Association of Hispanic Journalists and the National Association of Asian Journalists, and once elected as president, women gradually achieved parity with men regarding the presidential count.

Founded in 1987, the Association for Women in Sports Media (AWSM) is a volunteer-managed support network and advocacy group for women who work in sports media, including media relations; membership is now also open to men. AWSM (pronounced "awesome") particularly tries to promote diversity and fair portrayal of women professionals in sports media by serving as both watchdog and bully pulpit. For example, in 1990, two New England Patriots football players complained that sports reporter Lisa Olson was "a looker," a complaint that the Patriots' general manager investigated and determined was unfounded. The players sexually harassed Olson in their locker room by walking naked in front of her and making vulgar comments and lewd gestures. Olson filed a civil suit against the team, which was settled, but Olson moved to Australia after Patriots fans made threats on her life. AWSM gave interviews and wrote about the controversy to raise awareness of the sexual harassment of women sports journalists.[64]

Two other major lawsuits illustrate the significant impact that courageous individuals can have if they are willing to subject themselves to the economic, physical, and mental demands of legal action. *Sports Illustrated* reporter Melissa Ludtke was denied access to the New York Yankees locker room while covering the 1977 World Series. The clubhouse is where reporters get important interviews with players and see how they react to the game's outcome. Los Angeles Dodgers players voted to allow Ludtke into their locker room. However, midway through the first World Series game, Bowie Kuhn, the Major League Baseball commissioner, overturned the Dodgers' decision and prohibited all women journalists from accessing either team's locker room, either before or after the game—

allegedly, lest Ludtke see the players naked. News of the sex discrimination suit that Ludtke filed against Kuhn drew enormous attention but nearly always missing that the point, as was also the case with Olson, was equity. Just before the next year's World Series, judge Constance Baker Motley ruled that Ludtke's Fourteenth Amendment rights and her fundamental right to pursue a career had been violated.[65] In her 2024 memoir, Ludtke suggests that *Ludtke v. Kuhn* pushed locker room doors open for women and inspired many women to enter sports-related careers, including sports journalism; women are network sports producers and directors, including on ESPN.[66] Nonetheless, it is worth remembering that, like Olson, Ludtke suffered the emotional toll from the sports writers' innuendo and ridicule, echoed in television comedy sketches and newspaper cartoonists, who depicted Ludtke as "peering up at hulking, hairy-legged men," a "temptress who'd misuse her equal access to seduce ballplayers."[67] Sports journalism continues to be dominated by men and resistant to women, making Lisa Wilson's presidency of the Associated Press Sports Editors remarkable.

Using her married name, Betsy Wade was the lead plaintiff in the landmark sex discrimination lawsuit *Elizabeth Boylan, et al. v. The New York Times*. Wade's (1929–2020) *New York Times* obituary described her as "revered among peers for her role in the 1974 class-action suit against *The Times*, one of the industry's earliest fights over women's rights to equal treatment in hiring, promotion, pay and workplace protections."[68] Her career went up and down. The *Herald Tribune*'s women's page editor fired Wade in 1953 because she was pregnant. A few years later, the *New York Times* hired Wade as its first woman copy editor,[69] but after four weeks of training, she was assigned to the Women's Department. Finally, at her insistence, she was eventually transferred back. In 1972 Wade joined a women's caucus to study gender (in)equities at the *Times*. The caucus sued after finding that women earned significantly less than men and that no women were on the editorial board or had top corporate jobs or the highest-prestige reporting jobs.

In 1978, the suit was settled when the *Times* agreed to hire and promote more women, and that same year, Wade became president of the New York Newspaper Guild, the largest local in the national union now known as The NewsGuild. Linda Greenhouse, a Pulitzer Prize–winning reporter who covered the U.S. Supreme Court for the *New York Times*, literally credited the lawsuit for her career.[70] The *New York Times* appointed Le Anne Schreiber as its assistant sports editor and a couple of months later as its sports editor, making her the first woman to run a major newspaper's sports section (although she had never covered sports for a daily newspaper). She apparently told the *Times* from the start she would only stay two years: "I was, depending on one's view, the bitch, the saint, the amazon, the token, the recipient of awards and death threats and, ultimately, the ingrate, for insisting upon my pre-agreed release after two excruciating years."[71]

Until the 1970s, the relevant unions ignored discrimination and sexism. Now that communications and media-related union leaders are more active on this, women are closing the gender gap in union membership generally. A few local shops even have women leaders. For example, Diana Mastrull, an editor at the *Philadelphia Inquirer*, is president of The NewsGuild of Greater Philadelphia as well as The NewsGuild's international chair. Both wings of the Writers Guild have a few women officers. But women have not achieved parity in terms of leadership. The Screen Actors Guild—American Federation of Radio and Television Artists has no women in top leadership.

Gender Differences in Leadership

The concept of the "glass ceiling," coined in 1978 by the management consultant Marilyn Loden, describes cultural barriers to the advancement of women across a host of professions and more recently also of minoritized people that left them stalled in the middle. The issue became such a concern that the Glass Ceiling Act of 1991 established a commission to study how to eliminate artificial barriers to the advancement of women and minorities. Psychologists Eagly and Carli explain the problems with the glass ceiling metaphor in ways that are relevant to media, beginning with the fact that barriers are neither invisible nor absolute.[72] Furthermore, the metaphor of a single, unvarying obstacle ignores the complexity and variety of challenges at many points, not only at the very top.[73]

Loden went on to write *Feminine Leadership or How to Succeed in Business Without Being One of the Boys*.[74] As the title indicates, Loden was one of many to equate femininity and women and to associate women with consensus-seeking, collaborative management styles and intuitive and empathic approaches to problem-solving. In yet another arguably oversimplified dichotomy, Loden urged women to "be themselves" instead of imitating corporate men.

Again, in the 1980s and 1990s, many scholars cast women as the preferred and perfect counterpart to men as leaders. Helen Fisher, a prominent and much quoted biological anthropologist who presented her research on women's executive skills to the American Press Institute and the American Society of Newspaper Editors, suggested that because of their opposite primordial jobs, men and women have evolved over millennia in opposite ways. As a result, men use focused, compartmentalized, incremental reasoning ("step thinking"). In contrast, women think contextually, holistically ("web thinking"), Fisher insists, adding that women's mental flexibility, verbal skills, long-range forethought, and "uncanny ability to embrace ambiguity" were advantageous in the news business.[75] When making decisions, women weigh more variables, recall more viewpoints, and consider more options.[76] While large news organizations won't eliminate all hierarchy, Fisher has predicted, natural selection ultimately means that the companies that promote women will triumph.

Others offered analogous dichotomies, with women consistently said to value information-sharing and networking. Sally Helgesen observed that women managers typically posit a circular "web of inclusion" that appreciates ideas from all employees, fits jobs to individuals' talents; they work at a steady pace, value flexibility, and normalize unscheduled interruptions."[77] Several scholars contrast men's transactional leadership to women's transformational, interactive approach—that is, using relational skills to motivate and influence followers.[78]

This romanticizing of women's styles almost certainly overstates women's preference for consensus and concord. Overall, women and men television news directors and print and online managing editors manage their newsrooms in similar ways. When the *Sarasota* (FL) *Herald-Tribune* had an all-women management team, it placed a high value on teamwork, collaboration, and family-work balance, which Tracy Everbach properly identified as characteristic of a "feminized" organizational culture.[79] Yet, scholars have shown that editors' gender does not significantly influence which topics get covered, although women-headed newspapers have tended to run more positive stories and treat reporters with gender equity more often than newspapers headed by men. Sylvia Banderas Coffinet had been an executive at Vox Media and Hello & ¡Hola! Media Inc. before being named in 2023 the first CEO of the Latino Media Network, founded and owned by two Latinas. For the year Banderas Coffinet stayed at LMN, she was excited that only Latinas were in the C-suite, but this did not seem to affect decision-making at the network.

Margaret Gallagher, who has written several reports on gender in journalism, argues that women have relatively little decision-making power either inside the media organizations themselves or in the larger political and economic institutions. In 2001, she explained, "It is as if one woman at the top is as much as the system can absorb without being thrown into a paroxysm of professional anguish about the potential effects—on status, salaries, self-esteem—of 'feminization.' . . . The 'one at a time' mentality vis-à-vis women in senior editorial management precludes the possibility of women building up the kind of power base necessary for real change—either in terms of journalistic output or in the way the institutions of journalism are organized."[80] A generation later, more than one woman executive is possible. But it's not as if women media managers hire or promote a flood of women, even when they reach what is known as critical mass.[81]

Very few of the women profiled here or mentioned in this introductory chapter set out to be executives. Joan Ganz Cooney, one of the first women executives in U.S. television, was an idealist who persevered despite sexism as well as doubts about her credentials and suspicions about her lack of high-level managerial experience and financial management skills.[82] Similarly, Daisy Veerasingham—the first woman and person of color to head the Associated Press—did not originally aim for the corner office. "It was just that I love that I could actually make a difference in terms of directions, strategy, taking people along with me."[83] One of the exceptions is Swati Sharma, the editor in chief of Vox. She says, "I started managing people when I was about 30. Stepping into that role, back when I was at the *Washington Post*, was pretty deliberate. And being in management, over time, has become an even more deliberate thing for me. Constantly, I'm trying to be better at this. Because the journalism is only as good as the culture of a newsroom. And management defines the culture."[84]

More typical is Karen Lincoln Michel, president and CEO of IndiJ Public Media and president of ICT (formerly known as Indian Country Today); she has had executive positions at several newspapers and magazines and was president of what is now the Indigenous Journalists Association. Michel said, "I didn't have a plan to be on the business side, or even to be a leader. Opportunities came my way. And when they did, I wanted to do my best in that particular job. And at every level of opportunity, I always thought, 'This is going to be the pinnacle, this will be as far as I rise.'"[85] Michel highlights another pattern for contemporary women: People helped prepare her up the ladder. Often these mentors have been men.

During the past decade, formal leadership programs in media have been developed, with mentoring, coaching, and so forth. It's worth noting that the Poynter Institute, a global nonprofit journalism training and research center, runs several five-day leadership programs. The workshop for women is not noticeably different from ones that are not gender-specific, except for the lesson on beating back imposter syndrome. Both the nongendered workshop and the one for women tackle how to delegate effectively, conduct difficult conversations, recruit and retain top talent who are diverse, achieve better work-life chemistry, "manage up," and use empathy to connect with team members.

Notably, since the 1950s, when public relations started expanding in tandem with the growth of consumer buying and white-collar jobs, PR has been unusually open to women. Women achieved more leadership positions compared to other media domains, at least for those first fifty years. Nevertheless, the field lacked gender parity in pay and executive status. Researchers posited that women's choice of "technician" roles over managerial ones represented socialization and the relative ease of women's home/work balance.[86] But PR scholars and practitioners were worried that PR would become a "Velvet Ghetto," meaning that so many women would enter the field that it would be perceived as "feminized" and thus salaries and status would drop, leading to a vicious cycle where men would avoid the field. The predictions did not come to pass, thankfully. Although women are not heads of PR agencies in the same percentages that they work for those agencies, salaries and access to CEOs did not decrease. Men still wanted and took PR jobs.[87]

Some women continue to express concerns that women are not getting the same opportunities to show leadership skills even in women-dominated spaces, making PR an "extra-feminized sector" with "extra-masculinized" decision-making.[88] For example, DeAnna Spoerl, who coleads Bear Icebox Communications with her husband, suspects that women focus more on the emotional side of work: "We want to do well and make sure others around us are doing well (not to say that males never feel this way). However, more males are driven by the dollar (whether it's to support a family or to climb up the corporate ladder). . . . Females tend to be more work-focused while males are more money-focused and therefore place themselves (and each other) in positions of power more regularly."[89]

Innovation and Entrepreneurship

Women have consistently been willing to experiment and innovate, including with new media technologies and platforms and sometimes with highly entrepreneurial interests. Occasionally these women grow wealthy, the most prominent case being Oprah Winfrey. Author of fifteen books, Arianna Huffington (b. 1950) made it to *Time* magazine's list of the world's one hundred most influential people, the *Forbes* Most Powerful Women list, and Winfrey's SuperSoul100 list of visionaries and influential leaders. She cofounded the Huffington Post, an early aggregator of blogs and news about politics, media, business, and entertainment; HuffPo also led in using search engine optimization based on trending keywords. In 2011,

AOL purchased HuffPo for $315 million; Huffington became head of the combined entity's editorial assets.[90] In 2016 Huffington stepped down to launch and lead Thrive Global.[91] (Among other things, Thrive's "wellness room" offers chair massages and a "nap pod."[92] Huffington herself hosts a mental wellness and resilience podcast.[93]) In 2018, Thrive Global was listed as one of "the 50 most sought-after startups in the United States."[94]

The newest (and youngest) media executives are highly entrepreneurial, launching their own organizations. Having first led mainstream news outlets and then working outside the system, for example, Mitra Kalita invented a whole new career trajectory for herself that became a model for other women. Other women have also successfully founded their own media businesses, often multiple ones, albeit for less glamorous profits than Huffington. Bonnie Bernstein (b. 1970) was a radio news and sports director before moving to television at ESPN, ABC, and CBS Sports. In 2013, Bernstein became vice president of Content and Brand Development for Campus Insiders; she created and hosted original programming for the network and designed brand extensions. Bernstein is now the founding CEO of Walk Swiftly Productions and a consultancy, Velvet Hammer Media. A former college gymnast, she has served in several capacities for nonprofits that promote youth sports. She partially credits her journalistic and entrepreneurial achievements to skills learned through sports: resilience, teamwork, patience, and willingness to take risks.

Michelle Ferrier, for another example, develops entrepreneurial ventures around online communities. Having received highly racist and violent hate mail about her newspaper columns, Ferrier founded TrollBusters, which she calls "online pest control for journalists."[95] TrollBusters monitors the social media accounts of journalists who have been attacked, collects the relevant digital evidence, coaches journalists on what to do when attacked, and provides reputation repair services.

Some women combine new and legacy media. In 1992 Maria de Lourdes Hinojosa Ojeda (b. 1961) cofounded *Latino USA* for National Public Radio; she still anchors the Peabody Award–winning show. Now the Mexican American Hinojosa has moved from television and radio journalism to producing podcasts. She is the founder, president, and CEO of Futuro Media Group, a nonprofit that creates multiplatform content from the perspective of people of color. *Hispanic Business* magazine designated her three times as one of the 100 Most Influential Hispanics. Robyn Moreno has also done work across platforms, as she says, "to stand up, speak out, and highlight the stories and issues that were not being told about women, Latinas, and people of color." The *Today* show contributor has been the founding contributing editor of *Cosmo for Latinas*; editor in chief of TheFetching.com; host of Pockets of Pretty, on the I Heart Radio Talk network; nominated for an Emmy as the host of a nationally syndicated lifestyle show; and the editor in chief and copresident of Latina Media Ventures, now a digital-first company.

Passion and Moral Commitment

Moral commitments come to the fore in the careers of nearly all the women journalism and media leaders. A 2023 report about twenty women of color who are prominent and transformational media executives highlights their shared agenda: creating inclusive and representative newsrooms by including diverse voices, experiences, and stories.[96] Perhaps it can also be said that diversity (using that term or some other word) of audiences, staffs, platforms, and so forth is no longer the purview of women and people of color and is instead widely celebrated at both individual and institutional levels, but certainly women are explicit about this. They embrace their power to transform news organizations and expand definitions of what constitutes news. Citing their own experiences, they often urge women to bring their "authentic," "whole" selves, knowledge, and perspectives to the job. The principle of authenticity is not new: decades ago, Ann Barkelew was discussing being "real" as opposed to always being right. And the moral passion is at odds with financial security, as it was with the feminist media projects of Frances Stevens. Now Iman Zawahry has dedicated herself to making stereotype-free films that show Muslim girls and women as they really are.

These commitments and principles come together in Amanda Zamora and Emily Ramshaw, the cofounders of The 19th*.[97] The site, whose content is free, reimagines politics and policy coverage through a gender lens. The language of The 19th* website emphasizes empowerment and passion: The staff is "a community of passionate people committed to serving women, LGBTQ+ and people of color"; it's a "passion project"; and Zamora is "passionate about dismantling systems of oppression."

Zamora and Ramshaw initially had not envisioned cofounding a newsroom. Then working at the *Texas Tribune*, they were theoretically trying to reimagine political journalism that didn't automatically foreground white men's perspectives.[98] Like many earlier feminist leaders, they "prioritized a different way of working together, with processes that centered our team and our audience in everything from hiring and internal workflows to budget setting, product design and development and our editorial strategy."[99] If all leaders face critical junctures, for Zamora and Ramshaw, it was the COVID-19 pandemic, which forced an end to their funding tour and made fostering a sense of community a challenge. They persevered, however, and launched in 2020.[100] When Zamora stepped down as publisher, she explained that she was "accustomed to assimilation and compartmentalization being requisite for 'success'" and had internalized "many conflicting lessons about the value of my voice and experience." But she essentially spelled out her leadership philosophy in thanking her staff for teaching her "persistence, courage, vulnerability, humility, accountability, allyship and so much more. . . . If I am a better leader today than 4 years ago, it's because of the space and grace you gave me."[101]

Robyn Moreno says, "'You can't be what you can't see' nor can we change what we don't acknowledge." Indeed, many minoritized people agree that having people like them in "critical, decision-making, shot-caller positions shows that 'if you can see it, you can be it.'"[102] This may underestimate difficulties. In the increasingly corporatized and bureaucratic context of the media industry, and given structural barriers at the societal level or economic constraints at the personal level, women and especially women of color may be stymied, even if they do see great role models. The best-intentioned top executive may not always be able to ensure a well-run workplace where people thrive, collaborate, and produce richly diverse content. Yet, as Veerasingham describes, it is important to understand that "'the only' actually can be a change agent."[103] Either way, without leaders with a vision for alternatives and committed to making efforts to bring about that vision, transformations will not happen. And the women profiled in this volume show how to be change agents.

Notes

1 Patricia Hill Collins, *Intersectionality as Critical Social Theory* (Duke University Press, 2019), 160–167.

2 Godwin served 2021 to 2024. The shortness of the tenure, however, says as much about general precarity in journalism and high turnover in new organization leadership as it does about women's place in journalism leadership.

3 Luba Kassova, *From Outrage to Opportunity: How to Include the Missing Perspectives of Women of All Colors in News Leadership and Coverage*, report for the Bill & Melinda Gates Foundation, 2022, 10.

4 Erika Falk and Erin Grizard, *The Glass Ceiling Persists: The 3rd Annual APPC Report on Women Leaders in Communication Companies*, Annenberg Public Policy Center, 2003. www.annenbergpublicpolicycenter.org/the-glass-ceiling-persists-the-third-annual-appc-report-on-women-leaders-in-communication-companies/.

5 Kirsten Eddy, Amy Ross Arguedas, Mitali Mukherjee, and Rasmus Kleis Nielsen, "Women and Leadership in the News Media 2023: Evidence from 12 Markets," Reuters Institute, March 8, 2023, https://reutersinstitute.politics.ox.ac.uk/women-and-leadership-news-media-2023-evidence-12-markets. The United States was the highest of the twelve countries. The Reuters researchers acknowledged that gender is not binary but ascertained that every editor in their sample identifies as either a woman or a man. I must note here that references to women and men here always refer to people who present or self-identify as women and men.

6 Women's Media Center, *Women of Color in U.S. News Leadership 2023*, December 2023, 28, https://womensmediacenter.com/reports/women-of-color-in-u-s-news-leadership-2023.

7 Paul Farhi, "'What a Stupid Question': Trump Demeans Three Black Female Reporters in Three Days," *Washington Post*, November 9, 2018, www.washingtonpost.com/lifestyle/style/what-a-stupid-question-trump-demeans-three-black-female-reporters-in-two-days/2018/11/09/272113d0-e441-11e8-b759-3d88a5ce9e19_story.html. A similar dynamic played when Donald Trump appeared at the 2024 conference of the National Association of Black Journalists.

8 Richard Maxwell Brown, "Timothy, Elizabeth," in *Notable American Women 1607–1950: A Biographical Dictionary*, ed. Edward T. James (Belknap/Harvard Press, 1971), 465–466.
9 Don Avery, "Franklin, Ann," in *Biographical Dictionary of American Journalism*, ed. Joseph P. McKerns (Greenwood Press, 1989), 236–237.
10 Karen A. Weyler, *Empowering Words: Outsiders and Authorship in Early America* (University of Georgia Press, 2013), 165–203.
11 Elizabeth F. Hoxie, "Walter, Cornelia Wells," in *Notable American Women 1607–1950: A Biographical Dictionary* Vol III, ed. Edward T. James (Belknap/Harvard Press, 1971), 536–537.
12 Maryland State Archives (Biographical Series), "Mary Katherine Goddard (1738–1816)," MSA SC 3520-2809, https://msa.maryland.gov/megafile/msa/speccol/sc3500/sc3520/002800/002809/html/2809bio.html.
13 Maryland State Archives, "Mary Katherine Goddard."
14 More family connections: Eleanor's father was journalist Robert Patterson, who succeeded his father-in-law as editor (Hoge 1966); Eleanor's brother Joseph Medill Patterson worked at the *Tribune* and in 1919 founded the *New York Daily News*. In 1939, Joseph Medill Patterson's daughter, Alicia Patterson (1906–1963), who began reporting for the *Daily News* in 1927, founded *Newsday*.
15 Paul F. Healy, *Cissy: The Biography of Eleanor M. "Cissy" Patterson* (Doubleday, 1966).
16 The two families also intersect as competitors. Eventually the Grahams bought the *Times-Herald*. Katharine Graham's son was the *Post*'s publisher from 1979 to 2000, her daughter Elizabeth Morris "Lally" Graham Weymouth (b. 1943) is senior associate editor, and her granddaughter Katharine Weymouth was publisher from 2008 to 2014. In 2021, the *Post* got its first woman executive editor, Sally Buzbee, previously the executive editor and senior vice president of the Associated Press.
17 Euell A. Dixon, "Linda Johnson Rice (1958–)," Black Past, March 29, 2020, www.blackpast.org/african-american-history/linda-johnson-rice-1958/.
18 Sarah Hale (unbylined editorial), "Introduction," *Ladies' Magazine*, January 1828, 3. https://babel.hathitrust.org/cgi/pt?id=nyp.33433081685715&seq=21.
19 Paul S. Boyer, "Hale, Sarah Josepha Buell," in *Notable American Women 1607–1950: A Biographical Dictionary* Vol I, ed. Edward T. James (Belknap/Harvard Press, 1971), 110–114.
20 Boyer, "Hale," 113.
21 Boyer, "Hale,"114.
22 Madeleine B. Stern, "Stephens, Ann," in *Notable American Women, 1607–1950*, ed. Edward T. James (Belknap/Harvard Press, 1971), 360–362. The magazine's title varied slightly over the years.
23 Susan Brownmiller was one of the sit-in's leaders.
24 Jan Whitt, *Women in American Journalism: A New History* (University of Illinois Press, 2008), 39.

25 Kimberly Wilmot Voss, *Re-Evaluating Women's Page Journalism in the Post World War II Era: Celebrating Soft News* (Palgrave MacMillan, 2018), 13.

26 Voss, *Re-Evaluating Women's Page Journalism*, 3–4, 12, 15.

27 Kimberly Wilmot Voss and Lance Speere, "Marjorie Paxson: From Women's Editor to Publisher," *Media History Monographs* 10, no. 1 (2007–2008), https://blogs.elon.edu/mhm/files/2017/03/mhmjour10-1.pdf, 7.

28 Voss and Speere, "Marjorie Paxson," 4.

29 Voss, *Re-Evaluating Women's Page Journalism*, 135–152.

30 Voss and Speere, "Marjorie Paxson," 8–10. Ironically, Paxson's first full-time job was covering hard news for United Press International starting in 1944, but she lost that position two years later having signed a waiver agreeing to quit when the war was over, 3.

31 Voss and Speere, "Marjorie Paxson," 8.

32 This does not necessarily entail pay equity. A NewsGuild–Communications Workers of America study of fourteen Gannett-owned unionized newsrooms found significant pay inequity on the editorial side. Women earned 83 percent of men's median salaries. Women of color earned 73 percent of white men's median salaries. The *Arizona Republic*, also the most diverse newsroom included in the study, had the largest gender and racial pay disparities. Gabby Miller, "New Union Study Claims Gender, Racial Pay Inequities in Gannett Newsrooms," *Columbia Journalism Review*, April 27, 2021, www.cjr.org/local_news/new-union-study-claims-gender-racial-pay-inequities-in-gannett-newsrooms.php. Meanwhile, in 2023, five white current and former Gannett employees sued Gannet, alleging that they were either fired or passed over for promotions in favor of less-qualified women or people of color in compliance with the company's diversity policy. Nick Robertson, "Gannett Sued for Alleged 'Discrimination Against Non-Minorities,'" *The Hill*, August 24, 2023, https://thehill.com/regulation/court-battles/4170321-gannett-sued-for-alleged-discrimination-against-non-minorities/.

33 Dorothy Butler Gilliam, "On the Cusp of Feminism with Dark Brown Skin," in *The Edge of Change*, ed. June O. Nicholson, Pamela J. Creedon, Wanda S. Lloyd, and Pamela J. Johnson (University of Illinois Press, 2009), 54.

34 Gilliam, "On the Cusp," 55.

35 Gilliam, "On the Cusp," 55–56.

36 Gilliam, "On the Cusp," 57–60.

37 Brooke Kroger, *Nellie Bly: Daredevil, Reporter, Feminist* (Three Rivers Press, 1995).

38 Black was similarly willing to engage in trickery and stunts to produce sensationalized exposés for the *San Francisco Examiner*.

39 "Manning, Marie," in *Notable American Women, 1607–1950: A Biographical Dictionary 1607–1950: A Biographical Dictionary*, ed. Edward T. James (Belknap/Harvard University Press, 1971), 491–492 (no author listed).

40 *Encyclopaedia Britannica*, "Elizabeth Meriwether Gilmer," updated December 12, 2024, www.britannica.com/biography/Elizabeth-Meriwether-Gilmer.

41 Cited in David Gudelunas, *Confidential to America: Newspaper Advice Columns and Sexual Education* (Transaction Publishers, 2008), 19.

42 Jean Lutes, *Front Page Girls: Women Journalists in American Culture and Fiction, 1880–1930* (Cornell University Press, 2006), 65–93.

43 Gudelunas, *Confidential to America*, 34.

44 Gudelunas, *Confidential to America*, 62.

45 Crowley also wrote a child-care column for the *Chicago Sun*.

46 Janice Pottker and Bob Speziale, *Dear Ann, Dear Abby: The Unauthorized Biography of Ann Landers and Abigail Van Buren* (Dodd, Mead, 1987), viii.

47 Marjory Louise Lang, *Women Who Made the News: Female Journalists in Canada, 1880–1945* (McGill-Queen's Press, 1999), 42.

48 Lang, *Women Who Made the News*, 42.

49 Ruth Westheimer, "Feb. 10, 1990: My Time as a Sniper," *New York Times*, September 24, 2010, www.nytimes.com/2010/09/26/opinion/etc-westheimer.html; James Barron, "Speaking, Not Sexually, with Dr. Ruth at 90," *New York Times*, June 3, 2018, www.nytimes.com/2018/06/03/nyregion/dr-ruth-westheimer.html.

50 Kate Storey, "How Dr. Ruth Made a Career of Sex—and Became a Cultural Icon Along the Way," *Esquire*, June 1, 2019, https://web.archive.org/web/20220103064604/https:/www.esquire.com/entertainment/movies/a27546207/ask-dr-ruth-westheimer-hulu-documentary-true-story/.

51 Jeannette Catsoulis, "'Ask Dr. Ruth' Review: Out of the Bedroom and into the Light," *New York Times*, May 2, 2019, www.nytimes.com/2019/05/02/movies/ask-dr-ruth-review.html.

52 "Erma Bombeck Biography: A Life of Humor," *Essortment*, https://web.archive.org/web/20131124210608/http://www.essortment.com/erma-bombeck-biography-life-humor-20298.html.

53 Stacey M. Robertson, *Parker Pillsbury: Radical Abolitionist, Male Feminist* (Cornell University Press, 2007). Revolution's publisher was Susan B. Anthony (1820–1906). George Francis Train, a controversial, eccentric entrepreneur, gave money to launch the paper in 1868, as did his friend, David Melliss. But after twenty-nine months and in debt for $10,000, Anthony gave the paper to Laura Curtis Bullard, a far less radical women's rights activist who had written for *The Revolution*. Bullard became editor; Edwin A. Studwell, a Quaker abolitionist and financier, was publisher. Stanton and Anthony had refused to run advertisements for patent medicines. Bullard's family had grown rich selling patent medicine, and "her" *Revolution* did advertise patent medicines. For its last four months, two men edited and published *The Revolution*.

54 "About *Ms.*," December 31, 2001, https://msmagazine.com/about/. In 2005, Steinem, Jane Fonda, and Robin Morgan cofounded the Women's Media Center, which "works to make women visible and powerful in the media."

55 Steve Kramer, "Uplifting Our Downtrodden Sisterhood: Victoria Earle Matthews and New York City's White Rose Mission, 1897–1907," *Journal of African American History* 91, no. 3, (2006): 243–266. Matthews was a prominent founding member of a national Black women's organization that hoped to improve Black women's image by inculcating middle-class domestic

values. In 1896, convinced that factionalism was limiting Black women's political effectiveness, the two organizations joined to become the National Association of Colored Women.

56 Elizabeth Bancroft Schlesinger, "Croly, Jane Cunningham," in *Notable American Women 1607–1950: A Biographical Dictionary*, ed. Edward T. James (Belknap/Harvard Press, 1971), 409–411. Croly was later editor of *Cycle Magazine* (which she founded) and *Home-Maker Magazine*.

57 White helped found the General Federation of Women's Clubs. She was elected president of the International Federation of Women's Press Clubs in 1891; after finishing her term as NEWPA president, she established the Boston Woman's Press Club, and the next year she was elected vice president of the International League of Press Clubs, a mixed-sex organization.

58 Elizabeth V. Burt, "New England Woman's Press Association, 1885–1982," in *Women's Press Organizations, 1881–1999*, ed. Elizabeth Burt (Greenwood Publishing Group, 2000), 153–163.

59 Burt, "New England Woman's," 159.

60 Burt, "New England Woman's," 160.

61 Gil Klein, "NPC in History: Women's National Press Club Centennial," March 3, 2019, www.press.org/newsroom/npc-history-womens-national-press-club-centennial.

62 Klein, "NPC in History." Hobby (1905–1995) herself had worked for the *Houston Post* and married the *Post*'s president, a former governor of Texas. Over the years, Colonel Hobby became in turn the *Post*'s executive vice president (as such, featuring more women's news), president, publisher, and co-owner (with her husband). Hobby also served in the Eisenhower administration as the inaugural secretary of the Department of Health, Education, and Welfare (later renamed).

63 www.jaws.org/.

64 Tina V. Hall, "Association for Women in Sports Media, 1987–Present," in Elizabeth Burt, *Women's Press Organizations, 1881–1999* (Greenwood, 2000), 21–26.

65 Anne Ritchie, oral interview with Melissa Ludtke. Interviews conducted February 21, 1993, March 2, 1993, January 15, 1994, and May 6, 1994, *Washington Press Club Foundation*, http://beta.wpcf.org/oralhistory/ludint.html.

66 Melissa Ludtke, *Locker Room Talk: A Woman's Struggle to Get Inside* (Rutgers University Press, 2024), ix, 307, 313, 321–325.

67 Ludtke, *Locker Room Talk*, x, 15.

68 Robert D. McFadden, "Betsy Wade, First Woman to Edit News at *The Times*, Dies at 91," *New York Times*, December 3, 2020, www.nytimes.com/2020/12/03/business/media/betsy-wade-dead.html.

69 One excuse for not hiring women was the assumption that women would quit journalism to devote themselves to child-rearing. Yet, women were fired upon announcing their pregnancies. Dorothy Gilliam described a related problem for her at the *Washington Post:* Gilliam, who did not know other women at the *Post* with children, initially got permission to work part-time

after her daughter's birth, but it was withdrawn after other reporters complained about this special treatment and asked to work part-time, too (including men who wanted to write "the great American novel)." Gilliam, "On the Cusp," 49–50. After Gilliam's second pregnancy, she left the *Post*.

70 Quoted in Peggy Simpson, "The Shock of Recognition," *Quill* 78 (February 1990): 34.

71 Le Anne Schreiber, *Midstream* (Viking, 1990), 5.

72 Alice H. Eagly and Linda L. Carli, *Through the Labyrinth: The Truth about How Women Become Leaders* (Harvard Business School Press, 2007).

73 Marilyn Loden said she coined the term to emphasize corporate structure and culture while speaking at a 1978 feminist conference on what thwarted women in the workplace—when other panelists emphasized women's poor self-image and self-deprecation. Others have also claimed credit for the concept, including Hewlett-Packard executive Katherine Lawrence, who said she mentioned it at a 1979 conference. The coinage first appeared in print in 1984, when *Adweek* quoted *Family Circle* editor Gay Bryant referring to the "glass ceiling." Penelope Green, "Marilyn Loden, Who Championed a Feminist Metaphor, Dies at 76," *New York Times*, September 3, 2022, www.nytimes.com/2022/09/03/us/marilyn-loden-dead.html.

74 Marilyn Loden, *Feminine Leadership or How to Succeed in Business without Being One of the Boys* (Times Books, 1985).

75 Helen Fisher, "The Female Mind," in *The Edge of Change: Women in the Twenty-First-Century Press*, ed. June O. Nicholson, Pamela J. Creedon, Wanda S. Lloyd, and Pamela J. Johnson (University of Illinois Press, 2009), 27–41, 31.

76 Fisher, "Female Mind," 33.

77 Sally Helgesen, *The Web of Inclusion: A New Architecture for Building Great Organizations* (Currency Doubleday, 1995). She deemphasizes gender differences in this book, in which the *Miami Herald* is one of five cases. In contrast, in *The Female Advantage: Women's Ways of Leadership* (Currency Doubleday, 1990), which draws from analysis of women-led organizations, Helgesen developed the notion of the spiderlike web of inclusion she specifically associated with women.

78 Judy B. Rosener, "Ways Women Lead," *Harvard Business Review* 68, no. 6 (1990): 119–125; Alice H. Eagly and Linda L. Carli, "The Female Advantage: An Evaluation of the Evidence," *Leadership Quarterly* 14, no. 6 (2003): 807–834. Eagly and Carli comment that people usually judge leadership based on what they deem appropriate—given their cultural perceptions—behavior for men and women.

79 Tracy Everbach, "The Culture of a Women-Led Newspaper: An Ethnographic Study of the *Sarasota Herald-Tribune*," *Journalism & Mass Communication Quarterly* 83 (2006): 477–493.

80 Margaret Gallagher, "Reporting on Gender in Journalism," *Nieman Reports*, Winter 2001, https://niemanreports.org/articles/reporting-on-gender-in-journalism/.

81 Kay Graham's becoming publisher did not bring a significant increase in the number of women at the *Washington Post*. In 1970, its 272 reporters, columnists, and editors included 33 women.

82 Michael Davis, *Street Gang: The Complete History of Sesame Street* (Viking Penguin, 2008), 124.

83 WMC report, 2023,18.

84 WMC report, 23.

85 WMC report, 14–15.

86 Carolyn G. Cline, *The Velvet Ghetto: The Impact of the Increasing Percentage of Women in Public Relations and Business Communication* (IABC Foundation, 1986). See also, Elizabeth L. Toth, Carolyn G. Cline, and IABC Research Foundation, *Beyond the Velvet Ghetto* (IABC Foundation, 1989).

87 Parallel worries about journalism turning into a pink ghetto, but without any hope of women getting top leadership positions, also turned out wrong.

88 Michal Rakowski and Joanna Broniewska, "Women in Public Relations," March 6, 2023, Enterie, https://enterie.com/women-in-public-relations/.

89 Rakowski and Broniewska, "Women in Public Relations."

90 Jeff Bercovici, "AOL Buys the Huffington Post for $315 Million," *Forbes*, Feb 7, 2011, www.forbes.com/sites/jeffbercovici/2011/02/07/aol-buys-the-huffington-post-for-315-million/?sh=198df1015ed8.

91 In 2021 Danielle Belton, who is Black, became HuffPost's editor in chief. She increased the number of Black newsroom employees. Kate Palmer is co–executive editor.

92 Bryan Robinson, "How Arianna Huffington Is Transforming America's Workplace to Benefit You," *Forbes*, January 15, 2020, www.forbes.com/sites/bryanrobinson/2020/01/15/how-arianna-huffington-the-meryl-streep-of-businesswomen-is-transforming-americas-workplace/?sh=54abbee73bb4.

93 Huffington apparently once collapsed from exhaustion and awoke seriously injured.

94 Robinson, "How Arianna Huffington."

95 Michelle Ferrier, "TrollBusters: When Passion and Purpose Meet the World's Needs," Srfreedex, November 25, 2021, https://srfreedex.org/journaliststoo-trollbusters-when-passion-and-purpose-meet-the-worlds-needs-michelle-ferrier-united-states.

96 Women's Media Center, "Women of Color," 5, 28, 30–32.

97 The asterisk signifies that the Nineteenth Amendment remains unfinished given that it primarily benefitted white women.

98 Amanda Zamora, "A New Chapter for Leadership at The 19th," The 19th*, September 29, 2023, https://19thnews.org/2023/09/amanda-zamora-stepping-down-publisher/. Zamora, now advising The 19th News Network, hopes to invent new paths for co-reporting and collaborating with "partner publishers" who republish The 19th stories. She has founded Agencia Media, a consultancy focused on civic engagement that uses user research and participatory design.

99 Zamora, "A New Chapter."

100 Abby Johnston and Amanda Zamora, "The 19th Is Building a Network for More Equitable News," *The 19th**, January 23, 2024, https://19thnews.org/2024/01/announcing-the-19th-news-network/.

101 Zamora, "A New Chapter."

102 Women's Media Center, "Women of Color."

103 Women's Media Center, "Women of Color," 17. She also acknowledged the "negatives" of being the only woman of color in a room.

Mary Ann Shadd Cary

Embodying Intersectionality through 1850s Newspaper Publishing

Tracy Everbach

Mary Ann Shadd Cary defied the conventions of her time, ignoring the social expectations for women, Black people, and newspaper publishers, and bravely forging her own identity in the pre–Civil War 1850s.[1] She was the first Black woman to publish a newspaper in North America. Although she was born in the United States, she believed Canada was the most hospitable place for Black people to live freely, and she published the *Provincial Freeman* in Canada West (now known as Ontario, Canada). Her legacy as a Black press pioneer has been overshadowed by other Black women activists and abolitionists such as Harriet Tubman and Sojourner Truth. This is partially because her barrier-breaking occurred outside the United States, but also because she was a complex figure whose independence and outspokenness angered those within her own communities; she often drew ire. Many of her peers believed women should remain silent and support men, should not have a public role, and certainly should not publish a newspaper. Mary Ann Shadd Cary clearly did not care what they thought.[2]

Seventy years before women earned the right to vote in the United States, when women were expected to maintain a domestic role and be "ladies," and Black people were considered less than whole persons, Shadd Cary gained an education, founded and taught in schools, published pamphlets and newspaper pieces, spoke publicly, and eventually became a suffragist and lawyer. From a modern theoretical lens, she was the embodiment of intersectionality. As noted by Patricia Hill Collins, Black women's political activism is a response to social problems facing a community of people,[3] in this case, free Black people and those who escaped enslavement. Black women have long been involved in community activism aimed at the needs of groups harmed by social injustice.[4] After centuries of assaults on Black men and expectations for women to fight for solidarity and loyalty, Mary Ann Shadd Cary's journalistic work epitomized the intersectionality of race, sex, social class, and opposition to injustice.[5] Her actions reflect how Black women have always brought a lens and perspective to activism and advocacy that reflected their perspectives and political needs as Black women.

Background

Mary Ann Shadd came from a Delaware family of free Black abolitionists who helped enslaved people escape from the American South via the Underground Railroad. Her father, a community activist, worked as a shoemaker. The Shadds were free, light-skinned, and middle class; therefore, they possessed more privilege than many Black Americans. Mary Ann, born in 1823 in Wilmington, Delaware, was one of thirteen children. When she was ten, Abraham and Harriett Shadd moved their family to West Chester, Pennsylvania, about thirty-five miles from Philadelphia, so she, the eldest daughter, could attend a private Quaker school.[6] Her father instilled in her his philosophy that educated Black people should work to uplift others less fortunate.[7] Graduating six years later, she returned to Wilmington and opened a school for Black children, offering them an opportunity unavailable to her in Delaware. Mary Ann Shadd later taught in Norristown, Pennsylvania; Trenton, New Jersey; and New York City—places with strong Black communities.

In 1849, Shadd became involved in politics when she wrote a letter to Frederick Douglass, expressing her thoughts on improving conditions for Black people in northern states. She argued for Black education, investment in agriculture, and interracial political action. She also railed against those she described as corrupt Black ministers.[8] As a Black woman in a society that oppressed both her race and sex and required her public silence, this was provocative. The same year, Shadd wrote a twelve-page pamphlet, *Hints to Colored People of the North*, which encouraged Black people to work against factors she believed led to their oppression. The pamphlet lamented Black people's displays of expensive goods and practices, such as costly entertainment and public dinners, which Shadd said did not advance equality. She advocated for "education, moral refinement, and economic self-sufficiency" to fight racism and argued these elements were key for Blacks to be accepted by white society.[9]

In 1850, the United States passed the Fugitive Slave Act, which required the U.S. government to cooperate with slave hunters from the South to catch and return formerly enslaved Black people who had escaped, even in northern states that had outlawed slavery. Outraged that people could be returned to enslavers and that the federal government participated in capturing them, Mary Ann Shadd and her brother, Isaac, left the United States for Canada, where slavery had been outlawed since 1833. At the time, hundreds of other Black people were emigrating to Canada West. One newspaper estimated that three thousand Black people fled northern U.S. cities after the passage of the act.[10] Some abolitionists viewed Canada as friendlier to Black people than the United States. Starting in the 1920s, Black Americans established several settlements near the U.S.-Canada border, in part because the Canadian government offered them inexpensive land. The Canadian government also welcomed Black American fugitives from slavery as laborers.[11]

Henry Bibb, a formerly enslaved person who escaped from the South, had emigrated to Canada around the same time as the Fugitive Slave Act was ratified. He and his wife, Mary Miles Bibb, founded Canada's first black newspaper, the *Voice of the Fugitive*.[12] Shadd became friends with the couple, who helped persuade her to move to Windsor, Canada, and to raise funds to establish a school. She started her school with the help of the American Missionary Association (AMA). However, she eventually had a falling out with the Bibbs and the AMA. Shadd opposed these groups' advocacy and charitable donations for refugees from the United States because she believed Black people should be independent and self-sufficient. She accused the AMA "of catering to the slave mentality developed by those who were owned by white Christians."[13] Shadd believed Black people should assimilate into Canadian society and that schools should be integrated, while the Bibbs and the AMA backed racially segregated schools and communities.[14] For daring to express her controversial opinions publicly and failing to bow to male leadership, she garnered the condemnation of the Bibbs and their allies. To further extend her voice, and to the outrage of the Bibbs, she wrote and published a pamphlet, *A Plea for Emigration or Notes of Canada West, in its Moral, Social and Political Aspect: With Suggestions Respecting Mexico, W. Indies and Vancouver.* Her pamphlet encouraged formerly enslaved people and other Black people to come to Canada West, by employing data, moral arguments, and persuasive language to recruit them.[15] Shadd cited evidence that contradicted portrayals of Canada West as a distant, frozen land in which crops would not grow and people would face perilous weather conditions.[16] She rejected the advice of other prominent Black leaders and others who felt warmer climates would be more hospitable to Black people and therefore encouraged emigration to Africa, the Caribbean, and Latin America. Shadd provided climate data, temperatures, soil and mineral analyses, crop and fruit growth, and livestock information that showed Canada offered resources and opportunities. In her pamphlet, she also advocated for racially integrated churches and communities and sought to educate her readers on laws and politics to inform and assist with their self-efficacy.[17] Her aim was to uplift, but as Jane Rhodes notes, the pamphlet also "romanticized British rule and elevated white institutions to the pinnacle of civilization."[18] Shadd believed that because of racism and racist policies in the United States, Canada was the answer for Black people, although she failed to acknowledge the extent of racism in Canada.

After she published *A Plea for Emigration*, the *Voice of the Fugitive* criticized her, taunting her for printing errors. The Bibbs' newspaper portrayed her as a hypocrite for condemning the AMA when she had accepted money from the association to operate her school. This led to a writing war between Henry Bibb and Shadd.[19] As she published unsigned letters in another newspaper criticizing Bibb, the *Voice* published criticism of her as less than honest, questioned her virtue, and called her "vile," among other labels.[20] As a consequence of the public disagreements and attacks, the AMA ultimately closed her school, saying that she was not sufficiently religiously evangelical.[21] Devastated and concerned about the *Voice*'s power, Shadd decided in 1852 to fight back by establishing her own newspaper.

Critical Juncture

Mary Ann Shadd knew she needed advice from influential Black men to start her newspaper, especially since "ladies" were expected to remain in the background of public life. She invited Samuel Ringgold Ward, an abolitionist and minister who had escaped enslavement, to join and advise her. Ward previously had published several newspapers, including the *Impartial Citizen*.[22] When the Bibbs caught wind of her intentions, they published slanderous insults in the *Voice*, accusing her of being a liar, manipulator, and of being deviant by failing to uphold the Victorian notion of womanhood.[23] Nevertheless, Shadd persisted, and the *Provincial Freeman*'s first issue was published on March 24, 1853, with Samuel Ringgold Ward listed as its editor. Because Ward lived in Toronto while the paper was published from Windsor, it quickly became clear that Mary Ann Shadd ran the operation. A statement under the masthead indicated that "all communications should be sent to the correspondence editor, M.A. Shadd," using her initials.[24] Eventually, in 1854, she signed her full name to editorials and dispatches from her travels, further reinforcing her leadership role. Also, when she traveled to fundraise, she often left her younger sister, Amelia Shadd, in charge, giving women powerful positions in society for this era. Her younger brother, Isaac Shadd, also assumed a role in the paper's operation.[25]

The *Provincial Freeman* eventually moved from Windsor to Toronto, where Shadd continued to publish controversial content, including articles highlighting the failings of the abolitionist movement, advocating for women's rights, and expressing a Black nationalist ideology that urged the unification of Black people.[26] Shadd also became instrumental in forming the Provincial Union, an organized abolitionist group in Canada West, whose members "pledged themselves to the common purpose of self-help, racial uplift, and abolition without the involvement of white antislavery leaders."[27] Samuel Ringgold Ward was elected the union president in 1854; other leaders included Toronto activist Thomas F. Cary (Shadd's future husband). By this time, Shadd revealed that she was the M. A. Shadd listed under the *Freeman*'s masthead.

The newspaper published editorials calling for Black, white, and other activists to bond together for racial equality; Black people could and should assimilate into Canadian society, which Shadd claimed would treat them as equals. It aimed to serve as a conduit for abolitionists to communicate with each other.[28] Shadd wrote, "If a sound moral and religious influence, when exerted by individuals, can accomplish great good, surely the influence of large communities, such as this, for instance, in its character of a liberal, powerful, well-sustained Province, can do more."[29] She also used the *Freeman* for criticism—of the poor writing submitted by some of the readers, of shortcomings in the abolitionist movement, and of denial of women's rights.[30] She lashed out at both men and women for failing to support her as a woman editor, noting a double standard in which men newspaper editors could behave "peacock like" and call "public attention to their individual merits and high importance," while she was forced into a secondary role.[31] At a time when most women remained in the domestic sphere, Mary Ann Shadd traveled freely around Canada West and northern U.S. states, serving as the spokesperson and fundraiser for the *Freeman*. She published commentary lamenting the inequality of the sexes, reflecting feminist sensibilities. Although the abolitionist movement advocated freedom for all races, many abolitionist activists embraced the idea that women were inferior and should let men assume any public activism roles.

The newspaper was funded by investors and subscribers whom Shadd recruited during her travels in the United States and Canada. Other funds came from loans and business advertisements. The *Freeman* constantly needed to remind subscribers to pay their bills. Investors could buy shares of the newspaper for eight dollars each.[32] While Shadd controlled the paper and wrote much of the editorial content, the newspaper also carried other authors and letters to the editor from readers, and it reprinted articles from other publications. Samuel Ringgold Ward wrote for the first edition, and reprints came from writers and journalists such as Harriet Beecher Stowe, an advocate for women's rights, and Jane Swisshelm, a feminist who criticized the notion that "men were the best judges of proper behavior and activities for women."[33] Shadd also reprinted articles from the *New England Farmer*, including one about making girls independent.

For economic and practical reasons, including its location near several Black communities, Shadd moved the newspaper to Chatham, about fifty miles from Windsor, in 1856. Part of her attraction to the town was the fact that her parents and other relatives had settled nearby. Shadd took on the role of "agent" for the *Freeman*, which was a way for her to be in charge without being listed as the editor, deflecting criticism from those who believed women should not serve in such a public role. However, her strong watchdog writing continued to dominate its pages. She castigated the white founders of Dawn, a Black Canadian community, including the Reverend John Scoble, who had been involved in the AMA's withdrawal of funding to her Windsor school. She accused Dawn's white leaders of financial mismanagement and of having a white supremacist mentality; she encouraged Black residents to seize control of Dawn.[34] Retaliatory attacks in public meetings and lectures did not deter her. She continued to investigate and serve as a muckraking journalist. She exposed a white missionary, Rev. Hiram Wilson, alleging that the money used to pay for his home, a large brick mansion, came from funds designated for emigres.[35] When the U.S. Supreme Court issued the 1857 *Dred Scott v. Sanford* decision that declared Black Americans were not full citizens under the law, she argued the ruling was confirmation of the failure of the abolitionist movement in the states; it vindicated her support of Canada West as an optimal home for free and formerly enslaved Black people.

In 1856, when Shadd Cary was thirty-two, she married Thomas F. Cary. They had met when he invested in her newspaper. They had an unconventional marriage: Thomas lived in Toronto, where he worked as a barber, and Mary Ann lived nearly three hundred kilometers away in Chatham, where she published the *Freeman*. Thomas already had three children from a previous marriage. Despite their living separately, they had two children together, a daughter, Sarah Elizabeth, born in 1857, and a son, Linton, born in 1861. Thomas was supportive of his wife's public role. Unfortunately, he became ill and died in 1860, before their son was born.

Shadd Cary consistently faced difficulties financing her newspaper, largely because of a lack of paid subscriptions. By 1857, an economic depression in Canada led to further money problems. Due to the birth of her daughter and financial concerns, she stopped publishing the *Freeman*. The paper did reappear later with a few issues in 1858 and 1859, listing Isaac Shadd and Mary Ann Shadd Cary as editors. By then, the newspaper changed course and supported emigration to Africa and the West Indies in addition to Canada. Shadd Cary wrote that while racism and racial discrimination existed in Canada, she still believed the territory was more hospitable to Black people than the United States. Ultimately, the *Freeman* stopped publishing for good in 1859.

After Thomas's death in 1860, Shadd Cary and her sister operated a school in Chatham. As the Civil War broke out in the United States, Black people began leaving Canada to serve in the Union army. Shadd Cary returned to the United States for several years to recruit Black soldiers for the army.[36] Although she worked as a recruiter throughout the war, by its end she continued to consider herself Canadian and even held a Canadian passport.[37]

Resolution

In 1867, convinced that conditions had improved for Black people in the United States with the Emancipation Proclamation and Reconstruction, Shadd Cary returned, living in Detroit, across the river from Windsor, Canada. By 1869, she had settled in Washington, D.C., where she worked as a teacher in Black schools, eventually becoming a school principal. Concerned about a dearth of job opportunities in Washington for Black people, including her own children, she became a labor activist.[38] When Howard University established a law school in 1869, Shadd Cary became part of its first cohort, although she did not finish her degree until 1883, when she was sixty years old. In her later years, she advocated for women's rights, joining with white suffragists such as Elizabeth Cady Stanton and Susan B. Anthony to fight for the vote. She wrote about the suffrage movement in Black newspapers, urging Black people to join the cause and support women's rights. She even tried to register to vote in 1871 in D.C. (unsuccessfully). As Rhodes points out, "As a citizen, a resident of the District, a taxpayer, an African American, and a woman, she believed she had a legitimate claim to be heard."[39] Shadd Cary implored white women to recognize Black women as equals under the law. She eventually joined the temperance movement, which she considered a vehicle to work toward gender and racial equality.[40]

After earning her law degree in 1883, she practiced law in Washington, although she encountered obstacles in the white, male-dominated profession.[41] During her last decade of life, she lived in Washington, D.C., with her children. Her daughter, Sarah, worked as a teacher and later owned a dress-making business, and her son, Linton, worked as a messenger in the U.S. House of Representatives. Linton Cary died young, at thirty-two, even before Mary Ann Shadd Cary died of stomach cancer in 1893, at seventy.

Conclusion

Mary Ann Shadd Cary rebelled against traditional gender roles, social boundaries, social status, and conventions.[42] Her parents raised her to be an outspoken leader, and she did not care what people thought of her. She was willing to speak out when the conventions of the time dictated that women should be reticent and restrained. Women were viewed as passive and men as aggressive; Black people were considered ignorant and white people educated, and white people were accustomed to benefitting economically from enslaved Black people and Black poverty.[43] To amplify her voice and uplift her community, Shadd Cary founded the *Provincial Freeman* to share her writing, theories, and knowledge on how Black people could be successful by relocating to Canada.

Her actions reflected what Patricia Hill Collins refers to as the power of testimony: the actions of Black women to speak out for Black communities.[44] She was savvy enough to circumvent the social constraints of the time by listing a man as the editor, but those in her community knew she was the true brains and talent behind the dispatches in the *Provincial Freeman*. Shadd Cary was willing to endure condemnation and deprecation from different constituents, including those who thought her behavior was unladylike, those who told her to hold her tongue, and those who considered her arrogant and her behavior shameful. She defied the social structure and social mores for her race and sex. Not only did the white power structure criticize her, but so did people within her own community whose failings she critiqued. Despite the discrimination and oppression working against her, she continued fearlessly to resist expectations for Black women in the mid-to-late 1800s. Shadd Cary spoke out for the good of her community and the betterment of the people within it. Her social action within this framework thus reflects Collins's conceptualization of Black feminist activism.[45] As Collins notes, Black women's leadership and political activism have been essential to social change.[46] "Whether a moral, ethical tradition that encouraged African American women to relinquish the so-called special interests of issues as women for the greater good of the overarching community, or a survival politics that meant if Black women didn't do it, it simply didn't get done, Black women's reproductive labor was placed in service of Black communities."[47]

Shadd Cary's activism and journalism set a precedent for other independent and fearless activist Black journalists, such as Ida B. Wells-Barnett, a younger contemporary of Shadd Cary's who gained prominence forty years later, during the Jim Crow era, and indeed gained greater prominence in both scholarship and the popular imagination.[48] The younger journalist also published a newspaper and through her editorials called attention to racism and violence against Black people in the American South. During the 1890s in Memphis, Wells-Barnett chronicled the lynching and beating of Black people employing graphic language and straightforward data, methods Shadd Cary previously used in her pamphlet on the advantages of Canada. Like Shadd Cary, Wells-Barnett also fled north, first to New York City after whites burned down her Memphis newspaper.[49]

Although her groundbreaking work took audacity and courage, Shadd Cary did benefit from certain privileges because of her identities. These included being born into a free Black family, her economic status as middle class, her light skin that gave her social status, and her education that allowed her to work as a teacher, journalist, and lawyer. As Carol B. Conaway writes, Shadd Cary possessed blind spots about those who did not come from the same social class as she.[50] While she advocated for the financial independence and education of Black people and encouraged them to assimilate into middle-class society, she overlooked the fact that many were not able to achieve these goals, particularly those who had been enslaved and denied a formal education. Conaway notes that Shadd Cary's philosophy of Black self-efficacy was "not at all conducive to the needs of most black people in the lower and enslaved classes."[51] In addition, Shadd Cary saw Canada West as a bastion of freedom for Black people that would offer desegregated education by race and sex as well as economic opportunities, none of which materialized during her lifetime. While her reasoning sometimes was flawed, her work consistently offered hope and optimism to her community.

In her seminal book, *Ain't I a Woman*, bell hooks lauded Black feminists of Shadd Cary's era for their persistence, strength, and defiance: "The 19th century black female was a woman of action. Her suffering, the harshness of her lot in a racist, sexist world, and her concern for the plight of others motivated her to join the feminist struggle. . . . She did not rely on any group to provide her with a blueprint for change. She was a maker of blueprints."[52] Both using and circumventing the prevailing ideology, Shadd Cary challenged the narrative of the day. She became educated; founded, taught in, and led schools; didn't hesitate to share her opinion through written and spoken word; withstood harsh criticism; had an unconventional marriage; published a newspaper; became a suffragist; and earned a law degree. She never gave up her principles of uplifting her community.

Notes

1 Jane Rhodes, *Mary Ann Shadd Cary: The Black Press and Protest in the Nineteenth Century*, (Indiana University Press, 1998), 1–24.
2 Carolyn Calloway-Thomas, "Mary Ann Shadd Cary: Crafting Black Culture Through Empirical and Moral Arguments," *Howard Journal of Communications* 24, no. 3 (2013): 239–256; Carol B. Conaway, "Racially Integrated Education: The Antebellum Thought of Mary Ann Shadd Cary and Frederick Douglass," *Vitae Scholasticae* 27, no. 2 (2010): 86–101; Nneka D. Dennie, "'Leave That Slavery-Cursed Republic': Mary Ann Shadd Cary and Black Feminist Nationalism, 1852–1874," *Atlantic Studies* 18, no. 4 (2021): 478–493.
3 Patricia Hill Collins, *Intersectionality as Critical Social Theory* (Duke University Press, 2019), 167–168.
4 Collins, *Intersectionality*, 168.
5 The classic conceptualization of intersectionality comes from Kimberlé Crenshaw, "Demarginalizing the Intersection of Race and Sex: A Black Feminist Critique of Antidiscrimination Doctrine, Feminist Theory, and Antiracist Politics," University of Chicago Legal Forum (1989), 139–167. See also, bell hooks, *Ain't I a Woman: Black Women and Feminism* (South End Press, 1987).
6 Conaway, "Racially Integrated Education," 87.
7 Rhodes, *Mary Ann Shadd Cary*, 19.
8 Rhodes, *Mary Ann Shadd Cary*, 21.
9 Rhodes, *Mary Ann Shadd Cary*, 22.
10 Rhodes, *Mary Ann Shadd Cary*, 29.
11 Conaway, "Racially Integrated Education," 94; Rhodes, *Mary Ann Shadd Cary*.
12 Rhodes, *Mary Ann Shadd Cary*, 35.
13 Conaway, "Racially Integrated Education," 89.
14 Conaway, "Racially Integrated Education," 89.
15 Calloway-Thomas, "Mary Ann Shadd Cary," 239–246.
16 Calloway-Thomas, "Mary Ann Shadd Cary," 245–246.
17 Calloway-Thomas, "Mary Ann Shadd Cary," 246–253.
18 Rhodes, *Mary Ann Shadd Cary*, 44.
19 Rhodes, *Mary Ann Shadd Cary*, 47–49.
20 Rhodes, *Mary Ann Shadd Cary*, 57–66.
21 Rhodes, *Mary Ann Shadd Cary*, 68.
22 Rhodes, *Mary Ann Shadd Cary*, 71.
23 Rhodes, *Mary Ann Shadd Cary*, 72–73.
24 Rhodes, *Mary Ann Shadd Cary*, 74; Elizabeth Cali, "'Why Does Not Somebody Speak OUT?': Mary Ann Shadd Cary's Heteroglossic Black Protofeminist Nationalism," *Vitae Scholasticae* 32, no. 2 (2015): 32–48.
25 Rhodes, *Mary Ann Shadd Cary*, 93.
26 Cali, "'Why Does Not Somebody Speak OUT?,'" 33–34; Rhodes, *Mary Ann Shadd Cary*, 87.
27 Rhodes, *Mary Ann Shadd Cary*, 94.

28 Rhodes, *Mary Ann Shadd Cary*, 84–85.
29 Rhodes, *Mary Ann Shadd Cary*, 85.
30 Rhodes, *Mary Ann Shadd Cary*, 88–89.
31 Rhodes, *Mary Ann Shadd Cary*, 98.
32 Rhodes, *Mary Ann Shadd Cary*, 97.
33 Rhodes, *Mary Ann Shadd Cary*, 92.
34 Rhodes, *Mary Ann Shadd Cary*, 105–106.
35 Rhodes, *Mary Ann Shadd Cary*, 107.
36 Rhodes, *Mary Ann Shadd Cary*, 157.
37 Rhodes, *Mary Ann Shadd Cary*, 162.
38 Rhodes, *Mary Ann Shadd Cary*, 170.
39 Rhodes, *Mary Ann Shadd Cary*, 194.
40 Rhodes, *Mary Ann Shadd Cary*, 197.
41 Rhodes, *Mary Ann Shadd Cary*, 209.
42 Conaway, "Racially Integrated Education," 90.
43 Collins, *Intersectionality*, 164.
44 Collins, *Intersectionality*, 160.
45 Collins, *Intersectionality*, 158–159.
46 Collins, *Intersectionality*, 168; Carol B. Conaway, "Rhetorically Constructed Africana Mothering in the Antebellum: The Racial Uplift Tradition of Mary Ann Shadd Cary," *Journal of Pan-African Studies* 2, no. 1 (2007): 4–14.
47 Collins, *Intersectionality*, 169.
48 The next chapter in this volume is about Wells-Barnett.
49 Lori Amber Roessner and Jodi Rightler-McDaniels, *Political Pioneer of the Press: Ida B. Wells-Barnett and Her Transnational Crusade for Social Justice* (Lexington Books, 2018), xxix–xxxvii.
50 Conaway, "Racially Integrated Education," 93–95.
51 Conaway, "Racially Integrated Education," 100.
52 bell hooks, *Ain't I a Woman: Black Women and Feminism*, 193.

Ida B. Wells

Journalist Warrior for Justice

Michelle Duster

In 2020, almost ninety years after her death in 1931, Ida B. Wells was awarded a posthumous Pulitzer Prize Special Citation "for her outstanding and courageous reporting on the horrific and vicious violence against African Americans during the era of lynching."[1] Two years prior, the *New York Times* "Overlooked" series featured the decades-delayed obituary observing, "Wells is considered by historians to have been the most famous black woman in the United States during her lifetime, even as she was dogged by prejudice, a disease infecting Americans from coast to coast."[2] By the time she was well into her sixties, "she had been a firsthand witness to the realities of slavery, the freedom and hope of Reconstruction, the terror of post-Reconstruction, the implementation of Jim Crow laws, the Spanish-American War, World War I, segregation, mass migration, riots, and women fighting and winning the right to vote."[3]

Born in 1862, Wells came of age during a time when formerly enslaved people embraced their newfound freedom and worked to build businesses, institutions, and communities. The progress made within a few decades of freedom was followed by a violent backlash. She used journalism as a tool to fight against oppression, violence, lawlessness, and terror in order to effect change. Within this transformational time period, as a woman and African American, Wells had to contend with both racism and sexism. Describing herself as having a "tempestuous, rebellious, hard-headed willfulness" that sometimes got her in trouble,[4] she struggled to fit into the constricting Victorian-era role for women that emphasized "piety, purity, submissiveness, and domesticity."[5]

As an African American who refused to cower and a woman who refused to submit, Wells defied almost every social rule of her era at the turn of the nineteenth century. She was outspoken, independent, opinionated, feisty, and willing to fight for what she believed was always her rightful place at the front of the line. When the world told her to be afraid and settle for second-class citizenship, she fought with her pen to challenge hypocrisy and the status quo. During the peak of her journalism career, she gained national and international attention and was the most "widely known colored woman in the world."[6] Over a century later she is considered a pioneering investigative journalist and civil rights icon.[7]

Background

On July 16, 1862, Ida B. Wells was born into slavery in Holly Springs, Mississippi. The South was fighting to maintain its way of life: if the Confederacy had won, Wells would more than likely have been enslaved her entire life, as her parents and grandparents had been. As a result of the Emancipation Proclamation, Wells became free as an infant in January 1863. As the oldest of Jim and Elizabeth Wells's eight children, she helped with household chores and the care of her younger siblings. Her mother, a famous cook, was a deeply religious woman who maintained a strict and disciplined household. Ida mentioned in her autobiography how she "had tried to keep herself spotless and morally clean as my slave mother had taught me."[8]

During the Reconstruction period that followed the issuing of the Emancipation Proclamation, the Freedman's Bureau worked to rebuild the South and address the needs of the millions of formerly enslaved people, including by building schools. Wells's parents put a high value on education, and with the 1866 establishment of Shaw University (now Rust College) in Holly Springs she had the opportunity to attend school. Her father, a skilled carpenter, was a trustee at the school. Her mother also attended until she learned to read the Bible.[9]

Most of her teachers were white women, missionaries from the North who flooded the South after the war in order to teach the newly freed and largely illiterate population. Their teachings focused on religion, European history, culture, and home economic skills and emphasized Victorian roles and manners for women. As a voracious reader with limited reading choices, Wells read the Bible many times and novels written by white authors such as Louisa May Alcott, Charles Dickens, and the Bronte sisters that featured characters who overcame adversity. Being encouraged to focus on her studies was a privilege compared to the endless drudgery of forced unpaid labor that was the reality of slavery. Wells describes a carefree childhood and her young self as a "light hearted schoolgirl."[10]

Wells grew up in an atmosphere of great change, with a sense of hope and new opportunities. Her father enthusiastically embraced his newfound right to make his voice heard as someone who could cast a vote. He also became involved in political activism, attending and hosting meetings with fellow citizens. Despite progress in civil rights during this Reconstruction period, there was also backlash and danger, which Ida vaguely understood during her childhood given her mother's visible fear when her husband attended meetings.[11] Many former enslavers resented losing their "property," having to pay wages for what had before been "free" labor. Most of them considered themselves to be a superior race and were enraged at the idea of having to compete on an equal basis with those they considered inferior. After all, the Ku Klux Klan was founded in Pulaski, Tennessee, and a massive race riot had taken place in Memphis in 1866.[12]

In the midst of this atmosphere, Jim Wells encouraged Ida to read the newspaper to his friends. Because teaching enslaved people to read was illegal, there was high illiteracy among the formerly enslaved.[13] Newspapers exposed Ida to civic and political ideas and information at a young age. She was also influenced by her father's enthusiasm for embracing his rights to build a business, own property, and vote. She also watched her father rebound from attempts to intimidate or control him. His livelihood was threatened when he voted a different way than his former enslaver had demanded. In retribution his tools were locked away. Rather than give in to intimidation, Jim moved the family from the property of his former enslaver to a house across the street and purchased new tools.[14]

This willingness to stand up for one's convictions and suffer the consequences must have made an impression on Ida.

In 1878, both of Ida's parents and young brother died within a few days from yellow fever. At sixteen years old, she decided, despite the discouragement of well-meaning family friends, to take on the responsibility of caring for all five of her remaining siblings; the youngest was two years old. Because of her educational attainment, combined with the high demand for teachers, she concluded that teaching would be the best-paying job for her. She got a position at a rural school by passing an exam. With her paternal grandmother helping to take care of the children, she took on the job and all financial responsibilities. She managed to take care of everyone for a couple of years until her grandmother had a stroke. She soon accepted her aunt's invitation to move with her two youngest sisters to Memphis, where the aunt lived. Her brothers stayed in Mississippi to apprentice as carpenters; her other sister, who was disabled, lived with a different aunt and died young.

Black women worked outside the home much more than white women. Enslavement had denied them the luxury of not working. Meanwhile, Black men generally earned less than white men, so two incomes were needed. Many African American women in urban areas worked as unskilled laborers or as servants, laundresses, cooks, nurses, or seamstresses.[15] As a teacher, Wells became part of a small yet vibrant middle-class community in Memphis. She enjoyed an active social life and exchanged numerous letters with various "suitors" from different cities. She was a young woman who enjoyed nice clothes, the theater, attending lectures, outdoor activities, and traveling.

Early Journalism

Finding teaching to be monotonous, Wells sought creative outlets. She joined lyceums—social and literary clubs—where people recited poetry and essays, performed skits, and engaged in debates. One had a newsletter called the *Evening Star*, which she described as a "spicy" journal consisting of news, literary notes, and criticism, and was read aloud at the end of the meetings. After the editor moved to another town, Wells was selected as the editor. This was her first foray into writing and public speaking. She also was interested in acting and squeezed money out of her salary to take elocution classes to learn how to be an effective public speaker.[16] These gave her a creative and social outlet, and she developed a following as a writer and speaker.

During her twenties, Ida B. Wells gradually transitioned from a teacher into a full-time journalist, newspaper editor, and co-owner. The activities she was involved in gave her the training and preparation to handle what was to become of her life. The world she inhabited was going through enormous social change, with increasing violence against African Americans as well as the rolling back of rights that she had experienced during Reconstruction. She was not interested in marriage or motherhood. She had already spent years as a caretaker of her siblings, and although she still sent money for her siblings' care, she enjoyed the freedom that came with only worrying about herself. In this environment, she navigated the ever-present danger of physical attack as well as the attacks or insinuations that she had improper interactions with men, about her sisters really being her children, and other suggestions that she was "unladylike"; all these made her vigilant about protecting her reputation.

Wells had to navigate constrictive gender roles, and she suffered indignities specific to her race. As an African American, she had to navigate a post-Reconstruction era that was increasingly restrictive, humiliating, and violent. Although the social structure positioned white women as those who needed to be protected, Black women did not receive the same consideration. In fact, the popular debasing images represented in minstrel shows and vaudeville were those that Wells had to counter. Her feisty personality, strong-willed temperament, outspokenness, and independent streak put her at odds with the demure and deferential way women were expected to carry themselves. And her unwillingness to accept race-based second-class treatment put her in a state of constant frustration and tempered rage.[17]

Segregation laws were enacted in waves, such that the rights that Wells had grown up with were slowly dismantled. For example, Wells had ridden the "ladies' coach" between her home in Memphis and her job in Woodstock without issues until 1881, when Tennessee passed a law that segregated public transportation.[18] In 1883 and 1884, while commuting on the Chesapeake, Ohio, and Southwestern Railroad, Wells was ordered at least twice to move to the "colored car," which doubled as the smoking car, although she had purchased a first-class ticket.[19] In 1883, she put up a fight and three men forcibly removed her; in 1884 she left the train on her own accord. In both of these cases, Wells sued the railroad, arguing that these cars were separate and vastly unequal. In the 1884 case, she won her original lawsuit; but the railroad appealed to the Tennessee Supreme Court, which overturned the case in 1887.[20]

Most women writers wrote for church publications, which, because these were considered extensions of the gospel, provided no remuneration.[21] They tended to focus on subjects that fit with the dominant and expected role of hearth and home. Wells wrote a few articles about women's roles in society but quickly branched out to what would today be categorized as "hard news"—politics, social issues, and common sense issues that concerned the Black community.[22] During this time of rapid change and decreasing rights, she questioned and challenged leadership, laws, politics, and more. With her plain writing style and accessible language, she increased her following.

A minister soon asked her to write letters for the *Living Way*—a weekly Baptist newsletter. Writing under the pen name "Iola" about her indignity, the *Living Way* started her on the path to using journalism as a form of activism.[23] In *The Reason Why the Colored American Is Not in the World's Columbian Exposition*, a pamphlet she cowrote and edited a decade later, she outlined how Black women were not given the same level of respect as white women. Their conditions were unequal. "White men pass through these 'colored cars' and ride in them whenever they feel inclined to do so, but no colored woman however refined, well-educated or well-dressed may ride in the ladies, or first-class coach in any of these states unless she is a nursemaid traveling with a white child."[24]

She also constantly struggled with money. Usually, her only compensation was complimentary copies of the printed paper. In 1885, W. Calvin Chase, editor of the *Washington Bee*, rebuked her in his paper after she suggested that writers be paid for their essays.[25] Things changed in 1886 when she got the opportunity to write for *American Baptist*, which paid her one dollar a week and helped grow her reputation and audience.[26] Her articles were reprinted in numerous newspapers across the country—*New York Age*, the *Detroit Plaindealer*, *Indianapolis World*, and *Gate City Press* (Kansas City, MO), just to name a few. She gained such a reputation that she was nicknamed "Princess of the Press."

Wells attended the Afro-American Press Convention in Louisville in 1887—the first to include women—where she was elected assistant secretary. Two years later, at the National Colored Press Association convention in Washington, D.C., she met many well-known people such as Frederick Douglass, the renowned abolitionist, orator, author, and publisher and founder of the well-respected *North Star* newspaper; and T. Thomas Fortune, the influential publisher of the *New York Age*.[27] Gaining the attention and support of these leaders was pivotal in the ascendancy of Wells's career. Wells was so highly regarded that she was elected secretary of the organization. Fellow journalist Lucy W. Smith commented, "No writer, the male fraternity not excepted, has been more extensively quoted none struck harder blows at the wrongs and weaknesses of the race."[28]

Soon after the meeting, the Reverend Taylor Nightingale; a minister of a large congregation in Memphis, and J. L. Fleming, a newspaper publisher from Marion, Arkansas, asked Wells to become editor of the *Memphis Free Speech and Headlight*. The men had merged their two newspapers, Memphis *Free Speech* and *Marion Headlight*. She agreed on the condition that she also become part owner. She promptly shortened the name to *Memphis Free Speech*. Her partnership brought about scrutiny regarding her looks and suggestions she would never attract a husband; commentators suggested that "beauty and genius are not always companions."[29]

For financial reasons, Wells continued to juggle her full-time teaching job with the newspaper work, at least until she wrote an 1891 article about racially segregated schools. Black teachers were paid less than their white counterparts and typically worked in overcrowded and underresourced schools; Wells also argued that some teachers were less qualified and got their positions through questionable means. The response to her criticism was the nonrenewal of her teaching contract. Out of a job, she threw herself full-time into growing the newspaper.

Critical Juncture

In March 1892 Wells was in Natchez, Mississippi, selling subscriptions to her newspaper, when three of her friends were lynched. Thomas Moss, Calvin McDowell, and Will Stewart co-owned the People's Grocery in Memphis.[30] It rivaled a white-owned store, which irritated that owner. To eliminate the competition, a controversy was concocted, which led to the three Black men defending their property. They were arrested and lynched while in police custody.

Thomas Moss and his wife Betty were two of Wells's closest friends in Memphis; she was the godmother of their daughter. A letter carrier, Moss was an upstanding citizen who had invested in the grocery store as a second income. During his route, he brought Wells news about the community. Wells knew he and his partners were innocent and that they were murdered in order for white men to obtain social and economic control. Stunned by the cold-blooded murders, Wells responded in her *Free Speech*. One article encouraged retribution for the murders. Others urged the Black community to boycott streetcars and white-owned businesses and, for those who could afford it, to leave Memphis entirely for freedom and equality in other parts of the country. Thomas Moss's last words were, "Tell my people to go West." And Wells wrote, "The city of Memphis has demonstrated that neither character nor standing avails the Negro if he dares to protect himself against the white man or become his rival. . . . There is therefore only one thing left that we can do. Save our money and leave a town which will neither protest our lives and property, nor give us a fair trial in the courts, but takes us out and murders us in cold blood when accused by white persons." Sure enough, as many as six thousand people left the city, settling in many places across the country including Arkansas, Kansas, Oklahoma, and California.

The calls for boycotts were so successful that the managers of the streetcar company, which was losing money, visited Wells. Knowing how influential she was, they asked her to encourage people to resume riding the cars. Thrilled that the boycotts were having their desired effect, Wells decided to continue writing. She had armed herself, knowing that her life was in danger.

Wells investigated other lynchings. She found that many people who had committed no crimes had been lynched under the guise of protecting white women. In several instances, the liaisons between white women and Black men were consensual; rape was cried out only when their relationship was discovered. Wells asserted that white men used the accusation of rape to justify brutalizing Black men and thereby terrorize the Black community. Committing murder with impunity was a way to impose social and economic control over people who had three decades before been considered property. In an 1892 editorial, Wells asserted, "Nobody . . . believes the old thread-bare lie that Negro men assault white women. If Southern white men are not careful they will over-reach themselves and a conclusion will be reached which will be very damaging to the moral reputation of their women."

The editorial sent the city's white leadership into an uproar. Edward Carmack, the editor of the Memphis *Commercial Appeal*, questioned how the editorial's writer was allowed to live. The *Evening Scimitar* was even more precise: "It will be the duty of those whom he has attacked to tie the wretch who utters these calumnies to a stake . . . brand him in the forehead with a hot iron and perform upon him a surgical operation with a pair of tailor's shears."[31] Mobs set out to destroy both the paper that published the editorial and its authors. They tortured Rev. Nightingale. They would have tortured Fleming if he hadn't left town. The mob then destroyed the newspaper office. They never got to Wells because she was attending an African Methodist Episcopal Church convention in Philadelphia. She only learned about the violence to her partners and threats to her life when she went to New York City from Philadelphia and T. Thomas Fortune told her the news.

Wells realized she could never go back to Memphis. But, she was more determined than ever to tell an even bigger audience the truth about the lawlessness that was pervasive across the South. Fortune, along with his business partner Jerome Peterson, agreed that she would write for his *New York Age* and become a one-quarter owner in exchange for her *Free Speech* subscription list.[32] So, at the age of thirty, Ida B. Wells started a new life in a new city. She was a single woman with nothing but the clothes she had with her while traveling. Using the pen name "Exiled," Wells wrote about atrocities taking place in the South. She wanted people in the North to get firsthand accounts of the brutal reality of lynching. She wanted people to be horrified and to act on behalf of change.

The articles were compiled into a detailed pamphlet called *Southern Horrors: Lynch Law in All Its Phases* about cases of lynching and other levels of violence.[33] This led to speaking engagements arranged by Black women's clubs along the Northeast Corridor. A year later, Ida went international, giving speeches in the United Kingdom and elsewhere overseas. Frederick Douglass asked her to come to Chicago for a few months to help him write and produce a pamphlet to distribute at the 1893 World's Columbian Exposition. *The Reason Why the Colored American Is Not in the World's Columbian Exposition* pamphlet was a response to the absence of African American representation at the fair. The four contributors to the pamphlet—Wells, Frederick Douglass, Ferdinand L. Barnett, and Irvin Garland Penn—explained how African Americans were treated as second-class citizens and chronicled their contributions, which were excluded from the fair. Barnett was an established Chicago-based attorney who focused on civil rights issues as well as the founder and editor of the *Conservator* newspaper—the first Black-owned paper in Chicago. Penn was a well-known publisher of the *Afro-American Press* and secretary of the Freedman's Aid Society of the Methodist Episcopal Church.

Resolution

Although Ida B. Wells's journalism career catapulted her into international fame and she became an influential voice, she was chronically stressed about money. She had lost all of her income when her printing press was destroyed. All of her expenses were covered when she traveled to Great Britain, but she herself received no financial compensation.[34] She had no permanent or stable place to live: she had only been in Brooklyn for a year, Chicago for a few months, then traveled across the United States giving speeches; her aunt and sisters were in California, and she couldn't return to the South. This was unsustainable.

When she was asked to return to England in 1894, she found a way for more than her expenses to be paid. She asked her British host for two pounds a week.[35] Moreover, the editor of the *Daily Inter-Ocean* newspaper agreed to pay her to write a column ("Ida B. Wells Abroad") from England. This chronicle of her tour also gave her critics an opportunity to try to discredit her. She and her adversaries exchanged editorial debates in newspapers. Some insults hurled at her by Edward Carmack of the *Memphis Commercial Daily* included "notorious negro courtesan, disreputable colored woman, half-cultured hater of all things Southern, saddle-colored Sapphira . . . malicious wanton, and infamous slanderer."[36] Wells skillfully used the insults to hold a mirror to the United States and gain attention in the white press. She let her adversaries show themselves as vile, violent, and vindictive.

Moreover, she contrasted her experience abroad with that in her own country. She described how she felt free to move about in public spaces without being accosted or questioned, a level of freedom that she didn't enjoy at home. For example, in her March 24 article from Liverpool, she commented on how a "colored" person could enjoy transportation, hotels, restaurants, theaters, churches, and more in ways that were like "being born into another world."[37] The way Wells was treated and regarded with dignity and respect by the British was in stark contrast to the insulting minstrel depictions of Black women in the United States.[38]

Upon her return to the United States, she hoped to have a committee raise funds to support a year-long domestic speaking tour where she could help form antilynching leagues across the country. That did not happen, but she spent a year traveling throughout the country giving speeches, for which she charged a fee.[39] She also compiled information for her most well-known pamphlet, *A Red Record*, which documented lynchings of 1892, 1893, and 1894.[40]

Within three years after her entire world was turned upside down, she finally found a level of financial stability and emotional support. In 1895, she published her pamphlet, which is now considered to be one of her most substantial pieces of journalism, married Ferdinand L. Barnett, and settled in Chicago.[41] She hyphenated her last name to Wells-Barnett, and the couple had four children in eight years. From that point forward, until her death in 1931 at age sixty-eight, she juggled motherhood and marriage with her continued activism. Among other reforms in which she was a leader, she cofounded several organizations, including two that still exist: the National Association of Colored Women Clubs, and the National Association for the Advancement of Colored People (NAACP).

Wells-Barnett became a leader in the women's suffrage movement. She cofounded, in 1913, the Alpha Suffrage Club in Chicago. The organization promoted the enfranchisement of all women and was active in helping Black women to engage in the public sphere, including by working to elect African Americans to city offices. Indeed, Wells and other suffragists from Chicago went to Washington, D.C., to attend a parade organized by the National American Woman Suffrage Association (NAWSA) on the day before the 1913 presidential inauguration of Woodrow Wilson. On the day of the march, the head of the Illinois delegation told Wells that the NAWSA had decided to keep the delegation entirely white. The NAWSA leadership had decided that all African American suffragists, including Wells, should march at the end of the parade, not with the white Illinois women. Instead of going to the back, however, Wells waited with spectators. Then, as the delegation walked by where she stood, she slipped into the formation. She linked arms with her white suffragist colleagues and marched front and center.

Conclusion

Ida B. Wells (known as Ida B. Wells-Barnett after marriage) was a trailblazer who used journalism as a tool for activism. Because she chose to chronicle the details of the murders of her friends Thomas Moss, Calvin McDowell, and Will Stewart and investigate other lynchings, she put her life in danger. Her constant urging to boycott Memphis streetcars and white-owned businesses caused people to threaten her into silence. Still she spoke up, urging people to leave Memphis, and a mass exodus ensued. Her refusal to be silent and dedication to investigating, tabulating, and telling the truth about lynching in excruciating detail propelled her to a national and eventually international platform. She traveled throughout England and the United States over the course of several years in addition to distributing a pamphlet at the World's Fair in order to gain domestic and global attention to the realities of lynching and more generally of Black people's lives. Her goal was to effect societal change. She faced physical danger, economic loss, personal character attacks, and social alienation. Despite it all, she focused on using her voice to fight for justice and equality. She needed people to know that framing Black people (mostly men) as "dangerous" was an excuse to "justify" terror and violence on an entire community.

She subtly expressed in more of her private writings that she faced loneliness and suffered chronic financial stress but refused to compromise on her interests or principles. She forged ahead. As a single woman with an all-consuming career, she realized that she didn't fit the societal expectations of what women should be or aspire to be. She hadn't been particularly interested in becoming a wife or mother at the age when most women were focused on marriage and child-rearing. She clearly enjoyed travel and adventure, although she traveled for work, not leisure.

She followed her heart and principles to use journalism to counter false narratives and expose truths to impact laws, policies, and social structures. Her refusal to be silenced, her willingness to put herself on the line, and her incredible attention to detail and facts led her to appeal to the court of public opinion regarding lawlessness and terror. Her bravery, stubbornness, and commitment to making sure the world knew about the brutal and graphic truths about lynching made an impact during her lifetime and left firsthand accounts and data for later scholarship. The work of Ida B. Wells shows how southern political leaders in post–Civil War America enacted laws and turned a blind eye to mob violence that upheld a racial and economic caste system. She demonstrated how one voice could counter propaganda and use truth to impact change.

Notes

1 The Pulitzer Prizes, www.pulitzer.org/winners/ida-b-wells.
2 Caitlin Dickerson, "Ida B. Wells, Who Took On Racism in the Deep South with Powerful Reporting on Lynchings," *New York Times*, May 8, 2018.
3 Michelle Duster, *Ida B. the Queen: The Extraordinary Life and Legacy of Ida B. Wells* (Atria/One Signal Publishers, 2021), 93.
4 Miriam Decosta-Willis, ed., *The Memphis Diary of Ida B. Wells: An Intimate Portrait of the Activist as a Young Woman* (Beacon Press, 1995), 78.
5 Barbara Welter, "The Cult of True Womanhood: 1820–1860," *American Quarterly* 18, no. 2 (1966): 152.
6 "Ida Wells Married," *St. Paul Daily Globe*, June 28, 1895.
7 Barbara Allen, "Pulitzers Honor Ida B. Wells, an Early Pioneer of Investigative Journalism and Civil Rights Icon," Poynter.org, May 4, 2020.
8 Alfreda M. Duster, ed., *Crusade for Justice: The Autobiography of Ida B. Wells*, 2nd ed. (University of Chicago Press, 2020), 40.
9 Duster, *Crusade for Justice*, 8.
10 Duster, *Crusade for Justice*, 14–15.
11 Duster, *Crusade for Justice*, 8.
12 Mark Wetherington, "Ku Klux Klan," *Tennessee Encyclopedia*, https://tennesseeencyclopedia.net/entries/ku-klux-klan/.
13 Beth Barton Schweiger, "The Literate South: Reading before Emancipation," *Journal of the Civil War Era* 3, no. 3 (2013): 331–59, http://www.jstor.org/stable/26062071.
14 Paula J. Giddings, *Ida: A Sword Among Lions: Ida B. Wells and the Campaign Against Lynching* (Amistad Press, 2009), 26. Although the Fifteenth Amendment giving Black men the vote was passed in 1870, this incident evidently took place in 1867 because African Americans in Mississippi gained their right to vote before the right became federal law.
15 Claudia Goldin, "Female Labor Force Participation: The Origin of Black and White Differences, 1870 and 1880," *Journal of Economic History* 37, no. 1 (1977): 87–108, https://dash.harvard.edu/handle/1/2643657.
16 Wells kept detailed accounts in her diary of debts and expenditures. Because of her erratic pay, many times she borrowed money, then used a good portion of her pay against debts. For instance, on Tuesday, May 19, 1886, she wrote, "The schoolboard paid two months Sat. and I paid all outstanding debts except Menken's, Mrs. Thompson, Mr. Lott (elocution teacher); paid my board up to June 1st, sent aunt F[annie] $10 (to support her siblings), and today deposited $50 in the bank. Bought Mrs G[raham] a parasol for $2. nearly and have $15. with which to pay all others." Decosta-Willis Miriam, ed., *The Memphis Diary of Ida B. Wells: An Intimate Portrait of the Activist as a Young Woman* (Beacon Press, 1995), 66.

17 See chapters in Lori Amber Roessner, and Jodi L. Rightler-McDaniels, eds., *Political Pioneer of the Press: Ida B. Wells-Barnett and Her Transnational Crusade for Social Justice* (Lexington Books, 2018).

18 "(1866) Jim Crow Laws: Tennessee, 1866–1955," January 3, 2011, BlackPast, www.blackpast.org/african-american-history/jim-crow-laws-tennessee-1866-1955/.

19 The Chesapeake, Ohio and Southwestern Railroad Company vs. Ida B. Wells, Tennessee Supreme Court Cases, 1885 March 31, Tennessee State Library & Archives, Range 83, Section C, Shelf 6, Box Number 275, https://teva.contentdm.oclc.org/digital/collection/p15138coll18/id/121 (transcript of 1883 court case). For more information about these cases, consult Duster, *Ida B. the Queen*, 38–43.

20 *Appeal Avalanche*, "A Darky Damsel Obtains a Verdict for Damages Against the Chesapeake and Ohio Railroad: What It Cost to Put a Colored School Teacher in Smoking Car: Verdict $500" December 25, 1884, Wells, Ida B. Papers, [Box 8, Folder 11], Hanna Holborn Gray Special Collections Research Center, University of Chicago Library, https://www.lib.uchicago.edu/ead/pdf/ibwells-0008-011-01.pdf; Wells, Ida B. Papers, "Cases Argued and Determined in the Supreme Court of Tennessee," Shelby County, April Term, 1887 [Box 8, Folder 11], Hanna Holborn Gray Special Collections Research Center, University of Chicago Library, https://www.lib.uchicago.edu/ead/pdf/ibwells-0008-011-02.pdf. Indeed, the railroad complained that Wells was trying to harass the railroad, 615.

21 Gloria Wade-Gayles. "Black Women Journalists in the South, 1880–1905: An Approach to the Study of Black Women's History," *Callaloo*, no. 11/13 (1981): 143.

22 Ida B. Wells, *Ida B. Wells: The Light of Truth: Writings of an Anti-Lynching Crusader*, ed. Mia Bay (Penguin Books, 2014), xxii.

23 It is unclear why she chose that name, but family lore is that she saw her name written where the "d" looked like "o l." She liked it and decided to use it.

24 Ida B. Wells, *Ida in Her Own Words*, Michelle Duster, ed. (Benjamin Williams Publishing, 2008), 31. Mississippi, Louisiana, Texas, Arkansas, Tennessee, Alabama, Georgia, and Kentucky are the states to which she refers as enacting laws "making it punishable by fine and imprisonment for colored persons to ride in the same railway carriage as white persons unless as servants to white passengers," 30.

25 Linda O. McMurry, *To Keep the Waters Troubled: The Life of Ida B. Wells* (Oxford University Press, 1998), 93.

26 Duster, *Crusade for Justice*, 29.

27 Lerone Bennett Jr., *Before the Mayflower: A History of Black America; The Classic Account of the Struggle and Triumphs of Black Americans* (The Penguin Group, 1988), 160, 283. Some have argued that Wells was highly influenced by Fortune's social agitation philosophy. Tommy J. Curry, "The Fortune of Wells: Ida B. Wells-Barnett's Use of T. Thomas Fortune's Philosophy of Social Agitation as a Prolegomenon to Militant Civil Rights Activism," *Transactions*

of the Charles S. Peirce Society 48, no. 4 (2012): 456–82, https://doi.org/10.2979/trancharpeirsoc.48.4.456.

28 Duster, *Crusade for Justice*, 30.

29 Mia Bay, *To Tell the Truth Freely: The Life of Ida B. Wells* (Hill and Wang, 2009), 75–76.

30 Lisa A. White, "The Curve Lynchings: Violence, Politics, Economics, and Race Rhetoric in 1890s Memphis." *Tennessee Historical Quarterly* 64, no. 1 (2005): 43–61, http://www.jstor.org/stable/42628561; Linda Moore, "125th anniversary of People's Grocery lynching remembered," *Commercial Appeal*, March 9, 2017, https://www.commercialappeal.com/story/news/local/2017/03/09/125th-anniversary-peoples-grocery-lynching-remembered/98607052/.

31 Lisa A. White, "The 'Saddle-Colored Sapphira' Versus the 'Slimy Rattlesnake': The Rhetorical Melee of Ida B. Wells and Edward Carmack on the Subject of Lynching," *Tennessee Historical Quarterly* 62, no. 4 (2003): 321.

32 Duster, *Crusade for Justice*, 54; Rose Staveley-Wadham, "Ida B. Wells—Speaking Tour to Britain 1893 & 1894," *The British Newspaper Archive Blog*, March 24, 2021.

33 Ida B. Wells, *Southern Horrors: Lynch Law in all Its Phases*, 1892, https://www.gutenberg.org/files/14975/14975-h/14975-h.htm.

34 Duster, *Crusade for Justice*, 75.

35 Ida B. Wells in her April 6, 1894, letter to Frederick Douglass, *Ida From Abroad*, ed. Michelle Duster (Benjamin Williams Publishing, 2010), 113. Whether Wells ever received the compensation is unclear: in a series of letters to Frederick Douglass, Wells said that the main sponsor, Isabelle Mayo, pulled her support of the speaking tour. Wells also expressed in that April 6 letter what a huge personal and financial sacrifice the work was for her.

36 Linda O. McMurry, *To Keep the Waters Troubled: The Life of Ida B. Wells* (Oxford University Press, 1998), 214.

37 Wells, *Ida From Abroad*, 21.

38 Fannie Barrier Williams, "Great Britain's Compliment to American Colored Women," *Woman's Era* 1, no. 5 (August 1894): 1, https://search.alexanderstreet.com/view/work/bibliographic_entity%7Cbibliographic_details%7C2773974.

39 Duster, *Crusade for Justice*, 185.

40 Ida B. Wells, *A Red Record: Tabulated Statistics and Alleged Causes of Lynchings in the United States, 1892-1983-1894*, 1895, http://storage.lib.uchicago.edu/pres/2014/pres2014-0743.pdf.

41 "Ida Wells Married," *St. Paul Daily Globe*.

Mary Margaret McBride

A Journalist Finds Time, Space, and Her Pace

Sadie Couture

Throughout her forty-year career as a print journalist, writer, and radio host, Mary Margaret McBride came to many different crossroads: whether or not to continue her journalism studies despite the rescission of her aunt's financial support; whether or not to marry her college sweetheart and settle down in Missouri; whether or not to give up a grandmotherly persona and come clean about her identity to her radio listeners; whether or not to accept that her radio program was unsuited to television; whether or not to give up her show in the face of her manager's cancer diagnosis; and whether or not to continue broadcasting from her barn in the Catskills in her retirement. At all of these turning points during her long, decorated career in journalism, McBride went in the same direction—toward what she considered interesting, worthwhile, and enjoyable. However, no decision was more impactful for McBride, radio history, and the talk show format than when, in 1941, she made the difficult choice to return to a forty-five-minute program.

Background

Mary Margaret McBride was born in 1899, the eldest daughter of Missouri farmers. Due to her father's poor money management, the family frequently moved. From her rural upbringing, McBride made her way through journalism school at the University of Missouri and worked as a reporter at the *Cleveland Press* before coming to New York in the 1920s, working at the *New York Evening Mail*. She wrote sob stories and travel articles and took jobs as both a freelancer and ghostwriter.[1] McBride's early years were filled with both successes and failures, as the scrappy young journalist fought her way into a field dominated by men and characterized by precarity. Overall, however, she did well for herself throughout the 1920s: she wrote regularly for publications aimed at women, such as *Cosmopolitan*, *Good Housekeeping*, *Harper's Bazaar*, and *McCall's*, and more general interest magazines including the *Saturday Evening Post* and *Country Gentleman*. She was "one of the top (and best paid) feature writers of the decade."[2] After the stock market crash, however, like many, she found herself both out of work and out of savings. As a result, in 1934, she accepted a radio job despite her writerly ambitions.[3] She later explained, "I needed a job and I needed it quick."[4] Desperation led the thirty-five-year-old McBride to her second career, in radio, during which she hosted talk shows of varying lengths and formats from 1934 to 1954 and again starting in 1960 until shortly before her death in 1976.[5]

McBride flourished behind the microphone. She made her greatest impact on the media landscape of the mid-twentieth century as an interviewer, commentator, and radio personality. *The Mary Margaret McBride Program* (1941–1954) established, developed, and popularized many conventions of what we now know as the daily talk show format. McBride chatted with guests in a casual, unscripted way, fluidly discussing both their professional and personal lives. Her conversational style was rare in an era when tightly rehearsed shows dominated the airwaves; her approach defied the conventional genres and formats of the time.[6] McBride offered daytime listeners commentary about current events of political, social, and cultural importance; they also heard from celebrities and important figures. She became a daily presence for her millions of listeners—many of whom were women working in the home—and her relationship with these listeners was characterized by feelings of trust, closeness, and intimacy.[7] She advertised only products she was willing to endorse from her own experience (which meant that she rejected commercials for tobacco and alcohol). In any case, her commercials had the desired impact. Her fans also sent her an unprecedented amount of mail, writing to her about their personal lives and her role in them, and sending her food, gifts, and advice. She wrote a nationally syndicated column for the Associated Press, as well as numerous monographs about her life and career. Events celebrating her program pulled tens of thousands of fans—enough to fill Madison Square Garden and Yankee Stadium—and her popularity brought both financial stability and notoriety.[8]

McBride navigated, negotiated, and combatted a significant amount of gender-based discrimination throughout her career. Although many women worked on or for radio in the medium's early days, by the mid-1930s when McBride began hosting, the early flexibility in terms of gender roles had given way to institutionalized rigidity.[9] Women were mainly relegated to singing in variety shows, acting in serial dramas, or off-air support roles such as assistants, secretaries, or researchers.[10] Much of this exclusion was based on ideas about the sound of women's voices. Starting at least as early as 1924, rumors circulated that women's voices were incompatible with radio technology, that listeners would not respond to the lack of authority in women's voices, and that women were otherwise unsuitable for on-air roles.[11] These [mis]conceptions were often applied to McBride, whose voice was not deemed pleasant or fitting for radio. The press often maligned McBride's voice as well as her age, weight, marital status, and upbringing.[12] For instance, an otherwise complimentary *New Yorker* profile of McBride described her voice as sounding as if it belongs to a "naïve," "corn-fed ingenue."[13] Prominent radio critic and columnist Ben Gross characterized McBride as "*the worst* radio speaker he had ever heard."[14]

Meanwhile, a persistent gendered hierarchy between daytime and nighttime radio ensured McBride's program would be aired in the early afternoon, which was considered a challenging time slot. By the 1930s, types of programs deemed feminine, commercialized, frivolous, or irrelevant to public life were relegated to the daytime. Programs deemed important for the public good were aired during the evening. Women and "women's topics" were demarcated as daytime content, while the evening hours were allocated for men and "masculine" content despite limited evidence that listenership was starkly split along these temporal and gendered lines.[15] This balance allowed radio executives to de-emphasize and delegitimize women listeners, yet simultaneously providing content that spoke to many women and relying on these women to sustain their business models. McBride perceived her time slot as "an hour when tired young mothers nap with children, suburban matrons are on the way to the bridge club, and older women are gadding to matinees or shopping."[16] When she told her boss she wanted a morning time when people could hear her, he replied, "You've been given that time just because it is dead. If you can get listeners, we want you. If you can't, we don't."[17]

McBride occupied a feminine sphere on the radio; her program was "typecast as a women's daytime show, not much higher in prestige than the soap operas."[18] She was both restricted and enabled by her time slot, free to experiment and innovate while her style and content were critiqued according to gendered norms. Despite these obstacles, McBride persevered, making hard choices and using her skill, intuition, and dedication to her craft to carve out a place for herself in American radio.

Critical Juncture

McBride's first radio job was hosting the program *Martha Deane* on WOR six afternoons a week.[19] She was hired to play a grandmotherly figure and to wax on her fictional children, grandchildren, favorite recipes, and household tips.[20] The facade didn't last long. She forgot several of the details she was supposed to memorize, including her "grandchildren's" names. After a few weeks, although she remained Martha Deane, the thirty-five-year-old unmarried McBride revealed her true identity on the air in an outburst she later characterized as "I killed off Grandma."[21] However, her fans connected to her new, more transparent approach. As one commentator put it, "To these hundreds of thousands of women, Martha Deane is not a radio broadcaster; she is a friend, a confidante, a good neighbor who happens to communicate her jolly thoughts and ideas and gossip to them by radio."[22]

A condition of her employment was that she would recruit and sustain her own sponsors—a daunting task and unusual for the era, when it was common for a single company to sponsor a program.[23] At first, given her journalistic training, McBride was uncomfortable with the commercial aspect of *Martha Deane*.[24] However, she found the sponsors she needed and eagerly promoted them on the air, eventually growing very comfortable in her hybrid role of hosting, editorializing, and advertising, a key instance of the complex entanglements of consumerism and cultural production typical for mid-century U.S. radio.[25] Over the years McBride's commercials became legendary; "one of her casual remarks once sold eight freight-car loads of carrots!"[26] and The Mary Margaret McBride Collection in the Library of Congress is jam-packed with thank-you notes from individuals, organizations, and establishments that McBride promoted on the radio. The praise at times verges on the extreme. For instance, in a letter to McBride's manager Stella Karn, Walter Bruce of Bohack's grocery stores writes, "Dear Miss Karn: I should have known—after all, you warned me. But even then I was amazed at the response we had from Mary Margaret McBride's audience on our recent butter contest. . . . We gave up counting after 40,000 and we say again 'Mary Margaret McBride sure can pull them in.'"[27]

McBride, her guests, and her listeners came to welcome discussions of her sponsors' products. Guests could be expected to chime in. As one commentator wrote, "A three-way benefit evolves when special guests for the day support the enthusiastic endorsements of Miss McBride, add some of their own; and she, in turn, discusses the latest book of the obliging guest."[28] And when McBride ran out of time to discuss each product in-depth, she simply asked her listeners to help out, telling them, "I will just name these products and I trust you loyal people so much that I just name 'em and I know you'll go out and buy everything double because I'm not doing much commercial, see?"[29]

And listeners responded. From 1934 onward, McBride's following grew. Her fans enthusiastically organized parties at which they listened to and discussed the show, tried out the household tricks and recipes McBride mentioned, and purchased the advertised products in an effort to ensure the show's continuation.[30] *Martha Deane* was also popular with critics. Despite his initial harsh comments, Ben Gross came around and praised McBride in writing as early as 1936.[31] McBride enjoyed *Martha Deane* and its success, but she had additional ambitions. Not only did she consider herself a writer first and foremost, but she also hoped to be nationally syndicated rather than merely locally broadcast. The program was time-consuming, and although she no longer pretended to have a fictional family, she wasn't broadcasting under her own name. McBride wasn't satisfied.

In 1937 she experimented with a short-format, national show in addition to her local longer-format one. Broadcast on CBS, she used her own name on the fifteen-minute program. She ultimately dropped the new show in 1939 for multiple reasons: overwork, conflict with sponsors, and difficulty with the brief amount of time allotted to her.[32] Her discomfort with a shorter format is why it's surprising that in 1940 McBride decided—somewhat abruptly—to stop hosting *Martha Deane* and to move to another fifteen-minute program called *Columnist of the Air*, produced and sponsored by the Florida Citrus Commission. This program would be different from *Martha Deane* (but similar to her CBS show) on several registers: it was shorter, nationally broadcast, she would use her own name, and it would have a single sponsor. The program was somewhat of a disaster from the beginning: McBride immediately regretted her decision; she hated the short format and the control her sponsor wanted to have over the show.[33] The fifteen-minute slot was "so harried by young men with stopwatches that the easy geniality of her program began to wither."[34] McBride described it as her "measly fifteen minutes," adding, "Perhaps I should add that time on the network is so expensive that fifteen minutes seemed a fine big chunk to everybody but me, accustomed to three times as much."[35] As one columnist put it, "The advantage of being herself . . . was offset for Mary Margaret by the fact that 15 minutes barely gave her time to pull herself together. Once a person has talked three-quarters of an hour daily, one-quarter tends to bring on oral claustrophobia."[36]

Columnist of the Air was canceled before McBride's first contract was up; both McBride and the citrus commission considered it a bust.[37] In one of her many memoirs, McBride characterizes her time in Florida working with the citrus commission as "the beginning of disaster"[38] and "too painful to tell in detail."[39] For the second time in a decade, McBride found herself out of a job. This time, however, she didn't take the first thing that came around: "I didn't want anything except my lovely forty-five minutes back. . . . I just longed to feel warm and snug around me again the approval of the listeners who had been with me from the beginning."[40] Experiments with shorter-format programs made her realize what she was best suited to, what she enjoyed, and what her listeners responded to. McBride held out for a longer program.

Resolution

In 1941, she breathed a sigh of relief when manager Stella Karn landed her an afternoon slot on WEAF, the NBC flagship station in New York City, every weekday. After some uncertainty and tumult, she gladly settled into a steady show. McBride wrote, "I'm the happiest WOMAN in the world. . . . I'll be back at work again—back with my beloved forty-five minute program! . . . I was homesick for my forty-five minutes even before I'd finished saying goodbye to them."[41] Her relief was palpable to others: "Mary Margaret returned joyously . . . to her old 45-minute schedule, tears streaming unabashedly down her cheeks during her first broadcast."[42] *The Mary Margaret McBride Program* brought her the most stability, popularity, autonomy, and financial success of her career. Most commentators gloss over her experimentation with a shorter format, chalking it up to an erratic moment of poor judgment or a small bump in the long road to the inevitable.[43] Others ignore it.[44] However, this episode reveals much about McBride's life, her ambitions, midcentury radio, and the challenges she faced in a male-dominated industry.

First, while McBride came to love radio and the opportunities it afforded her, throughout her life she harbored an ambition to be a novelist. This girlhood calling fueled her throughout her schooling and her print journalism career; her memoirs are filled with references to "that great novel I was going to write."[45] She explained that when she was young, her two grandfathers "agreed that I certainly would be a great writer and I firmly believed them. We had it all planned out that first I would be a reporter and from that I would go on to CREATE novels."[46] McBride seemingly never quite gave up this dream, although she never produced a full-length work of literary fiction. She produced a long stream of articles, memoirs, cookbooks, and other print materials. These were mostly related to her program: memoirs and lightly fictionalized memoirs, recipes from the show, and nonfiction articles about radio. She didn't have time for much else. McBride was renowned for her detailed research, and her guests were often shocked at how much she knew about them. For instance, in 1950 radio commentator H. V. Kaltenborn proclaimed, "Gee, you remember all these things! Mary Margaret, do you do that with everybody you have as a guest? You've actually read the book!"[47] When she was producing her show, she would often stay up very late researching guests, then get up again at 5:30 A.M. to prepare. She and her manager Stella Karn spent their weekends and evenings on activities that would produce a good story for the next day.[48] This hectic schedule didn't allow for much time for personal life or leisure and certainly didn't allow much time to write.

Secondly, the highly ambitious McBride had big dreams. Dominating New York's daytime airwaves was not enough for her—she wanted to be heard throughout the country and beyond. She often couched this desire in a sweet-sounding wish that her mother in Florida could hear her program—on one of her earliest national broadcasts she talked directly to her mother.[49] Nevertheless, in other venues, McBride wasn't shy about wanting national fame. Presumably this was also fueled by a desire for legitimacy and respect that McBride sometimes lacked due to the gendered perceptions about her program.

In the radio landscape of the late '30s and early '40s, these priorities were often in conflict, forcing McBride to negotiate between them. Her daily show brought her fame and good fortune, but it was too time-consuming for her to simultaneously write the great American novel. The shorter program was nationally syndicated but much too brief to allow her personality to shine. *Martha Deane* had a fan base, but the name was the property of WOR, and she had to hide behind a character rather than truly being herself. Having a single sponsor was simple, but that simplicity came with a lack of control. In an already hostile industry, McBride's choices were not infinite, but choose she did. From 1937 to 1941, McBride chose her preferred pace over national syndication, she spoke as herself rather than as *Martha Deane*, she focused on radio over writing, and she produced her show independently rather than being safely ensconced by a single sponsor. For that brief period, she chose to take risks, betting on herself and what she considered to be the best qualities of her radio program.

These decisions allowed McBride to further develop one of her characteristic contributions to broadcasting—what she famously called the "forty-five minute tempo."[50] To contemporary listeners, the tempo of McBride's show might sound very slow. Each program mainly consisted of McBride talking at great length about seemingly unrelated topics. She did not appear to keep track of time, nor was she afraid of silences or pauses. There was little identifiable "content" in the way of guests, topics, or segments. As one commentator proclaimed, "I was convinced that Miss McBride wasn't conducting a radio program but a filibuster."[51] A December 2, 1946, *Time* magazine article about an award McBride was getting asserted, "Mary Margaret is a brilliant interviewer. With a well-controlled gush she can 'soften up' almost anyone to just the sticky consistency her listeners love. She does it with an air of dithery, appreciative interest that soon has most guests babbling as if they had known her for years. Once she had Jimmy Durante telling such pitiable stories about his youth that, before the program's end, both were sobbing."[52]

McBride often delved into a story and only after some moments of confusion did it become clear that she was tying that story in with a previous point, a plug, or a guest. For example, on her program in 1943, McBride told a long story about a radio announcer and only later linked it to one of her sponsors. Incredulous at this method, her guest—film writer and producer Fred Finklehoffe—exclaimed, "You mean to tell me that you went through that whole thing, that entire procedure there about the fellow with the blonde wig and the girl with the red hair just to get to Bohacks?!"[53] Another McBride trademark was losing her train of thought, forgetting certain details, or making mistakes. For instance, McBride once stumbled on her words and then dug deeper into her forgetfulness, laughing about it. That said, she was able to get many impactful people on her program, including Eleanor Roosevelt, President Harry Truman, Governor Thomas E. Dewey, Frank Lloyd Wright, Bob Hope, Carl Sandburg, Margaret Bourke-White, Zora Neale Hurston, Tennessee Williams, Joe DiMaggio, and the fan dancer Sally Rand.

The structure (or lack of it) of the show also contributed to the atmosphere that many listeners loved dearly. The program had very few orienting elements: the opening music and beginning few sentences, and then a brief mention of the station around the thirty-minute mark were the only real moments of regularity. Mainly, familiarity on the *Mary Margaret McBride Program* was produced by people, stories, and phrases that recurred throughout the programs. As one commentator noted, "A day's broadcast is as unpredictable as April weather."[54] The show had very little segmentation or pattern of when or how the stories, interviews, and ads would happen. Once the program began, talk flowed without any meaningful interruption. An especially notable aspect of this flow was McBride's refusal to orient the listener. As a rule, she did not announce her guests ahead of time.[55] Often, she began an interview without any warning and only later revealed details about the guest. For example, at the top of a 1945 program, after chatting with her announcer Vincent Connolly about how to structure a speech, McBride said, "Whenever I make a speech, I wonder which to do: leave 'em laughing or leave 'em crying. What do you think, David McCord?"[56] This quick pivot from meditations on speechwriting to an interview with a famed poet is typical of McBride's technique: she signaled to her listeners that she expected them to be active and engaged, that they should trust McBride to provide the necessary information, and that McBride trusted them, in turn, to listen from the beginning to the end. Through her insistence on a longer-format program and its pace and flow, she was able to charm listeners and bring them into the fold of her program.

While listeners ultimately loved McBride's pace and flow, success wasn't a guarantee when she opted for a longer-format program in 1941. McBride made many risky decisions throughout her career. Most of these ended up paying off, but all of them should be regarded as the courageous breaks with convention that they were. But she didn't do it alone. She referred to staff and guests as her "radio family."[57] Manager Stella Karn, announcer Vincent Connolly, longtime secretary and producer Mrs. D., research assistant Janice Devine, and personal friends not only were discussed on the show but also regularly appeared on the show. Her radio family filled in when guests canceled or got sick. McBride invited them on the air to chat during frequent "jam session programs," and her radio family attended all the celebratory events and shows.[58] These relationships sustained McBride, who never married or had children.

The most important relationship was with her manager Stella Karn: "Stella was my chief booster, frequent deflator, and head of my radio family."[59] Karn and McBride met while working for a church organization in 1922 and became roommates. When McBride's manager on *Martha Deane* was fired after an alcohol-fueled outburst, Karn stepped in and confidently and competently managed the program.[60] Karn organized McBride's bookings, sponsorships, and schedules but doesn't seem to have been directly involved in the conceptualization of the show, which was already established when she became manager.[61] McBride and Karn sustained an exceptionally close working and personal relationship until Karn's death in 1957. The exact nature of their bond remains a matter of much speculation.[62] Once they could afford their own apartments, Karn and McBride did not live together, but they spent most of their time together and were devoted to each other. When Karn bought a house in the Catskills in upstate New York, the women remodeled the barn for McBride to live in.[63] It was Karn's diagnosis of terminal cancer that led McBride to cancel her show.[64] Karn was the center of McBride's (radio) family. When asked, "If you had your life to live over again, what would you want to be?" Karn replied, "The manager of Mary Margaret McBride!"[65] McBride likely shared the sentiment. In both her personal and professional life, McBride did things differently from others. With the support of her chosen family, she was able to take risks and make her mark in radio.

Conclusion

While she isn't typically regarded as a household name, McBride's impact on the media landscape of today is noteworthy, and—as with many historical figures—her legacy is complex. Many conventions she developed and popularized have become beloved and mainstay features of much broadcast and audio media. For instance, conversational tone, direct address, and host-delivered ads have been appropriated widely across time and space. She actively participated in the development of America's mediated consumer culture and the media's deep entanglement with commercial interests. McBride's professional impact includes features that are loved and others that could be happily discarded.

With regard to social justice, Mary Margaret McBride led by example rather than through her words.[66] She wasn't a loud voice for women's rights, but she showed women that other worlds were possible. She both reinforced and challenged the hegemonic femininity of her era; while she supported and offered counsel to women on homemaking and child-rearing, she herself didn't choose that path, and the most important relationship in her life was with another woman. She dressed modestly and conservatively while living an independent, cosmopolitan life in New York City. She also quietly exposed her audience to the civil rights movement, winning praise from the head of the NAACP Walter White, who characterized her as having "stood courageously for principle."[67] She never discussed sexuality on her program but had guests who were rumored or known to have same-sex relationships—for instance, actress Tallulah Bankhead. Connolly—her announcer—was a "confirmed bachelor," code at the time for nonheterosexual men.

McBride's legacy is most felt where she spent most of her time: behind the mic. While women's contributions to radio history have been overwhelmingly underemphasized, women "invented and sustained some of broadcasting's most central innovations and served in key decision-making roles, and furthermore participated in the development of entire genres that spoke to them as a specific group about the interests and concerns of women's lives."[68] Mary Margaret McBride is a part of that legacy. McBride's program was experienced by some as a "magic spell right into your own heart."[69] But it resulted from the hard work, dedication, and talent of McBride and her radio family, and her decision to take up time on the airwaves.

Notes

1 Susan Ware, *It's One O'clock and Here Is Mary Margaret McBride: A Radio Biography* (New York University Press, 2005).
2 Ware, *It's One O'clock*, 139.
3 Ware, *It's One O'clock*, 137.
4 Mary Margaret McBride, "Words and Music," *The Radio Daily*, August 28, 1941, Mary Margaret McBride Papers 1926–1975, Box 8, Library of Congress, para. 4.
5 Hilmes, *Radio Voices*; Ware, *It's One O'clock*.
6 Hilmes, *Radio Voices*; Ware, *It's One O'clock*.
7 Sadie Couture, "Forging a Format: Advertising, Attention and Intimacy on the Mary Margaret McBride Program, 1941–54," *Radio Journal: International Studies in Broadcast & Audio Media* 21, no. 2 (2023):155–170.
8 Hilmes, *Radio Voices*: 277-278; Beverly Merrick, "Mary Margaret McBride, Talk Show Host: The Perfect Proxy for Radio Listeners," *Journal of Radio Studies* 4, no. 1 (1997): 151–70; Curtis Mitchell, "Mary Margaret's Magic," *Coronet*, January 1954, McBride Papers 1926–1975, Box 4.
9 Hilmes, *Radio Voices*, 132.
10 Hilmes, *Radio Voices*, 132.
11 Susan J. Douglas, *Listening In: Radio and the American Imagination* (University of Minnesota Press, 2004), 102, 135; Hilmes, *Radio Voices*, 59, 141–42; Ware, *It's One O'clock*, 52.
12 Merrick, "Mary Margaret McBride," 152, 153; Ware, *It's One O'clock*, 6–7; Allen Churchill, "Mary Margaret McBride," *American Mercury*, January 1949, McBride Papers 1926–1975, Box 4; R. C. Ruark, "Mary Margaret," May 16, 1949, Mary Margaret McBride Papers 1926-1975, 0316F, Box 8.
13 Barbara Heggie, "Profiles: The Forty-Five Minute Tempo," *New Yorker*, December 19, 1942.
14 Merrick, "Mary Margaret McBride," 151–152. Emphasis in original.
15 Hilmes, *Radio Voices*, 141, 151, 154.
16 Mary Margaret McBride, *Out of the Air*, 1st ed. (Doubleday, 1960), 24.
17 McBride, *Out of the Air*, 24.
18 Ware, *It's One O'clock*, 26.
19 Ware, *It's One O'clock*, 160–61.
20 Hilmes, *Radio Voices*; Merrick, "Mary Margaret McBride"; Ware, *It's One O'clock*.

21 McBride, *Out of the Air*, 19.
22 "Dear Martha Deane," *New York Woman*, October 28, 1936, 13, McBride Papers 1926–1975, Box 4.
23 Cynthia B. Meyers, *A Word from Our Sponsor: Admen, Advertising, and the Golden Age of Radio*, 1st ed. (Fordham University Press, 2013): 79; Timothy Dean Taylor, *The Sounds of Capitalism: Advertising, Music, and the Conquest of Culture* (The University of Chicago Press, 2012): 20.
24 Ware, *It's One O'clock*, 89.
25 Kathy M. Newman, *Radio Active: Advertising and Consumer Activism, 1935–1947* (University of California Press, 2004).
26 "Mary Margaret Zips to New High with Listeners," *People*, McBride Papers 1926–1975, Box 7.
27 W. Bruce, "Correspondence from Walter B. Bruce to Estella Karn," December 17, 1945, McBride Papers 1926–1975, 0316F, Box 1.
28 M.B.S. Parker, "Mary Margaret McBride: Her Broadcast," McBride Papers 1926–1975, Box 4.
29 "The Mary Margaret McBride Program," June 6, 1946, The Mary Margaret McBride Collection, Library of Congress Recorded Sound Research Center; "The Mary Margaret McBride Program," January 20, 1943; "The Mary Margaret McBride Program," June 6, 1946.
30 Ware, *It's One O'clock*, 161.
31 Mary Margaret McBride, *Here's Martha Deane* (Garden City Publishing Co. Inc., 1936), 19–20.
32 Ware, *It's One O'clock*, 165.
33 Ware, *It's One O'clock*, 168–169.
34 Heggie, "Profiles," 32.
35 McBride, *Out of the Air*, 102.
36 Philip Hamburger, "Mary Margaret McBride: A Supersaleswoman Shares Adventures of Mind and Stomach with a Host of Radio Listeners," *Life*, December 4, 1944, 51, McBride Papers 1926–1975, Box 4.
37 Ware, *It's One O'clock*, 170.
38 McBride, *Out of the Air*, 104.
39 McBride, *Out of the Air*, 107.
40 McBride, *Out of the Air*, 107.
41 McBride, "Words and Music," para 2–3.
42 Hamburger, "Mary Margaret McBride," 51.
43 McBride, *Out of the Air*, 98; Ware, *It's One O'clock*, 165–170.
44 Hilmes, *Radio Voices*; Merrick, "Mary Margaret McBride."
45 Mary Margaret McBride, *A Long Way from Missouri* (G.P. Putnam's Sons, 1959), 23, 161, 232.
46 McBride, *Long Way from Missouri*, 12.
47 "The Mary Margaret McBride Program," November 11, 1950.
48 McBride, *Out of the Air*, 44; Merrick, "Mary Margaret McBride," 155.
49 "The Mary Margaret McBride Program," December 23, 1938.
50 Quoted in Heggie, "Profiles," 32.

51 "But Will She Meet Billie Pep?" McBride Papers 1926–1975, Box 5.
52 "Radio: Goodness," *Time*, December 2, 1946, https://time.com/archive/6823482/radio-goodness/.
53 "The Mary Margaret McBride Program," January 21, 1943.
54 "Mary Margaret McBride, Here Nov. 22 Is 'Specialist in Friendship,'" *Mexico Evening Ledger*, McBride Papers 1926–1975, Box 5.
55 Ware, *It's One O'clock*, 55.
56 "The Mary Margaret McBride Program," October 31, 1945.
57 Ware, *It's One O'clock*, 28.
58 McBride, *Out of the Air*, 32.
59 McBride, *Out of the Air*, 32.
60 Ben Gross, "Looking and Listening with Ben Gross: Manager's Job Is Hard; You Can't Be a Softie; Estella Karn Speaks Up," McBride Papers 1926–1975, Box 8; McBride, *Out of the Air*, 23; Ware, *It's One O'clock*, 161.
61 McBride, *Out of the Air*; Ware, *It's One O'clock*.
62 Ware, *It's One O'clock*, 130–31.
63 Beverly Merrick, "Mary Margaret McBride: At Home in the Hudson Valley," *Journalism History* 22, no. 3 (1996): 110–118.
64 Ware, *It's One O'clock*, 212.
65 Gross, "Looking and Listening."
66 Ware, *It's One O'clock*, 191.
67 Walter White, "A Party for Mary Margaret McBride," McBride Papers 1926–1975, Box 8.
68 Hilmes, *Radio Voices*, 132.
69 Rosalind Siegel, "The Message: Personalities on Parade," McBride Papers 1926–1975, Box 7.

Katharine Meyer Graham

A Complicated Person Confronting Complicated Problems

Linda Steiner

The assertion that Katharine Graham was the most powerful woman since Queen Victoria was undoubtedly overblown.[1] Whether her title was Katharine the Great, president, publisher, or CEO of the *Washington Post*, however, the woman who broke through journalism's glass ceiling, albeit not by choice, was powerful.[2] Graham had a significant impact on the country not only because of the elite status of the *Post* per se but also because of the executive decisions she made, earning her a reputation as legendary. Gloria Cooper, who served in various editorial capacities at the *Columbia Journalism Review*, explained the flattering reviews of Graham's memoir: "Everyone's a sucker for transformation stories, and the make-over of an insecure, dowdy, poor little rich girl into The Most Powerful Woman in America, framed within the parallel tale of how a puny third-rate daily changed into a fearsome giant, is not to be resisted."[3]

More to the point, Graham was filled with contradictions. As a *Post* staff writer put it when Graham died in 2001 at the age of eighty-four (she was born in 1917), she was "riddled with insecurities, awkward in many unfamiliar situations. . . . She could scare the bejesus out of staff members who didn't normally deal with her."[4] On the one hand, as Cooper notes, Graham always felt inadequate (and explicitly confessed this in *Personal History*), a belief "planted by Agnes Meyer, her egocentric, hard-drinking, depressive, demoralizing mother, and cultivated by Philip Graham, her egocentric, hard-drinking, depressive, demoralizing husband." On the other hand, in part by consulting smart business leaders and journalists, she made crucial decisions that had impacts not only on her own paper but that protected certain press freedoms and responsibilities as well as the rights, otherwise threatened, of journalists in the United States. A teaser to a profile of Graham summed this up immediately underneath the profile's title: "On an August Morning in 1963, a Shy, 46-Year-Old Housewife Nervously Walked into a World of Balance Sheets and Powerful Men. Suddenly, She Was in Charge of a Media Empire That Included the *Washington Post* and *Newsweek* Magazine. . . . Katharine Graham Transformed the *Post* into a Remarkably Influential and Profitable Newspaper and Herself into One of the Nation's Toughest Business Executives."[5]

Background

In 1933, when the nation's capital had five daily newspapers, Katharine's father Eugene Meyer, a major financier and, later, chairman of the Federal Reserve, bought the *Washington Post* at a bankruptcy auction. Her rather self-absorbed mother Agnes was briefly the *New York Sun*'s first woman reporter. Kay Meyer worked for the school paper at her private girls' high school in Washington, D.C., and at Vassar, which she attended before transferring to the University of Chicago.[6] One summer she worked for a suburban chain newspaper, although the Newspaper Guild objected to her unpaid status; she sarcastically called that objection her "introduction" to union politics. After graduation, Kay briefly worked for the *San Francisco News* to prepare for the newspaper business. With his only son intent on becoming a doctor and his other three daughters being uninterested in journalism, Eugene needed Kay to "go through the whole mill."

Kay doubted her ability to take on the *Washington Post*, however. Moreover, she detested what newspaper executives spend most of their time worrying about—that is, advertising and circulation. In any case, in 1939, just when she was worried that the *News* needed to let some staffers go, her father brought her back to D.C. to work for the *Post*, first in the editorial department and later in circulation. Upon marriage to Philip Graham, then a brilliant Supreme

Court clerk, she continued to write for a while, even joining the Women's National Press Club. For several years, she wrote a weekly column for the *Post*. But she primarily stayed busy with raising four children and managing the family's active social life.

In 1946, when the couple had been married for six years and Don had been deputy publisher for a couple of years, Meyer handed over the newspaper to his son-in-law. Katharine Graham explained in her Pulitzer Prize–winning memoir, *Personal History*, why she did not mind her father's decision: "Far from troubling me that my father thought of my husband and not me, it pleased me. In fact, it never crossed my mind that he might have viewed me as someone to take on an important job at the paper."[7] Indeed, to illustrate what she referred to as her "sense of inferiority," Kay recalled that much later, when her husband was quite ill, she mentioned to a friend the possibility of "hanging on to the paper until the children, especially the boys—since in those days that's how I thought—were old enough to run it." The friend insisted, "You can do it. . . . You've got all those genes. It's ridiculous to think you can't do it. You've just been pushed down so far you don't recognize what you can do." She quotes her response: "That's impossible. I couldn't possibly do it. You don't know how hard and complicated it is. There's no way I could do it."[8]

Made chairman of the Washington Post Company after Eugene's death in 1959, Philip Graham grew the company by investing in radio stations and buying their morning rival, the *Times-Herald* (thereby doubling the *Post*'s circulation), *Newsweek* magazine (very much a money-maker), and two television stations.

Katharine Graham Takes Over the *Post*

At age forty-six, Kay became president of the company in 1963, after Philip died by suicide at the couple's Virginia estate. He had long struggled with alcoholism, manic depression, and nervous breakdowns, as well as infidelity (his last liaison involved a *Newsweek* stringer). Graham suffered insecurity and decreasing confidence that were the long-term results of belittlement by her mother, condescension from her husband (seeing herself as "tail to his kite"),[9] and a long-standing tendency to self-tormenting self-criticism. That said, she stepped up to the job as a matter of family loyalty. In 1969 Graham became publisher; she held the title of chairwoman of the board from 1973 to 1991. She was the first woman to be a Fortune 500 CEO and the first woman elected to the Associated Press Board of Directors. Initially, Graham wisely relied on a circle of men who had worked with her husband; she later made hires of her own. She continued to attribute some of her success to luck. Yet she took responsibility for her mistakes and faced up to her weaknesses; she sought out formal and informal training, hiring coaches and consulting with people she trusted.

While slow to appreciate the women's liberation movement, Graham said she eventually tried to raise the consciousness of men executives. Sensitized by her friend Gloria Steinem, Graham backed Steinem's brave move in launching *Ms.* magazine, giving her $20,000 in seed money.[10] But that was about the extent of Graham's feminist activism. She may have ultimately appreciated the importance of increasing women's visibility, but she stayed out of nonexecutive hiring decisions and did not fight for hiring women. In 1970, some forty-six women *Newsweek* staffers sued their employer for sex discrimination. Women could be researchers or, rarely, reporters. By 1970, however, only one woman at *Newsweek* had been promoted to junior writer, Lynn Povich, who later wrote a book about that class action suit.[11] In 1972, more than one hundred women employees of the *Washington Post* filed a sex-discrimination complaint that was settled only eight years later. The agreement provided for $104,000 in monetary awards and a five-year affirmative action plan requiring the newspaper's editorial and commercial departments to fill at least one-third of jobs with women.[12]

The memoir recounts many difficult moments. The importance of luck and chance is a major theme. In 1989, Graham described her "exhilarating journey from inexperienced housewife to whatever it is I am today. It's been rather like having a good seat on a roller coaster."[13] Notably already in that 1989 speech, Graham expressed concern about threats to press freedom; she presciently warned about the "general dislike of the media, which could lead to further restraints," and the problem of audiences' short attention spans and disinterest in complex, abstract issues.[14]

Critical Juncture

Graham is most famous for two decisions. The first was her 1971 decision to publish the Pentagon Papers—classified documents about the Vietnam War that were leaked by Daniel Ellsberg, a military analyst—and that the *New York Times* had been enjoined from publishing. Because the Graham's company was just on the brink of going public, several trusted advisers (especially lawyers) opposed publication: accusations of criminal activity would have jeopardized the *Post* and the entire company.[15] On instinct, however, she authorized publication. Second was agreeing to back the Watergate investigation of President Richard Nixon's reelection campaign, despite the threats to the company. Attorney general John Mitchell warned that Graham was "gonna get her tit caught in a big fat wringer" if she allowed publication of a single Watergate story. The threats failed. The *Post*'s Watergate reporting won a Pulitzer Prize. After Watergate, elite journalists called Graham not only "the symbol of the Press but also "the most powerful woman in America."[16] Eventually, Richard Nixon resigned. Graham did not agonize over either of these questions. She simply acted as a good publisher, protecting journalists' independence and journalism's public service role. That said, for Graham, one of the important lessons of Watergate was that financial strength is essential to an aggressive news organization.[17]

The critical juncture, albeit less heroic, controversy of interest here was a pressmen's strike that lasted over four months. Indeed, the length of Graham's discussion in her memoir of labor issues suggests the extent to which these bothered her. Notably, while at the *San Francisco News*, she helped cover a couple of strikes. In 1937, she had said she wanted to be a labor reporter. Her memoir, however, is unsympathetic to the thirteen unions at the *Post*. The *Post* management ignored the unions' "guerrilla warfare" only because of what Graham called a shortsighted focus on competition with the *Washington Star*.[18] Years of inadequate labor relations and poor management allowed unions to exploit the paper's weaknesses, take control and assert authority, refuse automation, and commit or threaten acts of expensive sabotage. Labor won huge increases in pay and other benefits, as well as concessions. The paper had about twice the number of printers than it needed.[19] But now the *Post* was accountable to stockholders. Indeed, Graham told Wall Street analysts in 1972 that to maximize profits, her primary goal, she would cut the costs "imposed by archaic union practices that deprive the company of the savings we ought to have from modern technology."[20] Moreover, she insisted the company's commitment to journalistic excellence and integrity was consistent with its commitment to profitability: "You cannot have one without the other."[21] She hoped the labor problem could be resolved amicably, in a "constructive spirit," but she never promised this.[22]

To prepare for strikes, the company sent some nonunion personnel to what unionists called "scab school" to learn how to operate the equipment. Still, in 1973, when printers went on strike, management quickly agreed to demands. In 1974, in response to the aggressive toughness of a new management team, the Washington–Baltimore chapter of the Newspaper Guild went on strike, albeit without setting up a strike line. The other unions did not support the strike. Although they committed minor acts of resistance, the pressmen easily justified continuing to work since there was no picket line to cross (nor had they promised not to cross a line).[23] Senior editors worked long exhausting hours, even enjoying the experience of proving "their legs were still good."[24] Graham pitched in by writing stories, taking ads, and hearing complaints.[25] She argued that management needed to hold the line to make the paper profitable and that most *Post* readers either thought the paper was unaffected by the strike or was better during the strike, which also ended quickly.[26]

The crucial 1975 strike began when Local 6, Newspaper and Graphic Communications Union, set fire to a press, beat up a foreman, and shut down the paper's nine presses. This created, Graham said, "a siege atmosphere on the outside, produced cohesion on the inside, and . . . forced us to make decisions."[27] Much of the warfare was tactical and logistical: figuring out how to airlift by helicopter photo-composed pages to new, remote places for printing the paper (a task that relied on Graham's personal clout), repairing the damaged presses, and dealing with exhaustion and low morale. J. Walter Thompson public relations experts helped with the propaganda battle. This time, a few top *Post* people criticized Graham's refusal to yield to the pressmen's demands: experienced pressmen remained critical to publishing, unlike the printers in the composing room, whose jobs could be automated. Many friends told her to make a deal. Disturbed by the pressmen's ability to wrangle overtime and bonus pay, however, Graham refused. Although the *Post* missed one day of publishing, a week later the paper was delivered at near-normal levels.

On orders of the local guild chapter, about 275 guild members initially went out on strike with the pressmen (mostly from the business side).[28] But most of the paper's news and commercial workers were outraged at the "knee-jerk" demand for union solidarity and decided "to spurn old loyalties, defy their own leadership—and cross a picket line."[29] Over five hundred guild members crossed the picket line, consistent with a tradition that reporters/writers frequently see themselves as having more in common with management (i.e., "elites") than with craftspeople, and regard themselves "as professionals, if not intellectuals."[30] One scholar suggests that the journalistic triumphs of the Pentagon Papers and Watergate may have solidified writers' loyalty to the *Post* over loyalty to fellow unionists.[31] Meanwhile, reporters were clearly bothered by the extensive and presumably premeditated vandalism and destruction of the presses. Guild members were further alienated when a striker beat up a reporter. As one *Post* historian put it, "For most of the news staff Fort Sumter had been fired on, the Maine sunk, Pearl Harbor bombed. They rallied around Old Glory."[32] One guild member who sympathized with the union said that if the reporters stayed out, "I don't think anybody really believes that a handful of top *Post* editors and some people trained at the scab school could have put out a credible newspaper."[33]

Graham said that she would have been happy if most of the guild members (reporters) who refused to cross picket lines never returned, but she clearly went to pains to assure nonstriking guild members that she was bargaining in good faith. Her memoir quotes vicious personal attacks on her, especially by union leaders and the *Star*. She was particularly stung by criticism from Ben Bagdikian, a former *Post* national editor and then ombudsman and later an expert on media economics and political economy, of her focus on maximizing profits and "executivism."[34] In her push to reduce spending and please investors, he said, Graham could have cut executive salaries; in the previous four years, the *Post*'s administrative costs had more than doubled.[35] One account of the *Post* "news empire" quotes an unnamed *Post* reporter saying, "Mrs. Graham set out to prove she was a better newspaper publisher than Phil. Having done that, she then set out to prove she was a better businessman than her father."[36]

Resolution

Graham didn't flinch when people said that the blood of a pressman who died by suicide was on her hands or when pressmen's wives stood vigil outside her home; indeed, those wives were misguided in thinking they could appeal to Graham as a woman.[37] But Carol Felsenthal's biography of Graham also quotes *Post* executives who worried, at least during the beginning of the strike, that she would back down because of her fear (even hysteria) that the *Star* would take advantage of a weakened *Post*.[38] For a couple of weeks the low-quality and far slimmer paper lost $300,000 in advertising revenue a day (to the benefit of its remaining rival, the *Star*). Graham herself said that the anxiety from the violence during the strike felt like being "pregnant with a rock."[39] In any case, Graham's backbone stiffened, adopting a take-it-or-leave-it stance. She became known as "the Iron Lady."[40] Moreover, as the paper grew larger and could take (and attract) more advertising, a quick settlement was decreasingly important. After four months, when the other craftworkers settled and the pressmen refused what the company said was its final contract offer, Graham hired replacement workers. Ever since, the pressroom remains nonunionized.

Some say her intention to break the union "is an opinion not much in dispute."[41] Graham herself insisted she neither wanted a strike nor intended to destroy a union but only acted to regain management rights to preserve the paper and the company. She claimed the strike achieved in one blow what management had intended to achieve over a period of years and proving that "sound management practices and a strong business organization are essential to a media enterprise."[42] Either way, she broke the grip of craft publishing unions with what Van Dyne called "wondrous effects": "Labor costs were cut, efficiency was improved, and profits went up."[43] Furthermore, although the death of the newspaper guild seemed imminent at the time, the Washington-Baltimore News Guild still organizes an open shop at the *Post*; its headquarters are across the street from the newsroom.

In 2018, a class analysis of the strike was titled "At the *Washington Post*, Did the Guys from Corporate Win After All?"[44] The author's answer was "yes": Graham was positioned as exerting class power on behalf of a conglomerate. Moreover, the reference to Graham as among the "guys" was intentional. During and after the time Graham was running the *Post*, commentators noted her gender. Graham did, too. But as much as she enjoyed being the only woman in rooms full of men, her decision-making was that of a corporate warrior. *Post* executives were certain Graham did the only thing that could save the paper and the company. The American Newspaper Publishers Association—whose members previously had condescended to her or worse—now "canonized" her.[45] Carol Felsenthal insists that Graham enjoyed emasculating men (the biographer speculates that once she felt settled as a leader, Graham felt free to lash out at people and fire them as payback for how her husband treated her) and enjoyed her new status as the one who successfully emasculated the pressmen's union. Felsenthal says that some men publishers simultaneously appreciated that she broke the union and resented the fact that it was a woman who did so.[46]

Graham relied for financial and business advice on a crucial and reliable mentor, Warren Buffett, whose Berkshire Hathaway owned a substantial stake in the *Post*. But even with this close, trusted friend, she warned Buffett to adopt a soft touch when advising her. Graham did not take kindly to critics, including the ones who called her a strikebreaker who helped usher in an anti-union wave; after all, she reportedly said she deserved a Pulitzer Prize for management.[47]

She objected strenuously to the *New Republic* and the *Washington Monthly* for their "demonstrably wrong," "outrageous" critiques. She complained about Ben Bagdikian, who had made "a cottage industry" of criticizing the *Post,* saying that his take on the strike made her "embarrassed to think this ignorant biased fool was ever national editor."[48]

Both her father, an honorary member of the pressmen, and husband had gotten along with blue-collar workers. But, Graham told the American Academy of Arts and Sciences that the strike gave the *Post* a sudden opportunity to correct "years of inadequate labor relations and poor management" and to redesign management practices, resulting in a stronger paper: "If we had started out with the intention to regain right away all the control we had given up over the years, we never could have succeeded."[49] George Meany, the president of the AFL-CIO, once asked her what she would have done if the pressmen had accepted that final (more than generous) offer. "Slit my throat," she replied.[50] After all, she was relieved that the company now had the opportunity to start fresh with workers. Local 6 was overwhelmingly white, so she could also brag that the new hires included women and minorities. That said, some Black employees commented that liberals at the *Post* had not complained about union racism before.[51]

Conclusion

Many have commented, reasonably, that Graham won the 1975 strike not because of her leadership skills but because of the pressmen's tactical errors, because Washington is not a union town, and because writers and editors very rarely identify with craftworkers (and so continued to work).[52] A motivational speaker whose business is promoting women's leadership used Graham's memoir more generally for a book touting Graham as a model for "female corporate success."[53] Yet, Graham would not seem to dramatize executive excellence. At least to her critics, her firing of multiple top business executives and editors showed that she was "an erratic decision-maker, a difficult boss, and poor handler of managerial talent."[54]

Likewise, the fact that Graham faced and sometimes resented sexism does not make her a feminist. Much later she admitted that she accepted women's second-class citizenship "a little bit more than some others because of the strength of the men in my life and because of the particular way I grew up"—that is, in a world in which women thought of themselves as less bright and able than men.[55] The fact that she didn't always recognize when she was condescended to or resented turned out to be, she said, "bad in the sense that it was rather stupid, but it was good in the sense that I wasn't paranoid about how I was being treated."[56] A *Time* essay noted that her memoir "proved you can talk about humiliation with dignity, reach for help without being weak, be both vulnerable and powerful."[57] Notably, the essay, titled "The Accidental Feminist," neither says nor implies she was a feminist. In 2014, Knopf published a shortened e-book version of *Personal History*, titled *Progress: A Personal Journey in Feminism*, with an introduction by her granddaughter, Katharine Weymouth, publisher of the *Post* until 2014. But the claim that the book shows how Graham "became a feminist" is a stretch.

Nor did she anticipate the impact of feminism on and for other women. Apparently, she was late to understand the toll resulting from internalizing the gender scripts she had been taught; she speculated that women's *sense* of inferiority to men caused women to *become* inferior. Once she did understand that, in part by seeking out good mentors, she developed a sense of herself as a competent leader who avoided turning into an alpha-male authoritarian. (Notably, Graham never had a woman mentor, nor did she seem to act as a mentor, except perhaps to the children and grandchildren involved in the company.)

Another example of a decision that did not turn on what Graham thought was good for women or feminism was letting executive editor Ben Bradlee be the trailblazer among newspaper editors in killing off, in 1969, its daily stand-alone women's section. Judith Martin, who wrote for the *Post*'s For and About Women, acknowledges that journalists, including women, had long sneered at "women's pages" as silly, no more than "a treacly stream of flattery at the behest of 'society.'"[58] Recalling her experience as one of those former reporters on the society and party beat, Martin later observed, that the work was exciting and important; the section covered the feminist revolution of the '60s and '70s and the Women's Strike for Peace when otherwise these were rarely mentioned and then only as a joke.

Explaining the methods that her sister reporters on the *Post*'s women's page used to get scoops, Martin noted, "Truthfully, the sexism of the times gave us an advantage in gathering news that all of us on the party beat exploited." Martin noted that before attending an embassy party—part of her regular beat—she would ask the foreign desk what was happening around the world that day so that she could seek out the relevant ambassadors. "Having spent business hours avoiding the press, the targeted diplomat would nevertheless answer my questions, often also supplying recklessly un-spun background information of which he supposed I was ignorant. Inevitably, such a rich source would call the managing editor the next day, outraged at seeing his own words in print, to scream, 'How was I to know that girl was a reporter?'[59] And yes, Martin had identified herself as a *Post* reporter and had taken notes. "But how could anyone be expected to understand that a woman wearing a party dress was a working reporter?" Martin continued on with Style, later became a drama critic, and now is known for her "Miss Manners" syndicated column and books. The section's editor, Marie Sauer, who had been hired by the *Post* in 1936, three years after Eugene Meyer purchased it, simply retired.[60]

Officially Bradlee based his decision on his sense that contemporary women's interests were not different from men's. What he said was, "We had become convinced that traditional women's news bored the ass off all of us."[61] Speaking for herself, what Graham admired about the new section were the men who edited and wrote for it. Graham herself apparently missed at least some of the frothy content previously featured on the women's pages, telling Bradlee, "I am quite fed up with the really heedless eggheadedness of Style."[62]

As had many others, one former *Post* writer and editor described Graham "as tough as any man."[63] Graham did not fight for day care or maternity leave for employees, or even get to know them. The few employees allowed to work part-time (i.e., should they be trying to raise children, too) were ineligible for raises. The *Post* was required to pay out money to settle the EEOC suits. Judith M. Havemann, who served in several editorial positions at the *Post*, put it correctly: "Graham was sympathetic to women, but the pay, benefits, and day-to-day operations of the nation's most famous female-led company broke no feminist ground."[64]

Notes

1 Godfrey Hodgson, "Katharine Graham," *The Guardian*, July 18, 2001. According to this obituary, Graham disliked being called the most powerful woman in America (presumably, for bringing down Richard Nixon). But when British journalist Henry Fairlie, a *Post* columnist, interviewed her in a way that struck her as insufficiently respectful, she rebuked him by saying that a national security advisor to two U.S. presidents had said that she was the most powerful woman since Queen Victoria.

2 Citing many errors and unfounded allegations, in 1979 Harcourt Brace Jovanovich withdrew from publication Deborah Davis's book about Graham. Davis eventually published *Katharine the Great: Katharine Graham and Her Washington Post Empire* (Sheridan Square Press, 1991). Davis regards Graham and her newspaper as constituting a fourth branch of government.

3 Gloria Cooper, "The making of a publisher," *Columbia Journalism Review* 36, no. 1 (May/June 1997): 69. Cooper began her review for CJR by noting Graham's antipathy for that trade publication.

4 Robert G. Kaiser, "The Storied Mrs. Graham," Graham Holdings Company, July 18, 2001, www.ghco.com/historykaiser. Graham fell, struck her head, and died three days later.

5 Larry Van Dyne, "The Bottom Line on Katharine Graham," *Washingtonian*, December 1985, 128.

6 Given the number of people with shared last names, I refer to people by their first name until the death of Phil Graham and then refer to Katharine (known as Kay) as Graham. Any information not otherwise attributed comes from Graham's autobiography, Katharine Graham, *Personal History* (A.A. Knopf, 1997).

7 Katharine Graham, *Personal History*, 149.

8 Katharine Graham, *Personal History*, 319

9 Katharine Graham, *Personal History*, 231.

10 Katharine Graham, *Personal History*, 422.

11 Ironically, the same day the class action suit was announced (it was quickly settled without a hearing), *Newsweek*'s cover story, "Women in Revolt" (written not by a staffer but by a freelancer, Helen Dudar) featured the women's movement.

12 Stephanie Mansfield, "The Post, Women Workers Settle 1972 Sex Bias Case," November 19, 1980, *Washington Post*, www.washingtonpost.com/archive/local/1980/11/19/the-post-women-workers-settle-1972-sex-bias-case

/5f7a493f-6000-444f-8334-c11e00206b96/. Because Graham was eligible for a settlement payment, Van Dyne notes, she asked if she could refuse her share, but company attorneys replied she could not. Van Dyne, "The Bottom Line, 196.

13 Katharine Graham, "Learning by Doing," *Bulletin of the American Academy of Arts and Sciences* 42, no. 8 (1989): 37–53, 52.

14 Graham, "Learning by Doing," 53.

15 Going public had advantages and disadvantages for Graham and the company; ultimately, a lack of liquidity and a need for cash essentially forced Graham's hand. Moreover, around the same time, Van Dyne notes, many closely held news enterprises went public to finance technological modernization or expedite acquisitions, etc. Van Dyne, "The Bottom Line," 186.

16 Carol Felsenthal, *Power, Privilege and the Post: The Katharine Graham Story* (G.P. Putnam's Sons, 1993), 326.

17 Graham, "Learning by Doing," 48.

18 Graham, *Personal History*, 515.

19 Graham's critics agree. See, among others, Felsenthal, *Power, Privilege*, 341–342.

20 Ben H. Bagdikian, "Maximizing Profits at the Washington Post," *Washington Monthly*, January 1976, 29.

21 Van Dyne, "The Bottom Line," 188.

22 Richard Wells, "At the *Washington Post*, Did the Guys from Corporate Win After All?" *Labor* 15, no. 4 (2018): 59–76, 69.

23 Wells, "At the *Washington Post*," 69.

24 Howard Bray, *Pillars of the Post* (W.W. Norton, 1980), 245.

25 Graham, *Personal History*, 527.

26 Graham, *Personal History*, 528.

27 Graham, "Learning by Doing," 50.

28 Shirley Elder, "Journalists vs. the Unions at *The Washington Post*," *Columbia Journalism Review* 15, no. 1 (May 1, 1976): 42. Elder's husband, a *Post* reporter, crossed the picket line.

29 Elder, "Journalists vs. the Unions," 42.

30 Elder, "Journalists vs. the Unions," 42.

31 Wells, "At the *Washington Post*," 70.

32 Bray, *Pillars of the Post*, 261.

33 Pete Tucker, "Wash Post Busted Pressmen's Union in 1975 Strike. Why It Still Matters Today," Huffington Post, Aug 25, 2017.

34 Graham did acknowledge Bagdikian's role in getting the Pentagon Papers, however. *Personal History*, 446–447.

35 Bagdikian, "Maximizing Profits." Fairlie, while still a *Post* columnist, said much the same in the *New Republic* about Graham's required corporate mentality; in reviewing *Personal History*, he partly blamed Graham for the *Post*'s bad reputation—for unevenness, poor writing and editing, and arrogance—although he did not attribute this to money-grubbing per se. Henry Fairlie, "*Post*-Time (Again)," *Columbia Journalism Review* 22, no. 2 (1985): 50–52.

36 Bray, *Pillars of the Post*, 250.
37 Bray, *Pillars of the Post*, 286; Felsenthal, *Power, Privilege*, 345–346. The *Post* suggested this death stemmed from the man's fear that the union would punish him if he crossed the picket line. But his widow rejected that explanation.
38 Felsenthal, *Power, Privilege*, 346. Indeed, the *Star* suddenly became fat and profitable. Katharine's son Donald Graham, as the *Post*'s assistant general manager, led the strike-era publishing, which prepared him to be publisher (1979–2000).
39 Graham, *Personal History*, 550.
40 Felsenthal, *Power, Privilege*, 345.
41 Felsenthal, *Power, Privilege*, 348.
42 Graham, "Learning by Doing," 52.
43 Van Dyne, "The Bottom Line," 192. At least for some time, the case was studied at the Harvard Business School.
44 Wells, "At the *Washington Post*."
45 Bray, *Pillars of the Post*, 61.
46 Felsenthal, *Power, Privilege*, 349.
47 Bray, *Pillars of the Post*, 289.
48 Graham, *Personal History*, 570.
49 Graham, "Learning by Doing," 50, 51–52.
50 Bray, *Pillars of the Post*, 278.
51 Bray, *Pillars of the Post*, 280–281.
52 Felsenthal, *Power, Privilege*; Bray, *Pillars of the Post*.
53 Robin Gerber, *Katharine Graham: The Leadership Journey of an American Icon* (Portfolio, 2005). Gerber based a play about surviving domestic abuse on Graham's marriage.
54 Van Dyne, "The Bottom Line," 196. Van Dyne adds that her supporters said the firings demonstrated her high standards and willingness to acknowledge personnel mistakes.
55 Van Dyne, "The Bottom Line," 133.
56 Van Dyne, "The Bottom Line," 185.
57 Margaret Carlson and Janice M. Horowitz, "The Accidental Feminist," *TIME* 149 no. 7 (February 17, 1997): 24.
58 Judith Martin, "In Defense of 'Women's Pages,'" *Washington Post*, December 12, 2014, www.washingtonpost.com/lifestyle/magazine/judith-martin-in-defense-of-womens-pages/2014/11/25/f0fcc3a2-645c-11e4-bb14-4cfea1e742d5_story.html.
59 Martin, "In Defense of 'Women's Pages.'"
60 During World War II, Sauer, who had a master's degree in journalism from the Columbia University, a former president of the Women's National Press Club, joined the U.S. Navy WAVES doing public relations; she returned not to her previous job editing a weekly review of international news but to the women's section. Maurine H. Beasley, *Women of the Washington Press: Politics, Prejudice, and Persistence* (Northwestern University Press, 2012), 104.

61 Graham, *Personal History*, 414.
62 Quoted in Beasley, *Women of the Washington Press*, 151.
63 Judith M. Havemann, "Great Expectations: Women Now Hold Half of All Management Jobs in America," *Wilson Quarterly* 31, no. 3 (2007): 46–53, 47.
64 Havemann, "Great Expectations," 47. Noting that it was Graham's son Donald who added benefits such as family leave, Havermann's point is that both Grahams did what was necessary to keep the company healthy, including what was necessary to attract talent.

Joan Ganz Cooney

Television Pioneer

Amy Jordan

Joan Ganz Cooney is the visionary behind the quintessential educational television program *Sesame Street*. Together with cofounder Lloyd Morrisett, she imagined and designed the longest-running and most widely researched children's program. Now in its fifth decade, *Sesame Street* has taught generations of American children, and its international coproductions have reached a global audience. Cooney's vision, skill, and tenacity helped her rise to the highest position in an industry where, at the time of her ascension, few women held positions of power or influence. For her commitment to children's learning and growth and her pathbreaking role that helped women envision a different future, Joan Ganz Cooney has earned accolades and honors—from a Lifetime Emmy Award to the Presidential Medal of Freedom. Her complete story would fill volumes, but the key junctures highlighted below reflect her impact as a role model and inspired leader of the children's television industry.

Background

Joan Ganz Cooney was born in 1929, the youngest of three children, in Phoenix, Arizona. Cooney has said in interviews that she grew up "comfortable"—her mother was a homemaker, and her father was a banker. She also describes her adolescence as happy, enjoying the spotlight as a high school actor and receiving support from teachers who did not mind that she was "always reading and always arguing, forever trying to find answers."[1]

Like many women of her generation who went to college, she was encouraged to be a teacher. She did just that, earning a BA in education from the University of Arizona. The focus of her studies was primary school education—kindergarten through third grade was her specialty. But Cooney was not very interested in becoming a teacher. She told one interviewer, "I enjoyed that, but I never wanted to teach. I did not want a world of women and children. I wanted to get out in the world."[2] The education degree would later come in handy as she developed *Sesame Street*, albeit after many years and explorations into other careers.

Cooney's first job, in 1951, was with the Foreign Student Exchange, starting as a clerk/typist. After a year, she had saved up enough money to live in New York. Though she had been hoping for newspaper work, the only open shifts were overnights, so she instead took a position writing press releases at RCA, a position that she got through her friends' connections to the head of RCA, General David Sarnoff. Cooney's experiences at RCA mirror the experiences of many women at the time (and indeed still today). She recounted, "No one could understand why the General had brought me in. Rumors really attended me. And it was kind of miserable. I was this little innocent who was thought to be this manipulative, ambitious person probably sleeping with the General."[3]

After a few years, Joan moved to U.S. Steel, doing publicity for a CBS show the company sponsored. She did not envision a long-term future at U.S. Steel, and she kept her eye out for noncommercial television opportunities. She was able to leverage her connections to get a job producing documentaries and talk shows at Channel 13, New York City's public broadcasting station. Her new position allowed her to create television programs that tackled issues she cared about: civil rights, poverty, and injustice. One documentary she produced, *A Chance at the Beginning*, focused on an initiative that was the precursor to the preschool program Head Start. *A Chance at the Beginning* was a critical success—she won a local Emmy—and the program was later used to train Head Start teachers.

Critical Juncture

For Joan Ganz Cooney, 1966 was a turning point. As the story goes, Joan and her first husband Tim Cooney gave a small dinner party whose guests included the vice president of the Carnegie Corporation Lloyd Morrisett and his wife as well as Lewis Freedman, Joan's boss at Channel 13. The conversation turned to television and its untapped potential. Morrisett, an experimental psychologist by training, had noticed that his children were captivated by television, but nothing was really designed for them. Even at that very young age, Morrisett observed, his children could memorize advertising jingles. Together they wondered whether children's natural interest in television could be leveraged to be a force for good.

Cooney was immediately inspired by this idea. "I was plagued in my 20s that I was going to live and die without having made any difference. And when I heard educational television, I thought, 'that is where I can make a difference.'"[4] Morrisett was able to persuade the Carnegie Corporation to sponsor a study that would investigate its potential as an educational medium to help with cognitive development. Cooney persuaded him and her boss at Channel 13 to let her conduct the research. Over several months, she traveled the country interviewing experts in education and child development about the feasibility of creating a children's educational program. The result was a forty-seven-page report, *The Potential Uses of Television in Preschool Education*.[5]

What's remarkable about this document is the foregrounding of the importance of a curriculum as the basis of the series. The curriculum Cooney proposed would advance cognitive/intellectual learning but also cultural and emotional lessons. Built in are a nod toward the need to scaffold lessons, the importance of getting children to interact with the characters on the screen, and the value of using music and songs for engagement and retention. Additionally, Cooney argued passionately for the need to reach children and families who have fewer resources and limited access to preschool education.

The report was well received by Carnegie and went on to the head of the federal Office of Education and the Ford Foundation. On the basis of this research, Cooney created a detailed proposal that allowed her to raise $8 million from Carnegie, Ford, the Department of Education, and the Corporation for Public Broadcasting. With the funding secure, planning for *Sesame Street* began in earnest, guided by a set of lofty goals. "They hoped *Sesame Street* could function like a nationwide, economically efficient Head Start, exposing millions of underserved urban and minority children to cognitive skills that would help them succeed in school. Academic success would increase a generation's chances of escaping poverty, while a common television experience would help bridge cultural gaps that perpetuated prejudices."[6] Joan Ganz Cooney said, "This was the 60s, and every night you would turn your television on, and the news would tell you cities were burning, leaders were being assassinated, riots were being held at universities, anti-war riots. And so, it was as if people were saying 'so do something' to the television. One day, they turned it on, and television did something."[7]

Early in the visioning of what would become Children's Television Workshop (CTW), the production company behind *Sesame Street*, someone suggested that a man with more experience and visibility be put in charge. As Cooney told an interviewer, "Not many women were given this kind of responsibility. $8 million was a lot of money in those days. This would be about $30 million now or more. And of course, no one had ever heard of me."[8] Cooney was told that the project would not be seen as "important" if a woman were to head the organization. At one point, she was even told to write down the names of men who could take over the project, but that she could be the "number two." Joan responded, "No, you don't understand. I won't be number two. It was absolutely what I was born to do, and I knew it."[9] And so Joan Ganz Cooney became the number one. In 1969, when the Children's Television Workshop was formed, Cooney became its first executive director. She remained executive director of CTW until 1990, when she became the chair of CTW's executive board.

In her 1989 interview for the Television Academy Foundation, Cooney describes how being a top-level woman in a field dominated by men in some ways worked to her benefit. The late '60s and early '70s was a moment in U.S. history when the women's movement was underway, more public attention was being given to women in prominent positions, and more room was being made for women to participate in more sectors of society. "I gained real power because of this focus on me as a woman running Children's Television Workshop. I was asked to be on corporate boards because I was a woman—boards were just integrating in the '70s. That was immensely helpful to me in running this organization, to learn how corporations ran."[10]

Resolution

The *Sesame Street* team worked hard to create an educational program for preschool-age children that had a clear and focused mission to teach letters, numbers, vocabulary, and social-emotional skills, such as cooperation and tolerance. To ensure that children were learning the intended lessons, each "bit" in the program was carefully researched, including quasi-experiments to study children's attention to the screen and comprehension of the content. As one educational researcher wrote in 1976, "*Sesame Street* may be a researcher's dream. Who wouldn't want to be able to create a Snuffle-Upagus as a teaching device?"[11]

The *Sesame Street* research model requires both formative and summative research. Formative research, which evaluates content prior to airing to understand how children respond to such content, means that writers and researchers must work together (and quickly) to revise scripts, shoots, and even characters if it appears that it is missing its mark. Summative research examines the extent to which the program reaches its intended audience and whether, over time, *Sesame Street* achieves a measurable impact on children's learning. This was a completely novel approach to testing educational efficacy, but it was also necessary to ensure that the program was achieving its goals.[12] These are important goals, and important efforts to achieve these goals; nonetheless, the program was criticized.

From the start, the Children's Television Workshop (now Sesame Workshop) aimed to reach children who lacked access to preschool education, all the while knowing that because it aired on public television it would reach a broad audience, including children with more resources and school experience. Early studies showed that the program did move the needle on literacy. Less-resourced children were learning their letters and numbers, but so were middle-class children. Critics argued, however, that the knowledge gap between poorer and richer children was widening because children from higher-income households were watching *Sesame Street* more than those from lower-income homes.[13] The criticism stung, recalled Cooney, because "the aim was not to close the gap but to get all children above the literacy lines so they could go to school and hit the ground running and learn to read, which is key to education."[14] But after that critique, CTW invested heavily in conducting outreach to urban, low-income communities to raise awareness of the program among their highest-priority audiences. The cast even went on a national tour to build interest in targeted cities.[15]

The program was also initially criticized for what it might be doing to children's attention spans. It followed a format like the 1960s adult comedy program *Laugh-In*, a fast-moving, psychedelic program that was popular in the late '60s. Children were watching that show with their parents because it was funny and colorful. Moreover, the adult-directed humor on *Sesame Street* was seen as positive as it engaged parents, who could watch alongside their children and reinforce the lessons. As Newman writes, "*Sesame Street* episodes were an hour long, but they reached large audiences of young viewers who liked to see episodes and segments repeated. Part of their huge appeal was surely a credit to CTW's special effort to win the attention of these viewers. But, ironically, this effort and its public discussion in the popular press informed the development of a technophobic discourse of attention-catching media as a threat to children's ability to pay attention."[16]

Some critics argued that the fast pace and quick edits would affect children's attention spans and diminish their ability to read in the long run. Educational psychologist Jane Healy wrote, "Ideas in a book do not seize the reader's mind as do Ernie and Big Bird. Reading demands sustained voluntary attention from a mind that can hold a train of thought long enough to reflect on it, not one accustomed to having its attention jerked around every few seconds."[17]

Long-term studies of children's exposure to educational television, however, have found little evidence for this concern. One longitudinal study found that watching programs like *Sesame Street* in the preschool years was associated with academic success a decade later.[18] The researchers hypothesized that children who arrive at kindergarten and first grade having mastered their letters and numbers are more "ready to learn" and are more likely to be set on a path to success.

Moreover, studies have found that children are quite intentional in terms of what they give their attention to while watching TV. Far from being zombie-like in a television viewing situation, children actively monitor the screen for content that they think will be understandable and enjoyable.[19] Built into the DNA of *Sesame Street* is the very notion that if children do not pay attention, they will not learn. Debates about whether these efforts by producers to attract and maintain attention have a detrimental effect on children's cognitions have continued over the years. But many argue that today's media environment—where children consume most of their television content on YouTube[20]—largely exists of "bite-sized" bits of content.[21]

A third critique of *Sesame Street* turned on gender roles. *Sesame Street* has both Muppet and human characters on the show. In the earliest days of the program, the Muppets were predominantly male, and the humans had mainly traditional roles. The human character Susan was a particular target of criticism: observers complained she was too gender stereotyped as a wife at home, being supported by her husband. According to Cooney, "That got us into trouble with NOW [the National Organization for Women]. To say the least. It was so politically incorrect, but we thought it was a good idea to have a strong Black man supporting his wife. But it turned out to be a terrible idea, according to the feminists."[22] Susan's character was subsequently given an occupation as a nurse; this was also criticized for being a traditional occupation for women, but it remained a part of Susan's identity throughout her run on the show. Change regarding how women and girls have been portrayed in the series was slow, in part because of the dearth of female Muppeteers, but over the years more and more female humans and Muppets have taken up central roles, including the popular Muppets Rosita and Abby Cadabby. Storylines also have questioned gender stereotypes around toys, play, feelings, and occupations.[23] These changes have been significant, and Cooney was even invited to serve on the board of directors for NOW.

The historian Jill Lepore applauds early *Sesame Street* for how well it responded to its critics.[24] If a widening knowledge gap was a concern, researchers investigated ways to reach more children. If gender stereotyping was a concern, writers sought ways to portray counter-stereotypes. And while it might have been criticized for being socially conservative in some ways, from the start it pushed the boundaries of children's television. *Sesame Street* showed children and adults from different races interacting on an integrated street; this was both novel and controversial. Mississippi's state broadcast authority initially refused to air the program, citing viewers' preemptive complaints over the multiracial cast.[25] It dealt forthrightly with difficult topics, like divorce and death. Creating a children's show like *Sesame Street* took both a deep understanding of children's ability to manage complexity and a belief in the power and potential of television to address the needs of vulnerable children. Cooney had both. Her deep understanding of child development coupled with her commitment to addressing poverty and racism provided a backdrop against which the need for a television show like *Sesame Street* was evident.

Conclusion

Ultimately, the evidence for the success of Cooney's vision of *Sesame Street* was the program's popularity with children and parents. When it premiered on November 10, 1969, some 1.9 million households tuned in (although only two-thirds of U.S. televisions could receive it).[26] Within ten years, daily viewing by children under six had increased to nine million. Today, with the increasing fragmentation of the children's television landscape, official ratings have diminished but exposure has broadened.[27] *Sesame* has coproductions in over 150 countries around the world, reaching hundreds of millions of children worldwide, and the domestic version airs on PBS, Max, and YouTube. Sesame Workshop has extended its experience in reaching children with educational content and has brought its resources to communities experiencing trauma, military families, children with autism, children affected by incarceration, and refugee and displaced children.

Journalist and author Malcolm Gladwell says *Sesame Street* changed people's perceptions about television. Cooney showed that "TV could do more than merely distract. It could educate. And that seems obvious to us now, but that's a huge leap in 1968 and 1969."[28]

Separating Joan Ganz Cooney from the one program she dreamed up more than five decades ago is sometimes difficult. But her legacy to children extends beyond *Sesame Street*. Cooney and the Workshop have also produced shows geared toward older children teaching science, math, and literacy—including *The Electric Company*, *Square One TV*, *3-2-1 Contact*, *Ghostwriter*, and *The Not Too Late Show with Elmo*. In 2007, the Joan Ganz Cooney Center was established to help lead innovative thinking in a landscape becoming increasingly digital. In addition, the Joan Ganz Cooney Fund for Vulnerable Children supports Sesame Street in Communities (SSC). SSC reaches beyond television to work hand in hand with on-the-ground community providers to deliver resources to families in the United States who need them most.

Beyond the accolades that have showered the program (from Emmy to Grammy to Peabody Awards), Cooney has personally been recognized for her deep commitment to making the world better for children. In 1989, she received the Daytime Emmy Lifetime Achievement Award; that same year, she was inducted into the Television Academy Hall of Fame. President Bill Clinton endowed her with the 1995 Presidential Medal of Freedom Award, the highest civilian honor in the nation, saying, "Joan Ganz Cooney has proven in living color that the powerful medium of television can be a tool to provide reason, not reaction; for growth, not stifling; to help build young lives up, rather than tear them down."[29] She was inducted into the National Women's Hall of Fame in 1998, with this declaration: "Perhaps no other woman in the late 20th century has influenced the education of children as much as Joan Ganz Cooney."[30]

Cooney has received honorary degrees from the nation's most prestigious colleges and universities, as well as her alma mater. Indeed, in 2002, when Cooney was awarded an honorary degree from the University of Pennsylvania, I was humbled (and frankly, awed) to be her host during some of her time in Philadelphia. Cooney was gracious, attentive, and curious about the people and places around her and incredibly humble about her achievements. Fifteen years later, when I joined the Board of Trustees of Sesame Workshop, I was again inspired to be in her company. In the years that we have served together on the board, I have witnessed firsthand her earned wisdom, enduring vision, and unflagging commitment to using media to enrich and expand children's worlds. She is an inspiration to the field of children's television and women like me who work to ensure that the efforts we make to improve children's trajectories are meaningful.

Notes

1 Joan Ganz Cooney, interview by Shirley Wershba, Television Academy Foundation, The Interviews, https://interviews.televisionacademy.com/interviews/joan-ganz-cooney.

2 Joan Ganz Cooney, interview by Sharon Zane, Oral History Interview Project, Carnegie Corporation of New York Digital Archive, January 14, 1998, https://dlc.library.columbia.edu/carnegie/cul:3n5tb2rdbb.

3 Cooney, interview by Wershba.

4 Cooney, interview by Wershba.

5 Joan Ganz Cooney, *The Potential Uses of Television in Preschool Education*, report to the Carnegie Foundation, New York, 1966, https://joanganzcooneycenter.org/wp-content/uploads/2019/11/jgcc_1966report.pdf.

6 Kathryn Ostrofsky, "How 'Sesame Street' Persuaded Public Television to Act Like a Network." *The Current*, December 13, 2017.

7 Cooney, *The World According to Sesame Street*, directed by Linda Knowlton and Linda Costigan, 2006, Participant Productions.

8 Cooney, interview by Wershba.

9 Cooney, interview by Wershba.

10 Cooney, interview by Wershba.

11 Jim Warren, "Children's Television Workshop," *Educational Researcher* 5, no. 8 (1976): 8.

12 Shalom Fisch and Rosemarie Truglio, *G is for Growing: Thirty Years of Research on Children and Sesame Street* (Routledge, 2000).

13 Judith Haber Minton, "The Impact of *Sesame Street* on Readiness," *Sociology of Education* 48, no. 2 (Spring 1975): 141–151.

14 Cooney, interview by Wershba.

15 Jill Lepore, "How We Got to 'Sesame Street,'" *New Yorker*, May 4, 2020; Kristin Hunt, "Mississippi Banned 'Sesame Street' for Showing Black and White Kids Playing," *Washington Post*, February 5, 2023.

16 Michael Newman, "New Media, Young Audiences and Discourses of Attention: From 'Sesame Street' to 'Snack Culture,'" *Media, Culture & Society* 32, no. 4 (2010): 586.

17 Jane Healy, "10 Reasons 'Sesame Street' Is Bad News for Reading," *Education Digest* 56, no. 6 (1991): 63–66.

18 Daniel R. Anderson, Aletha C. Huston, Kelly L. Schmitt, Deborah L. Linebarger, and John C. Wright, "Early Childhood Viewing and Adolescent Behavior: The Recontact Study," *Monographs of the Society for Research in Child Development* 66, no. 1 (2001): 1–162.

19 Daniel R. Anderson and Stephen R. Levin, "Young Children's Attention to 'Sesame Street,'" *Child Development* 47, no. 3 (1976): 806–811.

20 Kate Knibbs, "The Future of Children's Television Isn't Television: Children's Media Is Its Own Universe, Where YouTube Sits at the Center—But Gaming Platforms Are Closing In," *Wired*, July 10, 2023; Christian Dankl, "Kids and the Screen USA Study," September 13, 2021.

21 Newman, "From 'Sesame Street' to 'Snack Culture,'" 592.

22 Cooney, interview by Wershba

23 Erika Weisgram, "Reducing Gender Stereotypes in Toys and Play for Smarter, Stronger, and Kinder Kids," *American Journal of Play* 12, no. 1 (2019): 74–88.

24 Lepore, "How We Got to 'Sesame Street.'"

25 James Poniewozik, "'Sesame Street' Was Always Political," *New York Times*, December 12, 2021; Hunt, "Mississippi Banned 'Sesame Street.'"

26 Tim Gray, "'Sesame Street' Was First Brought to You by the Letters PBS 50 Years Ago," *Variety*, November 8, 2019.

27 Nicholas Zill, "Does *Sesame Street* Enhance School Readiness? Evidence from a National Survey of Children," in *"G" Is for Growing: Thirty Years of Research on Children and Sesame Street*, ed. S. Fisch and R. Truglio, 117–120 (Lawrence Erlbaum, 2000).

28 Cooney, *World According to Sesame Street*.

29 "Presidential Medal of Freedom," President Bill Clinton Award Presentation to Joan Ganz Cooney, September 25, 1995, www.c-span.org/video/?67407-1/presidential-medal-freedom.

30 "Joan Ganz Cooney," National Women's Hall of Fame, accessed November 11, 2023, www.womenofthehall.org/inductee/joan-ganz-cooney/.

Ann Barkelew

Leadership Lessons in Public Relations

Elizabeth L. Toth

Women make up the majority of public relations practitioners in both managerial and technical positions.[1] In the 1980s, however, only a handful of public relations women were chief communication officers in Fortune 500 corporations. One of these women was Ann Barkelew. This chapter shows how Barkelew achieved leadership roles in public relations and explains her leadership strategies and insights on leadership. Barkelew's success as a public relations leader provides timeless advice for both public relations women and men who want to excel in their careers.

Accredited as a public relations professional (APR), Barkelew has been recognized as one of the most outstanding professionals in public relations. Among her honors are the 1995 PR News Public Relations Professional of the Year; the 1999 City Business's Most Influential Women Award; the 2001 Fleishman-Hillard's Lifetime Achievement Award; the 2003 Arthur W. Page Society's Distinguished Service Award; the 2011 Plank Center's Milestones in Mentoring Award; and the Penn State Page Center's Lawrence Foster Award for Integrity in Public Communication in 2017, its initial year. She was president of the National School Public Relations Association; cofounder of the North American Public Relations Council; and 1993 chair of the Public Relations Society of America (PRSA) College of Fellows.

Ann Barkelew's leadership strategies included taking every opportunity that came her way; indeed, she never formally applied for a job. She launched the public relations programs for organizations that had none by finding advisors, hiring great people, learning from staff, and building a network of public relations professionals she met through public relations associations. Barkelew had men mentors because there were no women mentors; later, she became a mentor herself. The elected offices she held in public relations associations widened her connections to experts. Her leadership was collaborative and team-oriented. Thoroughly understanding how organizations relied on the goodwill and understanding of all of the people they dealt with, she mobilized communication efforts to maintain and cultivate those vital connections.

Barkelew's career well demonstrates how success in public relations requires many different kinds of skills, from producing messages in multiple forms, to conducting research on public opinions and behaviors, to counseling organizational leadership on how to build effective relationships with key constituent groups. Public relations for organizations centers on managing communications to achieve organizational goals. Moreover, Barkelew recognized that organizational success rests on achieving understanding through communication with often influential and active groups. One of the most quoted definitions of the field is, "Public relations is the management function that identifies, establishes, and maintains mutually beneficial relationships between an organization and the various publics on whom its success or failure depends."[2]

Background

Born in 1935 to Alexander Hamilton, an engineer, and Ruth Welsh Hamilton, a teacher, Barkelew grew up in Missouri.[3] She regards her mother as a role model: "I never really had a stay-at-home mom and I think that probably influenced me a lot." (All direct quotes from Ann Barkelew are taken from two conversations.[4]) During the war, when teachers were scarce, her mother was reassigned from teaching music to conducting morning and afternoon kindergarten programs. Her mother also volunteered as Barkelew's Brownie troop leader.

Already while just beginning her master's degree at Central State University of Missouri, Barkelew was offered her first job. A high school needed a substitute for a pregnant English teacher given that, in those days, a woman could not be a classroom teacher once she began to "show." Barkelew, in her twenties, taught high school English and journalism courses in Missouri before moving to Santa Barbara, California, with the encouragement of a friend who said teaching positions were plentiful and the climate was better there. Barkelew says that even during that early period of high school teaching she always asked a lot of questions of management. "I was sort of a militant teacher, not in a mean way, but I would ask questions about why we weren't being told about some of the issues that the district was facing because I thought we could help."

Working in Public Sector Public Relations

In the early 1960s, high school teachers needed a master's degree to get a permanent teaching credential in California. Therefore, Barkelew took a leave of absence and entered the University of Missouri, where she audited a course in school public relations in the College of Education. She was fascinated, she said, "by what you could do on purpose to influence how people felt about schools." Her master's thesis was titled "Organizing a Program of Public Relations for the Santa Barbara Schools." Without telling her, her thesis advisor sent the thesis to the Santa Barbara School district superintendent. On the basis of that thesis, the district created a position for her titled "coordinator of school community relations" so that she could put her thesis ideas into practice. Barkelew worked for the Santa Barbara school district as an administrator for five years. Meanwhile, she married a widower with two little girls. Although the marriage didn't last, Barkelew adopted the girls; she led their Girl Scout troop, among other things. This "central office" position eased her parenting challenges because she wasn't in the classroom. "I could leave the office to go help if there was an emergency." It's worth noting that when her two daughters were entering college and she was a corporate vice president, Barkelew married a single father with four children, the two youngest still at home. Asked about work-life balance, Barkelew described "a lot" of work-life balance issues given her high-powered job and the fact that her husband, a trial attorney, was often traveling: "Although it all seemed to work out. . . . I seldom went to bed before 1 in the morning and I was up at 5:30 or 6 A.M."

To create Santa Barbara's community relations program, Barkelew organized an informal advisory group of public relations professionals from Santa Barbara and beyond. She joined the professional public relations organizations such as the National School Public Relations Association (NSPRA) and the PRSA; these connected her with public relations practitioners in Los Angeles. Then, as Barkelew began to speak about the Santa Barbara program at conferences, she met the Los Angeles County School Superintendent, who asked her to talk to the Los Angeles County schools about the advantages of a good program of communication for schools. After talking with them, Barkelew was hired to work for the Los Angeles County Office of Education as their chief public information officer.

During her ten years of work in Los Angeles County, where there were more students in the public schools than some states' populations, Barkelew gained invaluable experiences that would change her career trajectory. She faced the communication issues that accompanied multiple controversies, including mandated collective bargaining for teachers, court-ordered desegregation of schools, bitter teacher strikes, declining enrollment that led to school closings, and the Jarvis-Gann Amendment, or Proposition 13, which capped local property taxes at one percent of an assessed value and thereby left some localities with significantly less tax revenue to spend on schools.

She had to build a team from scratch, starting with five or six people, and eventually coordinating thirty people in the largest districts. "They used to call me the Mother Flack because I was always watching out for them and being sure they were doing their jobs." To create this new communication function for schools, she relied on her network of area public relations professionals, other school public relations people, and outside advisors, such as Patrick Jackson, the 1980 president of the Public Relations Society of America at the same time Barkelew was the national president of NSPRA. Jackson and Barkelew would continue to work together to create the

North American Public Relations Association and the Public Relations Society of America College of Fellows.

Moving to Private Sector Public Relations

Barkelew faced a second leadership juncture because of her role as president of NSPRA. Representing NSPRA, Barkelew traveled throughout the United States speaking to public school officials on the importance of public relations in education, and in particular how to deal with declining enrollments and collective bargaining. A board member for Munsingwear, a Minnesota-based brand of underwear, heard her presentation and encouraged his CEO to consult with her about some of the communications challenges they were facing. Munsingwear was competing unsuccessfully with Polo, Izod, and "all the golf shirt manufacturers who manufactured most of their merchandise offshore whereas Munsingwear's plants were all in the U.S." Barkelew took a six-month leave of absence from her job in Los Angeles to "help Musingwear close about half of its U.S.-based plants without unions coming in and to help figure out how to make life better for their employees." She ended up staying because she loved Minnesota.

Barkelew stayed with Munsingwear for a year. She worked for an all-male C-suite. "So, the friends you would make right away were the men's secretaries. I learned early on that they were really the ones who ran the show, so I thought that was always a relationship to have. Some of them are my best friends still."

While she was working at Munsingwear, Dayton Hudson, a Minneapolis-based corporation with several subsidiaries, now known as Target Corporation, recruited Barkelew to be its first woman vice president of public relations. Barkelew joined Dayton Hudson in 1982, coordinating the public relations work of seven companies and attending, although initially as a nonvoting member, meetings of the senior management committee.[5] By 1992, Dayton Hudson was the fourth-largest retailer in the county, owning Dayton Hudson, Target, Mervyn's, and Marshall Field's.[6]

Dayton Hudson apparently had intended for Barkelew to take six weeks to learn the retail business and get acquainted with its various companies. But after two weeks on the job, Barkelew's CEO sent her to Detroit. Word had leaked out that Dayton Hudson was closing its seventy-one-year-old downtown store, with its perennial Thanksgiving Day parade. This "stung," causing hard feelings on the part of Detroiters.[7] Barkelew recalled saying to herself, "I've closed plants, I've closed schools, and so we did pretty much the same thing; we reached out to the community, met with the groups that you need to meet with. The most important thing was to explain why it was necessary."

Barkelew navigated the conflict, she said, by "educating the community to the needs, to what a public company is and what it can do, and its obligation to shareholders." She met with representative groups, the mayor's office, and leaders of arts institutions. "Everybody who had in any way interacted with the store had to know how they were going to fit into the new arrangement."

Allaying the concerns of Detroit community groups about that store, Barkelew says, helped her to build trust with the Dayton Hudson executives. "We kept the waters calm. We delivered on what was needed." She credited this first challenge as helping the executives of Dayton Hudson realize that public relations could make a difference. Barkelew enjoyed the support of her CEO, "who treated me like an equal; he always asked my opinion. But it took another four years for me to be named to the Dayton Hudson management committee; and again, it was twenty-six men and me."

Critical Juncture

In 1987, Dayton Hudson Corporation was one of the five largest retailers in the United States, with annual sales of over $18 billion.[8] Dayton Hudson had expanded to thirty-three states and operated 892 stores under its several subsidiaries. It employed thirty-four thousand in Minnesota alone. Dayton Hudson had a known community presence, donating five percent of its annual pretax profits to worthy causes.[9] So, it came as a surprise that it was subject to a hostile takeover attempt.

In June 1987, Dayton Hudson learned through rumors that a takeover attempt was underway. Its escalating stock price reinforced the rumor. Dayton Hudson reported that within three weeks, an unusual amount, thirty percent of its stock, had turned over.[10] Barkelew became part of the crisis team that gathered all the research possible on the situation, including new laws to deal with hostile takeovers. The team considered how to work with all concerned publics. She was the corporation's official spokesperson, handling countless inquiries. The story of how Dayton Hudson defended itself against this $6.6 billion corporate raid,[11] with Barkelew's leadership, has become a case study in the field of public relations.

Barkelew prepared the script and briefing paper for CEO Ken Macke to ask Minnesota governor Rudy Perpich to call a special legislative session to pass an antitakeover law that would protect all Minnesota-incorporated public companies. To convince Perpich to call the session and enact the protective law, Barkelew readied backgrounders, question and answer pieces, and discussions of the pros and cons of the legislation to encourage editorial support from Minnesota media. She organized CEO meetings with public affairs editors, meetings with business and community leaders, and wrote to Dayton Hudson's thirty-four thousand employees asking for their help in mobilizing legislative support. Meanwhile, the Dayton Hudson Foundation, which had donated $9 million that year to Minnesota nonprofits, urged two hundred community leaders to call their legislators. Other prominent Minnesota corporations, such as General Mills and Honeywell, issued supportive statements. On June 25, 1985, the state legislature passed a law protecting Minnesota corporations against corporate raiders, thereby ending the hostile takeover attempt.

Barkelew was aware that the corporate world had gendered norms that she had not experienced before. She said, "People were always very careful." For example, early in her corporate career, she was scheduled to meet in New York City with the reporters at *Women's Wear Daily* about a new product line. However, the CEO's secretary told her to reschedule her trip. "I asked why; I have this all set up with these reporters. She said that another male officer is going to be in New York at the same time and it is not a good idea for the two of you to be there at the same time. And, I thought, Why doesn't he have to reschedule his trip?"

According to Barkelew, "There was always concern among the men that having a woman in the mix would change what they did. Would they be free to, you know, tell jokes? I don't know what they were afraid of." She described that the gendered perceptions she experienced led to issues of appearance and "fit" in both figurative and literal terms: "There was always the concern about what it would look like. And here I was this divorced woman from California of all places, and I liked to dress in colorful things. I didn't wear the usual navy blue suits with floppy ties."

Realizing that public relations was not as well understood as finance, Barkelew had to find a way to communicate with financial experts so they would understand it. "As Patrick Jackson always used to say, 'When in China, speak Chinese.'" She knew that she was achieving success for Dayton Hudson. She thought that the reluctance to include her as a management committee voting member represented a combination of gendered perceptions and failure to understand public relations. For example, because finance people "always think in a straight line," she presented her work to them that way. "So, when I'd issue a news release, I would then take all the clips the next day and create a matrix of the key messages and then check off how many key messages we'd gotten in the *Wall Street Journal* and the *New York Times* or the Dow Wire or whatever. I'd just make a cover sheet and I'd say we did really well, our key messages got out, the numbers were all accurate in the coverage. I remember the day that the CFO came to my office and said, 'Gosh, this is really good.'"

Barkelew suffered salary inequity at Dayton Hudson. After her first performance evaluation, she told Dayton Hudson she wanted to be assured that she was paid the same as the man who headed the foundation and government affairs. She knew that he earned a lot more than she. Her supervisor replied, "Oh my goodness, Ann, he's married and has two little children." She recalled her reaction: "I was stunned. And I said, 'I'm divorced with two daughters in college. They cost a lot more than little kids.' And he just said, 'Let's talk about it later.' I'll never forget thinking to myself, Why aren't we worth as much? And a lot of perks came to the other division heads, all of whom were men, like a corporate car, or the kind of stock options."

When she joined Dayton Hudson, Barkelew organized an informal group of Minneapolis chief corporate communications officers, such as from Honeywell, 3M, and Cargill. The so-called group met monthly to learn about each other's companies. Barkelew asked the members to participate in a survey that she promised not to look at. They were to send to Dayton Hudson's human resources office their salary ranges and perks, such as life insurance, corporate car, and other benefits. Other members wanted to know the results as well. "We sort of helped ourselves." And Barkelew got a salary increase and new benefits.

Barkelew credits her leadership success to the networking she did with other women corporate communication leaders. She recounted that she was asked to join the Public Relations Seminar and the New York City–based Wisemen, invitation-only groups that usually included the same seven or eight corporate communication women leaders, including GE's Joyce Hergenhan and AT&T's Marilyn Laurie. "We shared a lot of information when we'd be at these meetings together." For example, in 1990, after Dayton Hudson's decision to stop funding Minnesota's Planned Parenthood became public, Barkelew immediately called Marilyn Laurie, who had also been dealing with the Planned Parenthood referendum. "And it was very important to guiding me through the Dayton Hudson situation."

The Planned Parenthood Issue

Barkelew also credited her relationships with journalists who covered Dayton Hudson on weathering the Planned Parenthood controversy. She said that she only learned about Dayton Hudson's withdrawal of funds from the Minnesota Planned Parenthood chapter when a local reporter called her for a comment. Having half an hour to get back to him, Barkelew called the Dayton Hudson Foundation executive in charge of social giving, who replied that he'd sent her a memo through interoffice mail regarding the withdrawal.

Barkelew anticipated that the public reaction would be swift and not all positive. The fact that Planned Parenthood of Minnesota knew the withdrawal of funding had been planned for two years and that the decision reflected employee concerns was ignored. Dayton Hudson's withdrawal became national news, leading to attacks from both pro-choice and pro-life activists. The Christian Action Council, an antiabortion group, called for a nationwide boycott of all Dayton Hudson stores on "Black Friday," the day after Thanksgiving.[12]

In that pre-Internet era, Barkelew acted as quickly as possible, preparing the official corporate response and shipping to all Dayton Hudson stores a brochure to be handed out to customers and picketers at the checkouts. The brochures pointed out how Dayton Hudson supported each of the thirty-eight states in which it operated in terms of payroll taxes, number of employees, and financial donations to local organizations. She brought together a group of community leaders to advise Dayton Hudson on how best to arrange grants that might be controversial. Based on the group's recommendations, Dayton Hudson backtracked and donated $18,000 to Planned Parenthood but clarified that the money was to be used for educational programs and not activities related to abortion.[13]

Dayton Hudson's CEO wrote an op-ed piece for the *New York Times* that stood by its commitment to charitable giving policies; to do otherwise would be "counterproductive to the needs of a society that values and encourages philanthropy."[14] Barkelew said, "We sort of lived through the issue, but we didn't want to back away from the things that we believed in" at a time when CEOs all over the country were saying "aren't you sorry that you give money to groups that you know are slightly controversial."

Protecting the Minnesota Children's Theater Viability

Barkelew's leadership ability was put to the test again when she joined, as a representative of Dayton Hudson, the Minnesota Children's Theater board of directors. At a dinner meeting she was attending, Barkelew learned from a reporter who was rushing to a 10 P.M. news conference that the artistic director of the Children's Theater had been arrested for sexually abusing young boys. Barkelew left the meeting and as soon as she could, talked to the organization's executive director about convening a public relations committee. "We need to take charge of this and not let it destroy the theater." She was elected chair of the interim executive committee that managed the crisis response. Her team pulled together representatives of the major area arts organizations and devised guidelines and policies on what to do if sexual harassment claims arose. "We had the I-Team [investigative team] of the CBS affiliate here going after us, demanding that we close the place down. We refused to do that. One thing we agreed on immediately was that we had to stop asking for money. We needed to go out there to meet the major donors. We needed to explain to them that we were in charge." In addition to sustaining these important relationships, Barkelew addressed the critical importance of the parents and children. As a board member, she openly questioned why the theater was operating a school—which had become the avenue for the artistic director to groom children from very young ages. "So, in order to clean up our act, we phased out the school."

Retirement, Public Relations Agency Head, Retirement Again

Barkelew retired at age sixty in 1994 from Dayton Hudson, a company worth $5 billion when she started and $28 billion when she left.[15] She had instituted Dayton Hudson's public relations arm and positioned the function as part of the executive team on an equal status with law, finance, and personnel.[16] Barkelew built key relationships between Dayton Hudson and employees, the State of Minnesota, Minneapolis, the national media, stockholders, and activist groups. She saw Dayton Hudson through buying and selling subsidiaries, defeating a hostile takeover attempt, and articulating a clearer understanding of support for Planned Parenthood despite criticisms. She kept a major arts organization viable after the arrest of its founder.

Upon retirement, Barkelew started consulting. Then, John Graham, CEO of Fleishman-Hillard, a national public relations agency, asked Barkelew to establish a new headquarters in Minneapolis for him. Barkelew recalled him saying, "'I want you to do it.' I said, 'No, you don't want me.' I'd never hired agencies, except for some highly specialized ones. I'd rather train my own people because it seemed to me like agencies always gave me all these young people and expected me to train them, and I figured I could train them and have them on my staff."

Graham was convincing, and over the next seven years, Barkelew built up Fleishman-Hillard's Minneapolis office until it was the third-largest in the Twin Cities. Then she retired again. Barkelew's leadership for Fleishman-Hillard included counsel to NYSE and NASDAQ corporations, professional sports organizations, and privately held companies. Barkelew described her leadership style as that of a teacher: "Even at the agency, I never asked my people to do anything that I wouldn't or couldn't do myself. I always sat in on meetings with them and offered suggestions, or I would help them with writing things or if they were frantically putting together a project or presentation. I was there helping them stuff envelopes or whatever. I like being a group leader; I like being a member of the group, but a participating member in the group. I like putting teams together and I like helping people grow."

Barkelew guided many others in their public relations careers. Beth Hemings, chief compliance officer for Rothschild Capital Partners, said, "I learned from Ann's style, her intelligence, the quickness of her; she was unflappable."[17] The head of public relations at Sears described Barkelew as "cool, calm and collected" and as helping him by sharing contacts and opening doors.[18] Fleishman colleague Rich Jennstedt described Ann's "giant wingspan" as wide enough for hundreds of family members (Barkelew has eleven grandchildren), friends, and colleagues.[19]

Barkelew has helped with fundraising for WomenWinning, formerly the Minnesota Women's Campaign Fund, which endorses and financially supports pro-choice women running for political office. She served on the Minnesota News Council, which adjudicates disputes between citizens and media. She is on the Board of Trustees of Ecumen, a nonprofit developer that operates living spaces for older adults and families. Barkelew used her retail contacts to help create the Ecumen Store, which sells medical equipment and supplies at reduced costs. She cochairs the Minnesota Women's Forum and the Twin Cities Communications Council.

Conclusion

Barkelew defines public relations as "performance recognized." She expanded on her definition to focus on public relations as building bridges between an organization and the people it deals with: "I think basically we are in charge of making people feel good about an organization; in other words, supporting it, understanding it, being willing to get involved with it, helping an organization have the kind of relationships with all the people it deals with." Barkelew emphasized the importance of bringing people together, especially in the public sector where less money is available. She commended public sector PR people for bringing together groups, not attempting to fly alone but to involve more people in a program or find a solution. For her, success means that even if people don't love an organization, at least they understand it and are not troubled by how it operates.

Public relations has always been at the forefront of crisis communications, where Barkelew found herself many times. PR professionals are crucial in a crisis, she says: "We know how to communicate the facts . . . and make sure that you have the facts before you start communicating and be sure that you've checked all the boxes. It's something that we've learned and that we do, wherever we practice, corporate America, private sector, public sector organizations." Inside the organization, Barkelew described the public relations function as "the common denominator in a company. . . . We speak all the languages and we always have the best interests at heart. We can always help people get to where they need to get to. We are who everyone comes to; we can see the whole apple. Other people may just look at pieces of it; we always look at the whole apple."

Barkelew partly attributes her leadership skills to things she learned as a Girl Scout. She described her scouting experiences in the context of World War II when children could play a meaningful role in helping the country with things like scrap paper drives, scrap metal drives, rummage sales, and volunteering in hospitals to deliver flowers and food trays to patients. She recalled working on badges in groups: she "always had lots of opportunities to be in charge." Her leadership also developed through working with many women in public school administration. "There were a lot of women in leadership roles such as elementary school principals, the many women in school system human resources and finance, not at the top positions, but at the next level. I always worked with a lot of women."

Barkelew's public relations leadership strategies spanned three very different types of organizations, indicative of successful leadership attributes that generalize no matter what the circumstance: collaborative thinking, taking initiative, and producing results that solve problems even in a gendered corporate environment that did not understand the gender inequities facing women. So, although Barkelew never formally applied for a job, she built an expertise that enabled her to take on new opportunities. "I found that once you have good general skills, then you can do it anywhere. A store manager is no different from a building principal; a CEO of a company is no different than a superintendent of schools."

Ann Barkelew originated public relations programs for organizations that had none. She succeeded by networking and collaborating with teams, staff, and professional colleagues and by building relationships of trust with management peers, journalists and communications professionals, and women peers. She relied on mentors to help her through issues and organizational crises. She worked her way through the gendered (and often sexist) culture of corporations by proving herself and demonstrating empirically the impact of public relations on solving organizational problems. As such, Barkelew constitutes a concrete example of public relations leadership in action.

Notes

1 U.S. Bureau of Labor Statistics, "Household Date, Annual Averages," 2021, www.bls.gov/cps/cpsaat11.htm.

2 Scott M. Cutlip, Allen H. Center, and Glen M. Broom, *Effective Public Relations* (Prentice-Hall, 1985), 4.

3 Brenda J. Wrigley, "Barkelew, Ann. H," in *Encyclopedia of Public Relations*, vol. 1, ed. Robert L. Heath (Sage, 2025), 60–62.

4 These were held on June 3, 2022, and August 25, 2022. The author is very grateful for Barkelew's participation and for the assistance of Linda Aldoory, now a dean at American University.

5 Paul Holmes, "Dayton Hudson Learns Issues Management Lessons from Merchandising," *PRovokeMedia*, December 7, 1992, www.provokemedia.com/latest/article/dayton-hudson-learns-issues-management-lessons-from-merchandising-(1992).

6 Holmes, "Dayton Hudson."

7 "Hudson's to Leave Downtown Detroit," *New York Times*, July 15, 1982, https://www.nytimes.com/1982/07/15/us/hudson-s-to-leave-downtown-detroit.html.

8 Allen H. Center and Patrick Jackson, *Public Relations Practices: Managerial Case Studies and Problems* (Pearson, 2003), 350.

9 Center and Jackson, *Public Relations Practices*, 350.

10 Center and Jackson, *Public Relations Practices*, 350.

11 Dennis Hevesi, "Kenneth Macke, Who Led Target, Dies at 69," *New York Times*, July 1, 2008, www.nytimes.com/2008/07/01/business/01macke.html.

12 Kenneth A. Macke, "Forum: Philanthropy as a Business Tactic . . . with Some Attendant Risks," *New York Times*, December 30, 1990, www.nytimes.com/1990/12/30/business/forum-philanthropy-as-a-business-tactic-with-some-attendant-risks.html.

13 Macke, "Forum: Philanthropy."

14 Macke, "Forum: Philanthropy."

15 "Ann Barkelew," Video, Arthur W. Page Center, Penn State University, https://pagecenter.psu.edu/resources/oral-history-collections.

16 Ann H. Barkelew, "Building Bridges: The Public Relations Challenge in the Public and Private Sector," Ball State University, 1993, http://schranzlecture.com/wpages/wp-content/uploads/2013/04/Barkelew_Ann_1993.pdf.

17 "Ann Barkelew: This Pioneering PR Executive Guided Many Careers with Her Example of Unflappable Calm," *Twin Cities Business*, April 1, 2020, https://tcbmag.com/honors/ann-barkelew/.

18 Ron Culp, "Ann Barkelew," October, 29, 2011, https://culpwrit.com/2011/10/29/ann-barkelew-a-mentor-with-wide-wing-span/.

19 Culp, "Ann Barkelew."

Oprah Winfrey

A Rise from Poverty to Talk-Show Host and More

Constance Mitchell Ford

Few Americans are better known or more widely admired in the United States and around the world than Oprah Winfrey, whose rise from poverty to talk-show host, magazine publisher, book enthusiast, actress, film producer, and founder of a cable network has prompted some to label her "The Queen of All Media."

Winfrey's rise to fame and fortune began with her eponymous talk show, *The Oprah Winfrey Show*, which debuted in 1986 and aired for twenty-five years from a studio in Chicago. At its peak, the show reached more than forty million viewers a week in the United States and was licensed to air in 150 countries around the world,[1] making Winfrey a household name. The show also made her very wealthy. In 1995 Winfrey's net worth of $340 million landed her on the *Forbes* magazine list of the four hundred wealthiest Americans.[2] Eight years later, she became the second African American on the *Forbes* list of billionaires (Black Entertainment Television founder Bob Johnson was the first). In 2023, *Forbes* listed her wealth at $2.5 billion, making her number thirteen among "America's Self-Made Women."

Winfrey was much more than a talk-show host. Through her show, she became a cultural icon who inspired Americans of different races and ethnicities—especially women—to improve their lives by embracing an optimistic self-help remedy. Academics sometimes criticized her belief that individuals have the power to change their own lives for the better as unrealistic for most people and as ignoring broader structural problems outside people's control. Yet the general public applauded her message. Some credit Winfrey for helping to seat the first African American as U.S. president when she officially endorsed Barack Obama in 2007 and campaigned for him. (She first endorsed him in 2006, before he declared his candidacy.)

The Smithsonian's National Museum of African American History and Culture opened an exhibit in 2018 called "Watching Oprah: The Oprah Winfrey Show and American Culture." Lonnie G. Bunch III, the founding director of the museum, grouped her with "women who did extraordinary things in their time—Harriet Tubman, Sojourner Truth, Ida B. Wells, Maya Angelou—women who worked to redeem the soul of America."[3] The exhibit, he explained, showed how Winfrey, inspired by major cultural changes, had challenged constraints and thereby encouraged her fans to transform their lives. "Just as Oprah Winfrey watched TV coverage of the Civil Rights movement and was shaped by the era in which she was born and raised, she has gone on to have a profound effect on how Americans view themselves and each other."[4]

In a country that has not always embraced African Americans, Winfrey's ability to transcend racial barriers to achieve such a high level of success reflects her strong sense of self (Winfrey always believed she was "special")[5] and perhaps a sixth sense that served her well when navigating pivotal business decisions combined with an inclination to seek advice from powerful and successful business leaders.

Background

Oprah Winfrey has discussed openly her difficult childhood. She was born in Kosciusko, Mississippi, in 1954 to an unwed teenage mother. Her early years were spent on a small farm with her nurturing maternal grandmother. Although they lived in deep poverty, her grandmother involved Winfrey in the church, taught her to read at an early age, instilled in her the importance of education, and gave her assurances that she was "gifted."[6]

At the age of six, she was sent to live with her mother, a maid residing in Milwaukee, Wisconsin. It wasn't a happy environment.

Winfrey felt neglected by her mother and unfulfilled academically. In 1986 she told the *Washington Post*, "I ran away from home. I started acting out my need for attention, my need to be loved. My mother didn't have the time. . . . I was smart and my mother, because she didn't have the time for me, I think, tried to stifle it."[7]

During the time she lived with her mother, Winfrey was raped by a cousin and molested by a family friend,[8] devasting events that she revealed on an episode of her talk show that focused on sexual abuse. But life in Milwaukee had some bright moments, including in 1964, when the ten-year-old Winfrey tuned in to watch *The Ed Sullivan Show*. "It was a moment that changed my life. When I saw The Supremes on TV that night, it was magical to me because I'd never seen black women on television . . . who conveyed such glamour and such grace. . . . And for years, I wanted to be like Diana Ross, or just somebody supreme."[9]

At the age of fourteen, Winfrey found herself pregnant. The baby died just two weeks after birth. As a result, Winfrey was sent to live with her father Vernon Winfrey in Nashville, Tennessee. He was a barber as well as a church deacon and strict disciplinarian. Under his tutelage, Winfrey began to thrive again as her father pushed her to excel academically. She later recalled this as a turning point. "I remember my father saying to me, 'You can't bring Cs in this house because you are not a C student. . . . You are an A student. So that's what we expect in this house.' And it was just so matter of fact. And I knew he was not faking it one bit. . . . I never tried to bring in a C because I realized that it's just not acceptable."[10]

Life in Tennessee was auspicious. At the age of seventeen and still in high school, after having been named Miss Black Nashville and Miss Tennessee, Winfrey began her broadcasting career. She took an on-air job at WVOL, an AM radio station serving Nashville's African American community. She won a full scholarship to Tennessee State University, a historically Black college, where she majored in communications. Two years later, while still a student at Tennessee State, Winfrey became the first Black woman news anchor at Nashville's WTVF-TV, an affiliate of CBS Broadcasting.

In 1976, before completing college, Winfrey relocated to Baltimore to coanchor the six o'clock news at WJZ-TV, the local CBS outlet. But things did not go well. Winfrey's bosses regarded her reporting style as too casual. Sometimes she became too emotionally involved in stories; she needed to fight back tears as she read sad stories and showed anger at stories that exposed unfairness.[11] Reportedly, she clashed with her more established coanchor.[12] She was soon demoted to a lower-profile position, cohosting WJZ's local talk show, *People are Talking*. It turned out to be a perfect fit. It highlighted Winfrey's strength as a compassionate and light-hearted interviewer able to connect with her guests in a way that resonated with her audience. During remarks at the 2023 inauguration of Wes Moore, the first Black governor of Maryland, Winfrey recalled finding her calling in Baltimore: "Though it wasn't the job that I moved here to do, it was the job that sparked my desire to use television to tell stories that would impact people's lives."[13]

In 1984, Winfrey moved to Chicago to host *AM Chicago*, a low-rated local half-hour morning program on WLS-TV, which was owned by the ABC television network, a division of Walt Disney Co. As such, she competed head-on with the reigning king of talk shows at the time, *The Phil Donahue Show*. That show was not only Chicago's top-rated talk show, but it was syndicated across the United States and was the top show of its kind nationwide. Winfrey's bosses at WLS never pressured her to compete with Donahue; they never believed that she *could* compete. Yet, in less than a year, *AM Chicago* had moved ahead of Donahue. The next year, the show was renamed *The Oprah Winfrey Show*.

Fame, Fortune, and a Good Lawyer

WLS paid Winfrey $230,000 in her first year. After her show quickly became a ratings blockbuster, Winfrey's agent negotiated a four-year contract with annual salary hikes of $30,000.[14] Most talk-show hosts would have been content with such a deal, but Winfrey wanted to weigh other options. Instead of accepting her agent's plan, Winfrey sought the advice of Chicago attorney Jeffrey Jacobs. In a stroke of genius and the first clue of Winfrey's business acumen, she fired her agent and signed on with Jacobs, who convinced Winfrey not to accept a salary as an employee and instead become her own boss.

The two then negotiated several stunning deals. First, they convinced ABC to give Winfrey the syndication rights to the show. That allowed Winfrey and Jacobs to negotiate a contract with King World Productions, at the time the nation's largest television syndication company and known for distributing hit shows including *Jeopardy!* and *The Wheel of Fortune*.[15]

Next, Winfrey sought ownership of the show. This required her to assume the production costs herself, a risky move for a novice television personality. To handle that responsibility, Winfrey created Harpo Productions, which was run by Jacobs, who also owned a small share of the company. It was an audacious business maneuver that seemed incongruous coming from a once-poor Black girl from the South. To make such a move, "I had to get rid of that slave mentality," Winfrey told *Forbes* in 1995. "That's where Jeff came in. He took the ceiling off my brain."[16]

Relaunched in 1986 under its new ownership, the show earned $115 million during its first two seasons of syndication, according to *Forbes*. This business ownership deal made Winfrey one of America's richest women and led to her becoming a media mogul. It was also a good deal for Jacobs, who became her longtime business partner. In 2017, Winfrey described taking ownership of the show as her "greatest" decision. "I said (to ABC executives) what if I own the show and you don't pay me unless the show makes money and we make money together so let's split it. So, I approach everything that way. If I'm going to be of value to you, it should also be of value to myself."[17]

A Different Kind of Talk

Owning her talk show gave Winfrey more control over the content. This proved to be critical during the talk-show wars of the early 1990s, when the success of Winfrey and Donahue ushered in dozens of additional shows led by hosts such as Jerry Springer, Geraldo Rivera, Ricki Lake, and Jenny Jones. To compete, hosts let the content on the shows degenerate into what some critics called "Trash TV" or "Tabloid TV." Shows featured family dysfunction, and guests exhibited antisocial practices, sometimes telling salacious or tawdry tales.

Following her rivals, Winfrey initially sought sensational themes. But as condemnation of talk shows escalated—and her ratings slipped—Winfrey announced she would cease focusing on dysfunction and start emphasizing uplifting topics. The turn began after Winfrey aired a show featuring members of the Ku Klux Klan, the longtime hate group that pursues a white supremacist agenda. She rationalized this on the premise that the KKK was newsworthy. But she soon realized the Klansmen were using the publicity to recruit new members: "I was interviewing the Ku Klux Klan and I thought, as an African American, oh, I'm going to get them; I'm going to [do this] for every Jewish person, for every person who's been discriminated against. And during the commercial break, I saw the Klan exchanging signals and looks at each other. And then . . . I thought I am doing nobody any good. They are loving this. They are using me. . . . I made a decision after that show: I'll never do anything like that again."[18]

By the end of the 1990s, Winfrey managed not only to survive the talk-show wars but to regain the top-ranked spot. This was partly due to her personality but also her style. Other talk show hosts at the time followed a detached journalist form—interviewing that showed little emotion. Winfrey was just the opposite. She often empathized or commiserated with her guests. She became teary eyed at particularly sad stories. She divulged intimate details of her own struggles, which encouraged guests to open up further and confess their feelings. At the time, this type of display was rarely seen on talk television. She also used self-deprecating humor about her weight and other shortcomings that allowed her to connect with the women in her audience as if she were a friend.

In 1998, Deborah Tannen, a Georgetown University linguistics professor, contrasted Winfrey's and Phil Donahue's techniques:

> [Donahue's] show was mostly what I call "report-talk," which often typifies men's conversation. The overt focus is on information. Winfrey transformed the format into what I call "rapport-talk," the back-and-forth conversation that is the basis of female friendship, with its emphasis on self-revealing intimacies. She turned the focus from experts to ordinary people talking about

> personal issues. . . . Oprah exhorts viewers to improve their lives and the world. She makes people care because she cares. That is Winfrey's genius, and will be her legacy, as the changes she has wrought in the talk show continue to permeate our culture and shape our lives.[19]

Felicia Stewart, a communications professor at Morehouse College, attributes Winfrey's ability to create a sense of unity among listeners of different races and backgrounds to her speaking style and discourse. "Her voice is one of empowerment, and she has used her voice on multiple platforms. Whether during television interviews, her own talk show, keynote addresses, or award acceptance speeches, audiences find Winfrey credible and persuasive."[20]

Famous for giving lavish gifts to her talk show audience, Winfrey gave each audience member at one 2006 taping a $1,000 debit card to donate to a favorite charity. She was famously generous with employees, giving iPads and $10,000 to all staffers of her lifestyle publication *O, The Oprah Magazine* to commemorate the magazine's tenth anniversary. One of the magazine's editors is Winfrey's long-time best friend Gayle King, who has hosted or co-anchored several talk shows, including *CBS Mornings* (formerly, *CBS This Morning*).

Winfrey's love of reading and her belief in the power of literature to enlighten and uplift people's lives was a frequent theme on her talk show and led to the creation of Oprah's Book Club in 1996, which, in turn, encouraged masses of women to launch local book clubs to follow and discuss Oprah's books. Each month, Winfrey selected a book, one that she thought would enlighten readers, to discuss on her show the following month. The books Winfrey recommended often became instant bestsellers, even old or obscure titles such as Leo Tolstoy's *Anna Karenina*, first published in 1878. The English translation that Winfrey chose of the novel, about a Russian high-society woman who has an extramarital affair, typically sold about twenty thousand copies annually. After Winfrey endorsed the book in 2004, sales surged; the publisher of that translation, Penguin Books, increased the print run to at least nine hundred thousand copies that year.[21]

This phenomenon came to be called the *Oprah Effect*. Fordham University professor Albert Greco estimates that the seventy books on Oprah's list sold fifty-five million copies during the fifteen years of the club's operation.[22] After *The Oprah Winfrey Show* ceased in 2011, the book club lived on, first as Oprah's Book Club 2.0 and again in 2019 as a joint venture with Apple TV+.[23] The long-lasting book club announced its one hundredth selection in 2023 and continues with several award-winning podcasts based on selections including *Caste* by Isabel Wilkerson and *The Covenant of Water* by Abraham Verghese.

Winfrey sometimes turned her favorite novels into films, including *Beloved*, the 1998 psychological horror drama about a former enslaved mother, played by Winfrey. The film, based on Toni Morrison's novel, was produced by Winfrey's Harpo Productions Inc. (Oprah spelled backward). Since 1989, Harpo has produced dozens of movies, television shows, and series; and Winfrey has acted in more than a dozen films. She was nominated for an Academy Award for best supporting actress in *The Color Purple*, released in 1985 and based on a novel by Alice Walker.[24] In 2014, she both coproduced and appeared in the film *Selma*, which was nominated for an Academy Award for best picture.

Winfrey has had her share of critics over the years. On several occasions, her show was blasted for allowing guests to promote speculative topics and unfounded health claims. For example, in September 2007 actress Jenny McCarthy asserted on the show that her son's autism began after he received the vaccine for measles, mumps, and rubella, a claim that the mainstream medical community disputes. Critics argued that Winfrey didn't push back against McCarthy's claims, which helped energize the antivaccination movement.[25]

Other critics take issue with Winfrey's confidence in the power of self-transformation. Janice Peck, a media scholar and former journalist, argues that such goals are unrealistic for most Americans given people's declining power over the material condition of their lives: "Oprah Winfrey has ascended to the position of culture icon of mainstream America by telling us we can do anything we put our minds to. This is a promise not unlike that of the lottery. Both are forms of wish fulfillment that owe their allure to the harsh reality of a go-it-alone world, both are ideological practices that help legitimize and reproduce the neoliberal order and forms of social (class) subjectivities appropriate to it."[26]

But Winfrey did have effects. During a 1996 show about mad cow disease and the risks of eating beef, Winfrey swore off burgers. This sent cattle prices tumbling and landed her in court two years later for "false defamation" of beef. The plaintiffs, four cattle ranchers in Amarillo, Texas, argued that her comments caused them to lose $11 million. After a six-week trial, the jury found in Winfrey's favor. Winfrey told a cheering crowd, "I will continue to use my voice. . . . I believed from the beginning this was an attempt to muzzle that voice. I come from a people who have struggled and died in order to have a voice in this country, and I refuse to be muzzled."[27]

One side benefit of the trial was that Winfrey's legal team hired Phil McGraw as a jury consultant. Winfrey was impressed by McGraw's work and invited him on her show, helping to launch his career as a television advice coach. Winfrey's Harpo produced McGraw's show, as well as the shows of Winfrey protégées Rachael Ray, who promotes cooking skills, and Dr. Mehmet Oz, who discussed medical matters and health.

Empowering Girls

Winfrey is often hailed for her philanthropy. Winfrey teamed up with Kraft Heinz Company, for example, on Mealtime Stories, which gives 10 percent of profits to food-related charities; its first was a line of soups and sides called O, That's Good! Her main tool for giving is the Oprah Winfrey Charitable Foundation, which supports schools, college scholarships, youth centers, and food distribution programs, among other things. Since its inception in 2010, the foundation has donated $400 million to a variety of individuals and organizations.[28]

Over $250 million has gone to The Oprah Winfrey Leadership Academy for Girls, a boarding school in South Africa that opened in 2007. Nearly all its graduates have gone on to attend college in South Africa, the United States, or Britain. In 2015, when being recognized for her philanthropy at *Variety*'s Power of Women luncheon, Winfrey gave a tearful speech, which has been viewed over three million times on YouTube. She explained that when she first came to Chicago and was earning more money than needed to pay bills, she considered launching something to help young girls in housing projects. She said that she could not really change the trajectory of those girls' lives because, after taking them out of the projects and spending time with them on the weekends, they would need to return to the same environment. "So by trial and error, I knew that in order to literally change the way a girl sees herself, I would need enough time to spend with her to be able to hire the right kind of teachers, the right kind of administration to be surrounded by a nurturing environment, to allow that girl to change the way she felt about herself and saw herself in the world."[29]

From this realization came the idea of creating a school for leaders in South Africa that would change women's lives and enable them "to break the cycle of poverty for themselves and their families forever."[30] The school had a rocky start, however. Soon after it opened, a woman staff member was accused of sexually and physically abusing students. While the episode was embarrassing, Winfrey generally won praise for dealing with the matter swiftly; she flew to South Africa to meet personally with parents and students and hired detectives to investigate the allegations. With its research-based holistic approach to education, the school continues to flourish.

Critical Juncture

Not everything Winfrey touched was an immediate success. Her leap from producing talk shows and film projects to launching an entire cable television network, the Oprah Winfrey Network (OWN), proved to be enormously difficult. Winfrey launched OWN in 2011 as a joint venture with Discovery Communications Inc., now known as Warner Brothers Discovery Inc. According to the parent company, OWN is the only network named for and inspired by a single person; it continues to be a leading destination for scripted and unscripted programming. Initially, Winfrey intended OWN to be a destination for the self-help, self-awareness, and be-your-best programming that she assumed her followers desired. After all, that formula worked phenomenally well for twenty-five years on her talk show. But the early programs, including a talk show featuring actress Rosie O'Donnell and a self-help reality show called *Oprah's Lifeclass*, where Winfrey offered lessons on how to maneuver different situations, never caught on. Ratings for the station were dismal.

Why Winfrey's fans didn't follow her to OWN is not entirely clear. Some critics argue that the original programming was dull and uninspiring. Some members of Oprah's team argue that viewers were accustomed to watching Oprah for free for twenty-five years on ABC. Moreover, when OWN launched, many of her fans did not have cable subscriptions. Others believe Americans had just grown exhausted with Winfrey and the talk-show format. "The industry had just become so wide and vast that people had other places to go," said Stewart, the Morehouse professor. "Some people may have thought she hit her pinnacle when she had the show and saw that as her peak. When she retired from the show, some people retired from her and moved on."[31]

Winfrey believes the problem with OWN was that she miscalculated the amount of self-reflection programs Americans really wanted. "I thought I was going to have people meditating in the morning, yoga classes midday, [spiritual guide] Eckhart Tolle on in the afternoon," Winfrey told *Fast Company* magazine. "I had a vision of what living your best life could look like. The people told me otherwise. I had to redo my vision."[32]

She similarly told *Vogue*, "I was so misled in my thinking. I thought I was going to create a network that was Super Soul Sunday all day long," referring to her show that interviewed top thought leaders. "I thought I was going to bring this spiritual consciousness–*awakening* channel! And I soon learned: Ain't *nobody* care about that."[33]

Resolution

The redo required rethinking what would attract viewers but without tarnishing her mainstream image. Winfrey had always appealed to a broad cross-section of America—all races, ethnic groups, and income levels, in all areas of the country. And her brand was decidedly traditional. In discussions with Discovery executives, she decided that OWN needed original, scripted programs.

For help, she turned to Tyler Perry, the Black Atlanta-based entertainment mogul and actor who created numerous movies and plays, many of which could be categorized as lowbrow comedies geared to African American audiences. Perry decided to ditch slapstick humor and create for OWN serious situational dramas about Black families, starting with *The Haves and the Have Nots*, a combination crime drama and soap opera. Shortly after it premiered in 2013, it became the most-watched scripted cable series among African American women. The show turned around OWN's fortunes. Although creating a network that appealed largely to African American women was not part of Winfrey's initial vision, this turned out to be an ideal audience. "It was an overlooked market," said Christopher Farley, a former *Wall Street Journal* culture editor and currently an executive editor at Audible who interviewed Winfrey several times over the years.[34] He added that many in Hollywood failed to understand this untapped market but "targeting black women is a very large and lucrative audience."

Leading OWN allowed Winfrey to break barriers for women in a way that had a profound impact on Hollywood. The most famous example is her 2016 decision to hire only women directors for a new OWN series, *Queen Sugar*, a family drama based on a novel by the same name. The series—which listed Winfrey and acclaimed film director Ava DuVernay as co–executive producers—centers on the lives of three African American siblings in rural Louisiana who must deal with the aftermath of their father's death and decide the fate of his eight-hundred-acre sugarcane farm. Over the course of its five-year run, *Queen Sugar* employed forty-two women as directors. Some were experienced film directors who nevertheless had trouble landing steady work in a field dominated by men. Others were newcomers looking for their first big break. During an interview for *Variety*'s 2022 Power of Women issue, which honored Winfrey and DuVernay, the two discussed their decision to hire only women directors. Winfrey said, "I remember getting the call from Ava saying 'I have this idea. What if we just have all women directors.' I go 'all women directors, can we do that?' She goes 'yeah, we can do that because you own the network.' Talk about an empowered idea."[35] DuVernay credited the support of a Black woman–owned network, saying the proposal would never have happened without a network to support it. She appreciated "being on a Black woman owned network that allowed us to not just let this be a trend or idea to launch the show, but a real movement that contributed to 42 women directors."[36]

All of the *Queen Sugar* directors were first-time television directors, and all of them went on to direct other television programs and films in Hollywood and elsewhere. A spokeswoman for Winfrey says the network has hired numerous women directors across all programming on OWN, although *Queen Sugar* was the only one to use only women.[37] By 2018, *Queen Sugar* and *Greenleaf*, a family saga about a Memphis megachurch controlled by the wealthy Greenleaf family, were two of the top five ad-supported cable dramas among women twenty-five to fifty-four years old.[38]

In 2017, Winfrey told a Bloomberg interviewer that her work on OWN was similar to her talk show: "Every day on my show for 25 years, I was the storyteller. You keep helping people to let their stories out into the world in such a way that enhances them or helps them see themselves. . . . Now I get to use drama as a platform to create stories that allow people, particularly African American people, to see and feel themselves in a way that shows us as people of value, as people who care about the things that everybody else cares about."[39] OWN was profitable and had approximately seventy million U.S. subscribers in December 2021.[40] In 2020, Winfrey announced that OWN would give staffers a paid day off for national election days and called on other business leaders to do the same. The network led a nonpartisan campaign called OWN Your Voice, hosting town hall conversations to encourage voting.

Conclusion

Winfrey empowered audiences to transform and uplift their lives, inspired people to embrace literature, hired and promoted women for high-level positions, and advanced educational opportunities for the disadvantaged. How long Winfrey will remain at the helm of

OWN is unclear. In 2020, Winfrey sold most of her remaining stake to Discovery. The transaction, according to Bloomberg, raised Discovery's stake to 95 percent and left Winfrey with 5 percent or less, although she remains CEO.[41]

She has very successfully invested in or even helped to launch mission-based businesses.[42] Winfrey invested $34 million in Weight Watchers (now called WW International), which supports sustainable weight loss by teaching healthy habits such as nutritional eating and exercise. In February 2024, however, she announced that to eliminate any perceived conflict of interest around her taking weight loss medications, she would not stand for reelection as a board of directors member and would donate her interest in the company to the National Museum of African American History and Culture.[43] She also invested in True Food Kitchen, founded by Dr. Andrew Weil. In 2020, with other celebrities she began backing new food startups, such as one that produces an edible coating that extends the shelf life of fruit, thus reducing wastage. With Natalie Portman, former Starbucks CEO Howard Schultz, and Jay-Z's entertainment company, Winfrey invested in an oat milk company that promotes nutrition and sustainability.[44]

Winfrey's accomplishments notably illustrate the power of leadership that comes through business ownership. By owning her talk show, she could determine the content. By creating her own cable network, she could cater to an untapped, underappreciated audience and permanently change Hollywood. Donating money to education and scholarships will presumably change the trajectory of thousands of lives and help to strengthen Black communities globally.

Notes

1 "Oprah Winfrey's Official Biography," Oprah.com, www.oprah.com/press room/oprah-winfreys-official-biography/all.

2 Jennifer Eum, "How Oprah Went from Talk Show Host to First African-American Woman Billionaire," *Forbes*, September 29, 2014 (based on 1995 reporting by Robert La Franco with Josh McHugh), www.forbes.com/sites /jennifereum/2014/09/29/how-oprah-went-from-talk-show-host-to-first -african-american-woman-billionaire/?sh=1db1a1316163.

3 "'Watching Oprah' Exhibition Opens at National Museum of African American History and Culture June 8," National Museum of African American

History & Culture, June 6, 2018, https://nmaahc.si.edu/about/news/watching-oprah-exhibition-opens-national-museum-african-american-history-and-culture.

4 "'Watching Oprah.'"

5 "Oprah Winfrey: Media Entrepreneur," Academy of Achievement, February 1991, https://achievement.org/achiever/oprah-winfrey/.

6 "Oprah Winfrey: Media Entrepreneur."

7 Jill Nelson, "The Man Who Saved Oprah Winfrey," *Washington Post*, December 14, 1986, www.washingtonpost.com/archive/lifestyle/magazine/1986/12/14/the-man-who-saved-oprah-winfrey/66d7b7b3-98af-4495-82a7-6b04827f1bd6/.

8 Thomas Morgan, "Troubled Girl's Evolution into an Oscar Nominee," *New York Times*, March 4, 1986, www.nytimes.com/1986/03/04/movies/troubled-girl-s-evolution-into-an-oscar-nominee.html.

9 "'Watching Oprah.'"

10 "Oprah Winfrey: Media Entrepreneur."

11 Anjali Becker and Jeanne Engelmann, *Own It: Oprah in Her Own Words* (B2 Books, 2016).

12 Anne Lies, *Oprah Winfrey: Media Mogul* (ABDO Publishing, 2011).

13 CBS Staff, "Oprah Said Eight Years in Maryland at WJZ Were 'Most Significant Years of My Life,'" *CBS News Baltimore*, January 18, 2023, www.cbsnews.com/baltimore/news/oprah-winfrey-wes-moore-governor-inauguration-maryland-wjz/#.

14 Jennifer Eum, "How Oprah Went from Talk Show Host to First African-American Woman Billionaire," *Forbes*, September 29, 2014, www.forbes.com/sites/jennifereum/2014/09/29/how-oprah-went-from-talk-show-host-to-first-african-american-woman-billionaire.

15 King World was acquired by CBS in 1999.

16 Eum, "How Oprah Went."

17 "The David Rubenstein Show: Oprah Winfrey," *Bloomberg*, March 1, 2017, www.bloomberg.com/news/videos/2017-03-01/the-one-question-oprah-winfrey-says-every-guest-asked.

18 Oprah Winfrey, "The Secret of My Success," Stanford Graduate School of Business, April 16, 2014, www.youtube.com/watch?v=6DlrqeWrczs.

19 Deborah Tannen, "Oprah Winfrey: The TV Host," *Time*, June 8, 1998, https://time.com/archive/6598176/oprah-winfrey-the-tv-host/.

20 Felicia R. Stewart, "Exploring Afrocentricity: An Analysis of the Discourse of Oprah Winfrey," *Journal of Black Studies* 51, no. 8 (2020): 832–833.

21 Edward Wyatt, "Tolstoy's Translators Experience Oprah's Effect," *New York Times*, June 7, 2004, www.nytimes.com/2004/06/07/books/tolstoy-s-translators-experience-oprah-s-effect.html.

22 Oprah Winfrey, author interview, January 2023.

23 "How Oprah's Book Club Came to Be," Oprah.com, www.oprah.com/oprahsbookclub/how-oprahs-book-club-came-to-be.

24 Winfrey's company did not produce that film.

25 Julie Gunlock, "Oprah's 'Truth' and its Potentially Deadly Consequences," *Wall Street Journal*, January 10, 2018, www.wsj.com/articles/oprahs-truth-and-its-potentially-deadly-consequences-1515628059.

26 Janice Peck, "The Secret of Her Success: Oprah Winfrey and the Seductions of Self-Transformation," *Journal of Communication Inquiry* 34, no. 1 (2010): 12.

27 Aman Betheja, "The Time Oprah Winfrey Beefed with the Texas Cattle Industry," *Texas Tribune*, January 10, 2018, www.texastribune.org/2018/01/10/time-oprah-winfrey-beefed-texas-cattle-industry/.

28 The Oprah Winfrey Charitable Foundation, www.oprahfoundation.org/.

29 Oprah Winfrey, speech at *Variety*'s Power of Women, www.youtube.com/watch?v=6Rfn94k717U. Oct. 20, 2015.

30 Winfrey, Power of Women speech.

31 Oprah Winfrey, interview, March 2023.

32 J. J. McCorvey, "The Key to Oprah Winfrey's Success: Radical Focus," *Fast Company*, October 12, 2015, www.fastcompany.com/3051589/the-key-to-oprah-winfreys-success-radical-focus.

33 Jonathan Van Meter, "Oprah Is on a Roll (Again)," *Vogue*, August 15, 2017, www.vogue.com/article/oprah-winfrey-vogue-september-issue—2017.

34 Winfrey, author interview, January 2023.

35 Angelique Jackson, "Oprah Winfrey Shares the Greatest Lesson She Took from Her 25-Year Talk Show: 'We Want to Know We Matter,'" September 28, 2022, *Variety*, https://variety.com/2022/biz/news/oprah-winfrey-greatest-lesson-talk-show-1235386739/.

36 Jackson, "Oprah Winfrey Shares."

37 Personal email exchange with OWN spokeswoman, March 2023.

38 Madeline Berg, "Oprah Winfrey Just Sold Most of Her Stake in Her OWN Cable Network," *Forbes*, December 22, 2020, www.forbes.com/sites/maddieberg/2020/12/22/oprah-winfrey-just-sold-most-of-her-stake-in-her-own-cable-network/?sh=fb93b4425468.

39 "The David Rubenstein Show: Oprah Winfrey," Bloomberg, March 1, 2017, www.bloomberg.com/news/videos/2017-03-01/the-david-rubenstein-show-oprah-winfrey.

40 Discovery Inc. 10-K filing with the U.S. Securities and Exchange Commission, February 2022.

41 Berg, "Oprah Winfrey Just Sold."

42 Jennifer Taylor, "Here Are All the Ways Oprah Winfrey Gives Back," GOBankingRates, January 29, 2021, https://www.gobankingrates.com/net-worth/business-people/how-oprah-winfrey-gives-back/.

43 "WW International, Inc. Announces Upcoming Oprah Winfrey Board Transition," February 28, 2024, https://corporate.ww.com/news/news-details/2024/WW-International-Inc.-Announces-Upcoming-Oprah-Winfrey-Board-Transition/default.aspx.

44 Hannah L. Miller, "Oprah Winfrey: The Business of Breaking Barriers and Becoming a Billionaire," *Leaders*, April 27, 2023, https://leaders.com/articles/leaders-stories/oprah-winfrey/.

Frances "Franco" Stevens

Raising Lesbian Visibility through Magazine (Re)Making

Stine Eckert

Frances "Franco" Stevens has long been adored and celebrated by readers of *Deneuve*, later called *Curve*, the national magazine she founded in 1990. Probably the most famous publication by and for lesbians in the world,[1] it became the most successful and longest-running lesbian magazine in the United States.[2] The magazine knew lesbians were cool well before the television shows *The L Word* and *Orange Is the New Black*. For many girls and women, *Deneuve/Curve* was the first time that they saw a magazine cover feature a lesbian; for others, it was their lifeline to a lesbian community.

Background

Frances Rene Stevens was born in Washington, D.C., in 1967 into a Jewish family. Growing up she said she never knew an "out" gay person and only *saw* a gay man in the TV show *Soap*.[3] In the 1980s she married a U.S. Army doctor, Blaine Stevens, moved to San Francisco for his work, fell in love with a woman, and divorced.[4] Before their wedding, Stevens said, she told her then-boyfriend about her feelings for women, but "he thought it was a phase."[5] Through taking a course on Variations in Human Sexuality at San Francisco State University, she said, she realized her identity as lesbian. But it was her husband who outed her to her family when, at a family gathering, he blurted out, "My wife is a d-ke!" Stevens said while the result of this was that she did not need to out herself, she also felt that it was her story to tell when she was ready; she resented that her story was "taken away" from her.[6]

After being outed to her family, Stevens lived in her car for about three months. When she called her mother for help and five hundred dollars, her mother said she could not support her. Stevens said she felt "completely alone" but later reconciled with her mother.[7] At the time, Stevens was majoring in biochemistry and microbiology at San Francisco State University.[8] Discovering that she was allergic to "practically every kind of animal," however, ended her plan to become a veterinarian.[9] Finally telling a university friend that she had no place to live, the friend and his roommate, both bisexual men, invited her to move in; they introduced her to the Castro, a gay neighborhood. They had a great time at Castro's gay bars. "But," she later said, "there's no women here. Where are the women?"[10]

Still, she was finally allowed to be herself. After meeting her first girlfriend, she also discovered the gay bookstore A Different Light. The store was a revelation to her: "Holy crap, there's books about this stuff, there's books where we're just normal people. And that's how I got sort of interested in resources that were there for me. I remember hiding in the San Francisco State library and looking for any queer stuff. And then when I found the bookstore, it just seemed immediately like home, like, OK, what do I have to do to get a job in this place? Because surely there's gonna be a wealth of information. I can read books when it's not busy and women are going to come in here."[11] She did get a job in the bookstore as a clerk—setting the course for more than just reading books about lesbians and meeting women.

Glossy and Coffee-Table Ready: A New Type of Magazine about, for, and by Lesbians

Not only was her search for a magazine about lesbians futile, but A Different Light customers also asked her for lesbian magazines: "The first week I worked there, there must have been about twenty women who came in and asked for a magazine like what I had envisioned."[12] One day it dawned on her: "I should be the one to create it. If you want things to change, you must take action instead of just complaining that someone else should."[13] At the time, the only glossy magazine for lesbians, *On Our Backs*, focused on porn; the *Lesbian News* in Los Angeles had a glossy cover but newsprint pages; all other publications for queer women were newspapers and zines.[14]

In 1990, at age twenty-two, Stevens founded *Deneuve* magazine, becoming a part of the beginning of the heyday of gays and lesbians in San Francisco and embarking on a publishing journey whose success was hard to foresee: "If somebody would have told twenty-two-year-old me that like twenty years later, this thing would still be going on, I'd be like, no way."[15]

Stevens had little journalism experience beyond a stint at her school newspaper and experiments with newsletters and a small lesbian tabloid.[16] She had to start from scratch: "I tried to seek out mentors and funding. I was a little kid and I wanted to put 'lesbian' on the front cover. . . . I wasn't taken seriously at all. There was no mentorship that I knew of for young people at that time."[17] She bought "about forty books on publishing," raised some money, and put a sign in the bookstore window calling for writers and photographers.[18] She received three hundred calls within one month, including from women who admitted they had no skills but thought the idea was so great that they would be willing to help in any way. More than one hundred appeared at a subsequent meeting.[19] A designer, who was also a student, got Stevens and her volunteers into her classroom after hours and on weekends to lay out the first issue of the glossy, colorful magazine that Stevens had envisioned: "I wanted a magazine that I could be proud to leave on my coffee table, even if my mom happened to walk by . . . a 'real' magazine, covering everything from news and politics to art and entertainment while celebrating lesbian women and their community."[20] Sick of seeing lesbian women treated like second-class citizens, Stevens ensured the magazine was printed on "nice paper."[21]

Stevens faced any number of challenges, she said, due to her gender: "You go on a press check at the printer and you're a woman, so they don't really care about your opinions when [something didn't] look right. . . . It . . . was definitely a man's world and I was not really welcome in it."[22] In 1991, the first issue of *Deneuve—A Lesbian*

Magazine was published. Its cover announced articles on "Lesbians Take Office," "Hot Spots & Hang Outs," "Previews & Reviews," a "Phranc Exclusive" interview with a singer-songwriter, and lesbian literature for high schools.[23] Named for Stevens's "first love,"[24] *Deneuve*'s thirty-two pages also contained poetry, tips on taxes, dating and travel advice, and an article on the comeback of an Olympic cyclist. Its three thousand print copies sold out in six days.[25] "When I held the first issue of the magazine in my hands, I felt as though I had given birth. It was one of the greatest moments of my life," Stevens reflected.[26] A woman camp cocounselor with whom Stevens worked when she was fifteen years had told Stevens that the kissing they had enjoyed was "not normal."[27] By founding *Deneuve*, Stevens tapped into San Francisco's lesbian community to create her own new normal: "We were in this little bubble of positivity, and everything around us was just full of negative energy: the economy's bad and the politics are horrible and everybody wants to kill us and/or hurt us. There were no lesbian rights. It was a very different time back then."[28]

Early Challenges: Raising Money during a Recession

When founding the magazine, financial challenges were her largest barrier. She worked extra hours at A Different Light, waitressed, promoted clubs, and invested in the stock market to build up the needed cash and credit. When she pitched her business plan, the economy was in recession and many print magazines were folding. Banks were reluctant to fund any new magazine, let alone a lesbian one: "Besides the homophobia, the misogyny in the business world was just brutal," Stevens recalled.[29] After getting denied despite having saved $70,000, she applied for several credit cards, cashed out nearly half a dozen at the same time, bet the money on racehorses, and won enough money to publish the first three issues.[30]

Moreover, getting the magazine into readers' hands was difficult: bookstores did not want to put the magazine on their shelves. Stevens therefore not only sent the first issue to magazine distributors and newsstands but also sold copies on the street outside A Different Light.[31] Finally, some mentors, such as Gina Gatta, who published city guides for gays and lesbians, saw the first issue and reached out to Stevens to express congratulations. Stevens responded to such appreciation by expressing her own respect and asking whether she could occasionally call them with her questions. Another mentor, Barbara Grier, cofounder of the lesbian book publisher Naiad Press, said she would support *Deneuve* if Stevens would send her five thousand flyers about the magazine to send to Naiad's mailing list.[32] By cleaning motorcycles, Stevens and her cofighters raised six hundred dollars to print the flyers, which Grier mailed to customers with an endorsement that *Deneuve* was the "greatest thing" for lesbians. Subscriptions arrived in droves.[33]

Growing *Deneuve* with Manila Envelopes and Lesbian Celebrities

Understanding that many women did not visit gay/alternative bookstores, Stevens leveraged knowledge gained from promoting dance clubs to spread the word about *Deneuve* through monthly dance parties.[34] In 1993, Stevens and colleagues even took a road trip across the United States to increase the magazine's visibility.[35] They visited a different city every day: going on radio shows, reading in bookstores, and going to coffee shops, clubs, and bars. "The magazine became a way for women to connect when they had no other way to meet each other. . . . That was deeply powerful validation that you're not alone," Stevens said.[36] Especially in rural areas, *Deneuve* offered a crucial connection for the lesbian community.[37] In 1992 about 40 percent of the copies were sold in rural areas: "A lot of women in these [areas] don't have any other contact with the lesbian community; we are it," Stevens said.[38] In the early days, the magazine, mailed in manila envelopes to hide the type of magazine, *Deneuve* received about a hundred inquiries a week from women who wanted to connect with other lesbians.[39]

Deneuve's first issue cost four dollars and contained two ads: for the computer business of Steven's father and A Different Light. Stevens realized she needed contracts with national advertisers, but this, too, was difficult: *Deneuve* wanted to allot only 40 percent of its space to ads rather than the 60 percent then common for magazines. But even by 2010 lesbians were not seen as a big market: "Gay men are seen as trendsetters and early adopters, whereas lesbians aren't. They aren't seen as cutting-edge in anything—fashion or technology—and the media has a lot to say about that. So, we feel it's our responsibility to help change the perception in the world and not just complain about it."[40] Nevertheless, *Deneuve/Curve* adhered to self-imposed policies on whose money it would take: "Beauty and fashion ads are rare; tobacco and fur ads are forbidden"; alcohol ads were permitted on the theory that alcohol is safe in moderation.[41] It refused sex advertisements except for sex toys and one sex store.[42] Eventually, big companies warmed to *Deneuve/Curve*; it ran ads for Bud Light, Subaru, Banana Republic, and United Colors of Benetton.[43] After Stevens made several cold calls to its ad agency, Anheuser-Busch suddenly agreed to take an ad, although the original copy showed a man's hand pulling a beer out of an ice cooler. Eventually, ads featured "real-life-like" women; compared to magazines targeting heterosexual women, its ads showed a broader range in body size, gender appearance, age, and dress.[44]

Deneuve continued to gain readers: by 1996 it had a circulation of sixty thousand copies, including fourteen thousand subscribers and an estimated two hundred thousand readers.[45] In 1993, it collected more than four thousand questionnaires from readers in big cities and farm towns across the country. Analysis of a 30 percent random sample showed that 86 percent of readers identified as lesbians; more than two-thirds had come out before the age of twenty-five and were out to parents and friends; only a third were out in their offices, schools, and organizations; 87 percent were feminists; and 11 percent had children.[46] The same survey showed that readers' favorite parts of *Deneuve* were the LesboFile—News, Rumors and Tidbits from the Lesbian Nation, Profiles of People, Features, D-ke Drama (a satiric view at lesbian life), and Book Reviews.[47]

From the beginning, Stevens strove to present the heterogeneity within the lesbian community. But former editor in chief Diane Anderson-Minshall said they should have featured Brown and Black women earlier and more often on the cover.[48] Additionally, ageism affected the magazine. When a 1991 *Deneuve* cover featured a lesbian over sixty years old—after previous covers featured lesbians in their twenties and thirties—the issue was a big financial loss: "Women wouldn't even pick up the damn thing!" Stevens recalled.[49] The magazine's concept of diversity was also intended to include celebrities as out-lesbian role models. But getting one on the cover was another challenge: Several stars known to be gay—tennis superstar Martina Navratilova and actor Lily Tomlin—were not then out publicly. The first one to be featured on *Deneuve* was singer-songwriter Melissa Etheridge, in December 1993, with the title "Melissa. Yes I Am!"[50] Stevens's magazine pioneered in putting prominent lesbians on the cover *as lesbians*.[51]

Critical Juncture

Perhaps the biggest challenge to the magazine came from a celebrity. Stevens remembers one day in 1994 or 1995: "I picked up this letter and I was like, oh no, no bueno. So, I opened it, and I was like, oh, this is just a joke. And then I was like, oh, I don't know that this is a joke. And then my heart just sank."[52] The letter notified her of a trademark infringement lawsuit filed by film legend Catherine Deneuve for the magazine's name. Although revered by lesbians for her portrayal of a lesbian vampire in the 1983 cult movie *The Hunger*, Deneuve did not want to be associated with a lesbian magazine. The lawsuits, one filed in Los Angeles and one in Paris, terrified Stevens, who called it "the most stressful time" in her life, causing her hair loss and insomnia.[53] The *New York Times* story about the lawsuit quoted Deneuve's lawyer stating that she wanted to protect a cosmetics line named for her: "It's not a political issue. . . . It's not an anti-lesbian thing at all. It's a trademark case but it's also a case regarding the right of a celebrity to market her own name and image."[54] The gay community disagreed. Anita Lofton, a DJ who helped with a magazine fundraiser, said it had more to do with homophobia than trademark infringement: "If it had been *Deneuve* the boating magazine, she wouldn't have minded."[55]

To keep the magazine going financially while raising funds for the legal battle, Stevens took money from a loan shark and organized the 1996 Alive & Kicking fundraiser in San Francisco. The event featured American celebrities such as writer Armistead Maupin and comedian-actor Lea DeLaria. Singer-songwriters Melissa Etheridge and k. d. lang donated autographed memorabilia for auctioning. Yet, despite this financial and community support, Stevens said she gave up after more than a year of battle. In order not to "die of legal fees" she settled with *Deneuve* out of court with neither party commenting on details.[56] "There's a gag order, like I've signed something saying I would never discuss this."[57] The biggest result: Stevens changed the magazine's name to *Curve*—it stood for not being "straight," for being "elegant," "exciting," "feminine," and implying "fullness."[58] The first issue with the *Curve* name appeared in 1996 with Martina Navratilova on the cover; a red band at the top stated, "Formerly Deneuve." After the name change, sales increased initially by 12 percent.[59]

With the magazine back on track Stevens continued to pour herself into it: "There was no family balance. There was no girlfriend balance. The magazine was my wife. It always came first." When she had a girlfriend, her girlfriend needed to figure out a way to get involved with *Deneuve* because this was where she was: "Everybody that I held close was somehow in one way or another affiliated with the magazine," Stevens reflected.[60] Stevens, then an avid boxer, described her daily routine as running three miles to work at 7 A.M., working until 5 P.M., going to the boxing gym, which closed at 8 P.M., then returning to the office to finish work. Stevens said boxing gave her a lot of discipline and confidence; the men-dominated environment taught her to "be one of the guys." She also found that sparring offered lessons applicable to the business world. For example, in one match she faced a woman—a very rare case. Following her trainer's instructions, she pummeled the other woman until she was "just a mess." The round was not over, but Stevens returned to her corner thinking her opponent was done. But her trainer thought otherwise and "chewed" her out:

> He was like, you keep throwing until I say you stop. If you were a man, do you think you would have just stopped? . . . This has to say a lot about my perception of men versus women in business at that time. . . . I thought, men will just go for the jugular, that's what they've been trained to do. I was trained that if somebody is

> hurting, you help them, you support them. And I was like, well, maybe I need to start looking at things a little differently; maybe I need to be more cutthroat. . . . Maybe when somebody's hurt, I need to go in for that final blow instead of checking to see if they're OK, and then I just realized, you know what? That's not me. That's not how I perform in life, that's not how I perform in the ring. And that's not how I want to perform in business.[61]

Then catastrophe struck. In 1997 she tripped and dropped a heavy box on her feet, breaking a bone and damaging nerves. Despite surgeries, she experienced ongoing physical pain: "It's like the nerve pain that just zings through your whole body like an ice pick."[62] During this difficult time, again the community came to help: "It was great how the people that were in my life rallied around me and held me and took care of me. There was a long time where I literally could not get out of bed. I did not leave my house. . . . My whole life changed in an instant."[63] Since the injury, Stevens has used a motorized wheelchair. She used a home health aide until this was denied after changes in California's workers' compensation system, which she has been fighting through the courts.[64] After her injury, she also met and married her wife, Jen Rainin. Rainin brought two sons into their marriage. The fallout from the injury and wanting to spend more time with her family led Stevens to conclude that she could no longer run *Curve*.[65]

Moreover, *Curve*'s financial troubles mounted, fueled by a global economic crisis, changes in the media industry, and an increasing acceptance of queer culture in mainstream media.[66] Stevens cut costs, running the magazine "crazy lean and mean" and holding fundraisers.[67] She also pleaded with readers in an editorial: "I admit the horrible truth: without your help, in the form of a subscription or even an outright gift or donation [*Curve*] may not continue."[68] In October 2010, Stevens sold *Curve* to Silke Bader, CEO of Australian lesbian publishing company Avalon Media; the purchase price remains confidential.[69] Avalon had already been publishing two lesbian magazines, for one of which Merryn Johns was the editor in chief. Johns took over the leadership of *Curve*, beginning with the

January/February 2011 issue. "It almost felt like when I sold the magazine, my child was going off to be married," Stevens said.[70]

Stevens remained deeply involved with the magazine. And *Curve* again landed in financial trouble despite a 2016 merger with a similar publication in the United Kingdom.[71] *Curve*'s circulation had dropped to 52,237 copies with 182,831 readers.[72] In 2020 Stevens and her wife bought back *Curve* for an undisclosed sum. They turned it into a nonprofit online publication, which launched in 2021 and appears occasionally, in conjunction with their newly created Curve Foundation. Stevens worked on the foundation's mission statement and serves as a sounding board and mentor. But the foundation has its own executive director. Moreover, her resources are limited by living with chronic pain. Part of *Curve*'s mission now is supporting journalists, for instance collaborating with NLGJA: The Association of LGBTQ Journalists. Since 2021 *Curve* has given $5,000 cash awards annually to five "emerging journalists whose work fosters fair and accurate coverage and elevates the voices of LGBTQ women."[73] An award launched in 2023 goes to seasoned journalists who cover lesbian social justice issues and communities.[74] The foundation also created a searchable, open-access archive[75] of all *Deneuve/Curve* issues.

Conclusion

Stevens used *Deneuve/Curve* to lead the way toward cultural change, covering issues well before mainstream media "discovered" them. Early on *Deneuve/Curve* highlighted issues such as workplace discrimination and benefits for partners in same-sex marriages, custody battles, and the genderizing of children's toys. It broke new ground on topics considered radical at the time, such as marriage equality, civil unions, adoption, pregnancy in the queer community, and gender transition. The *New York Times* called *Curve* "audacious."[76] For the lesbian community, DJ Anita Lofton best sums up the magazine's significance: "It's an awesome magazine and lesbians have so few things that are awesome. It's what *Life* is to white America or what *Ebony* is to black America."[77]

Stevens's journey demonstrates the personal risk, tenacity, and creativity that go into founding an alternative medium for women at a difficult time for LGBTQ+ folks. Her notion of leadership is that of a team player: "Maybe I empower people and then get out of the way. Or I try to, I don't know if I do that. I think being a good leader means picking the right people. One player can't do it all by themselves, and it was always a team effort with *Deneuve* and *Curve*. And I wish the other women who put their lives into it would get the kind of recognition that they deserve."[78] She credits the community for the long-term success of the magazine: That support is "why we're one of the few publications that have been able to survive for this long."[79] Stevens engages with younger queer activists. They in turn recognize her work: "Stevens is a part of the Gen X wave of queer women who were unapologetic, desired connection, and wanted to see themselves and each other reflected in media."[80] It perhaps shows intergenerational dialogue at its best, appreciating the chain of women and activists who built a movement, older generations learning from younger ones, and newer community members listening and understanding *herstory/queerstory* and its contexts. Stevens suggests that Judaism may have played a role in repeatedly questioning how to run *Deneuve/Curve*: "It is at the forefront of how I grew up, that it's OK to question what you believe. It's OK to question if something's right or wrong. Just because you're taught something or that's the way somebody's already always done something, it's not necessarily the way it has to be done."[81]

Franco Stevens has been the center of a nucleus of women who gave birth to a magazine that was repeatedly reborn, with new names, new owners, and new funding models. *Deneuve/Curve* became an important node for a counter-public feeding into a growing movement. Raising lesbian visibility and the visibility of LGBTQ+ women and nonbinary people was her greatest accomplishment, says Stevens, who claims she will close her magazine when full acceptance is reached.[82] The current moment with avenues for queer women to share their experiences through the Internet, social media, and mainstream media, stands in stark contrast with culture when Stevens launched *Deneuve*: "When we first started out, using the word lesbian was . . . verboten."[83] Putting the word "lesbian" on the cover was crucial for her: "I thought it was important to the community. And watching how terminology and the inclusion in our community has evolved over the years has been not only exciting . . . but it also continues to be a struggle to be inclusive.[84] With the exception of its 2018 issues, *Deneuve/Curve* carried the word "lesbian" in its tagline on the cover for each issue until its last print issue in 2019. For Stevens, new conversations about how feminism fits in with *Curve* and its movement remain necessary. But intersectionality remains hard to implement, something Stevens embodies: "As a lesbian, as a woman, as a disabled person, as a Jewish person, as this, the intersectionality is definitely sparse."[85]

Notes

1 Heather Cassell, "Publisher Sells SF-Based Curve Magazine," *Bay Area Reporter*, October 20, 2010, www.ebar.com/story.php?ch=news&sc=&sc2=&id=241082.
2 Lawrence Gross, "The Gay Global Village in Cyberspace," in *Contesting Media Power: Alternative Media in a Networked World*, ed. Nick Couldry and James Curran (Rowman & Littlefield, 2003), 759–272.
3 *Ahead of the Curve* [Documentary], 2020, www.imdb.com/title/tt8956926/.
4 Kate Brandt, *Happy Endings: Lesbian Writers Talk About Their Lives and Work* (Naiad Press, 2017), 151–160.
5 Brandt, *Happy Endings*, 152.
6 *Ahead of the Curve.*
7 *Ahead of the Curve.*
8 Franco Stevens, author interview, February 7, 2023.
9 Katherine Seligman, "Thrown for a Curve," *San Francisco Examiner*, May 12, 1996, www.sfgate.com/bayarea/article/Thrown-for-a-Curve-3144414.php.
10 Personal communication, 2023.
11 Stevens, interview.
12 Brandt, *Happy Endings*, 153.
13 Robin Lowey, "Frances 'Franco' Stevens," in Robin Lowey, *Gamechangers: Lesbians You Should Know About* (Epochalips Books, 2017), 32.
14 Heather Cassell, "Founder Stevens Buys Back *Curve* Magazine," *Bay Area Reporter*, April 21, 2021, www.ebar.com/story.php?ch=news&sc=news&id=304187.
15 Stevens, interview.
16 Brooke Levin, "Franco Stevens, Founder and Publisher of *Curve* Magazine," Autostraddle, March 28, 2010; Franco Stevens, "The Birth of *Deneuve*," *Deneuve* 1, no. 1 (1991): 2.
17 Stevens, interview.
18 Brandt, *Happy Endings*, 153.

19 Seligman, "Thrown for a Curve."
20 Lowey, "Frances 'Franco' Stevens," 32.
21 Brandt, *Happy Endings*, 155.
22 Stevens, interview.
23 Deneuve Premiere issue, *Deneuve* 1, no. 1 (1991): cover.
24 David W. Dunlap, "For Lesbian Magazine, a Question of Image," *New York Times*, January 8, 1996, www.nytimes.com/1996/01/08/business/for-lesbian-magazine-a-question-of-image.html.
25 Brandt, *Happy Endings*, 159.
26 Lowey, "Frances 'Franco' Stevens," 32.
27 Brandt, *Happy Endings*, 152.
28 Stevens, interview.
29 Stevens, interview.
30 *Ahead of the Curve*.
31 Levin, "Franco Stevens, Founder and Publisher."
32 Levin, "Franco Stevens, Founder and Publisher."
33 Levin, "Franco Stevens, Founder and Pubisher."
34 Brand, *Happy Endings*, 156.
35 *Ahead of the Curve*.
36 Jenn Rainin, "Franco Stevens and the History of *Curve* Magazine," *Gale Review*, July 13, 2021, https://review.gale.com/2021/07/13/the-history-of-curve-magazine/.
37 Polly Thistlethwaite and Daniel C. Tsang, "Lesbian, Gay, Bisexual, and Transgender," in Bill Katz and Linda S. Katz, eds., *Magazines for Libraries* (R. R. Bowker Publishing, 1995), 749, https://academicworks.cuny.edu/gc_pubs/208/.
38 Brandt, *Happy Endings*, 156.
39 *Ahead of the Curve*.
40 Levin, "Franco Stevens, Founder and Publisher."
41 Frances Stevens, "So Now We Know," *Curve* 3, no. 6 (1993): 6.
42 Katherine Sender, "Sex Sells: Sex, Taste, and Class in Commercial Gay and Lesbian Media," *GLQ: A Journal of Lesbian and Gay Studies* 9, no. 3 (2003): 331–365.
43 Thistlethwaite and Tsang, "Lesbian, Gay, Bisexual, and Transgender."
44 Diana Milillo, "Sexuality Sells: A Content Analysis of Lesbian and Heterosexual Women's Bodies in Magazine Advertisements," *Journal of Lesbian Studies* 12, no. 4 (2008): 390, https://doi.org.10.1080/10894160802278267.
45 Dunlap, "For Lesbian Magazine"; Seligman, "Thrown for a Curve."
46 *Deneuve*, "Expose Yourself. Survey Results." *Curve* 3, no. 6 (1993): 60.
47 *Deneuve*, "Expose Yourself. Survey Results," 60.
48 *Ahead of the Curve*, 2020.
49 Brandt, *Happy Endings*, 157.
50 *Deneuve*, "Melissa. Yes I am!" *Curve* 3, no. 6 (1993): cover.
51 *Ahead of the Curve*.
52 Stevens, interview.

53 Seligman, "Thrown for a Curve"; *Ahead of the Curve.*
54 Dunlap, "For Lesbian Magazine."
55 Seligman, "Thrown for a Curve."
56 Seligman, "Thrown for a Curve."
57 Stevens, interview.
58 Dunlap, "For Lesbian Magazine."
59 Seligman, "Thrown for a Curve."
60 Stevens, interview.
61 Stevens, interview.
62 Michael Grabell, "The Fallout of Workers' Comp 'Reforms': 5 Tales of Harm," ProPublica, March 15, 2015, www.propublica.org/article/workers-compensation-injured-workers-share-stories-of-harm.
63 Stevens, interview.
64 Cassell, "Founder Stevens Buys Back"; Grabell, "Fallout."
65 Cassell, "Publisher Sells."
66 *Ahead of the Curve.*
67 Cassell, "Publisher Sells."
68 Franco, "Step into the Honesty Box," *Curve* 20, no. 7 (2010): 6.
69 Cassell, "Publisher Sells."
70 Cassell, "Founder Stevens Buys Back."
71 Merryn Johns, "*Lesbian* Is Not Just an Identity—It's Something You Do," Slate, December 20, 2016, https://slate.com/human-interest/2016/12/why-curve-lesbian-magazine-will-not-drop-the-l-word-from-its-tagline.html.
72 *Curve*, "Curve Facts," 2020.
73 *Curve*, "2022 Curve Awards for Emerging Journalists," 2022, https://thecurvefoundation.org/2022/07/06/2022-curve-award-for-emerging-journalists/.
74 *Curve*, "Curve Programs," 2023, https://thecurvefoundation.org/programs/.
75 *Curve* Archive, n.d., https://www.curvemag.com/digital-archive/.
76 Dunlap, "For Lesbian Magazine."
77 Seligman, "Thrown for a Curve."
78 Stevens, interview.
79 Levin, "Franco Stevens, Founder and Publisher."
80 Cassell, "Founder Stevens Buys Back."
81 Stevens, interview.
82 Stevens, interview.
83 Stevens, interview.
84 Stevens, interview.
85 Stevens, interview.

Lisa Bell Wilson

A Calm, Confident Leader through Triumph and Tragedy

Shannon Scovel and Kevin Blackistone

For thirteen years, Lisa Wilson worked mostly evenings and nights at her beloved hometown newspaper, the *Buffalo News*. Serving on the copy desk, as a reporter, and as an assistant sports editor,[1] she rarely crossed paths with the paper's executives, such as its (first) woman editor-in-chief Margaret Sullivan. But in 2011, Sullivan summoned Wilson to her office. The sports editor's job was about to open. Sullivan wanted Wilson to consider it because, from afar, she had witnessed Wilson's leadership and had come to greatly respect it.[2] The meeting resulted in Wilson becoming the *Buffalo News*'s sports editor, making her the first Black woman to lead a major sports metro daily newspaper.

This was the first of many "firsts" for Wilson. Also the first Black woman president of the Associated Press Sports Editors and the first woman editorial director for *The Athletic*, Wilson navigates—with grit and grace—a U.S. sports media industry largely dominated by men, specifically white men, and embedded in a patriarchal culture.[3] Lifted up by other women, notably Margaret Sullivan, Wilson continues to write her legacy as history-making editor.[4] Being the first is never easy, and Wilson takes this responsibility seriously. She says she hopes her presence in sports media creates visibility, the kind that inspires increased belief in oneself among aspiring women journalists of color, in particular. This is because being a feminist alone is not enough to ameliorate these challenges for women journalists of color, an issue Alice Walker coined womanism to recognize the double punch of having to navigate sexism and racism.[5]

Indeed, visibility for women of color has been consistently lacking in sports journalism. The 2021 Associated Press Sports Editors (APSE) diversity report card showed that only 20.8 percent of sports editors in the country are people of color; just 19.3 percent are women. Women of color represent just 9.6 percent of all upper management in sports media.[6] Research has found that Black women in sports media in particular face increased discrimination and marginalization in the newsroom because they are fighting "two battles in the industry—both race and sex."[7] Wilson recognizes these challenges. She says that being a Black woman leader in this field is particularly meaningful because it shows the next generation that change is possible: "If I was a woman in leadership, it'd be great, but as a Black woman, that is profound. . . . When I meet other Black women, in sports media and out of sports media, they tell me how proud they are of me. It's hard to advance as a woman. It's really hard to advance as a Black woman."[8]

Her leadership and perseverance as one of the most prominent women of color in a sports media executive position remain a critical part of her story. Moreover, throughout her tenure as a sports media leader, Wilson has faced adversity, from personal tragedies to newsroom politics. Yet her coworkers and editors describe her as someone who has consistently remained calm, cool, and collected.[9] This steady, focused mindset has garnered her the respect of peers throughout the business and is one she has used to her advantage through trying times while managing a growing number of sports reporters at the *Niagara Gazette*, the *Buffalo News*, *The Undefeated*, and now *The Athletic*, where she is the editorial director for culture, opinion, and talent development.

Background

Born in Buffalo, New York, in 1969, Lisa Bell Wilson's love for sports developed early, although she says she wasn't much of an athlete.[10] As a member of the City Honors High School track and field team, Wilson jokes that twice she earned third place in the long jump, an event that had three participants. She also grew up watching football with her brothers on the family television set.[11] Wilson remembers the games as well as the broadcasters she saw and heard who analyzed the games, talked about football, and shared insights on the game. Specifically, Wilson remembers Jayne Kennedy, the first Black woman announcer on a nationally televised sports program, *NFL Today*. "That's the image I saw, a Black woman on TV talking about sports on the NFL pregame show," Wilson said. "I'm seeing her on TV and knowing 'Wow, you know, I could probably do this.' That was one of the first people I really saw doing it that made me think 'OK, there's a space for me.'"[12]

Journalism offered Wilson the chance to stay involved in sports despite her athletic shortcomings. Wilson says that she only joined her high school track team to bolster her college resume, though her most meaningful involvement in high school sports came as the statistician for the volleyball team. She also worked for her high school newspaper, a harbinger, no doubt, of her natural comfort in a newsroom.[13]

Another of Wilson's leadership role models was her mother: Ocie Bell supported her daughter's sports journalism passion while raising four children. Wilson's parents separated for several years, requiring her mother to transition from managing the household and working with the PTA, to balancing outside work with child-rearing. Wilson's parents ultimately reunited, but the strength Ocie Bell showed during the years in which she was a single mother greatly impacted her daughter. When Wilson earned a partial scholarship to Canisius College, her mother covered the difference. Her mother's selflessness stayed with Wilson and profoundly shaped her. Wilson said, "She made it work. It wasn't easy. She was making about $10,000 a year, and whenever I think about that and I do my bills, I thank the Lord for that woman. It was just a lot of sacrifice on her part."[14]

From Niagara Back to Buffalo: A Path toward Leadership

At Canisius, Wilson majored in communications while working at a Fotomat store and writing sports columns for Buffalo's Black newspaper, *The Challenger*. After graduating in 1991, Wilson planned to stay in Buffalo, where her family was an integral part of the community, and her father, the owner of a chain of dry cleaners, was a pillar in its Black community. She expected to spend her career covering local teams and retire after working at the newspaper she long admired.

But Wilson struggled to find a journalism job after graduating. She took a temporary job at a discount clothing store for a year before one of her college professors connected her with editors at the *Utica Observer-Dispatch*.[15] While Wilson did not get the *Observer-Dispatch* job, the editors there passed her information along to the *Niagara Gazette*. It offered her a three-month internship, which became her first full-time journalism job and lasted six years.[16] Wilson primarily described her daily grind covering local government and school boards as "horrible," but her determination to make it in journalism motivated her to stick with it.[17] This eventually proved fortuitous when the *Gazette* sports editor left. Accepting the "do-everything" job at the small paper meant Wilson would cover everything from high schools to the NFL.

Wilson grew as a person and a leader in Niagara Falls, near the Canadian border, as she took on more responsibility at the paper. She began working editing shifts on the layout team, making formatting decisions often just before deadline and selecting the stories she deemed most appropriate and important for the local audience. Wilson's confidence in her own leadership skills grew during those late-night layout shifts. Suddenly, she had a significant voice in the direction of the paper: "I found myself enjoying editing, like having the opportunity to lay out the section, decide what stories are most important, what you want to lead with, what you want to give the most weight to."[18]

Wilson's personal life changed in Niagara, too. She met her husband when they were covering a high school basketball game, he, for the *Buffalo News*. While sitting on press row, she struck up a conversation with Allen Wilson, who moved seats to chat with her.[19] He handed her his business card in case she "had questions about the business."[20]

In 1998, Wilson reached her first major career crossroads. A copy-editing job opened at the *Buffalo News*, the hometown paper she had always longed to work for and where her husband worked. This time, Wilson was not turned down. The transition, though, was far from seamless. To make this move, she left sports and shifted into a role on the copy desk in a top newsroom that she described as the gold standard but "intimidating."[21] In order to work for the larger paper, where all the major journalists whom she aspired to be like were working, she had to agree to be the rookie on a staff of veterans. But Wilson believed in her abilities, talents, and readiness for this next step: "I've always had to make these moves and bet on myself in my career. You have to make this choice: I was the sports editor at the smaller paper, but I could go to the larger paper . . . but I had to start over as a copy editor. I did it, just so I could get into the *News*."[22]

Colleagues quickly identified her as someone who would be "running the place" within a few years, Wilson said, and she embraced this leadership identity.[23] She held firm to her values, stayed composed in the face of adversity, and led with authority, compassion, and thoughtful decision-making skills. "I started as a copy editor. And then I was doing some layout shifts because I had that background," Wilson recounts.[24] "And I ended up being the backup as the Sunday layout editor. And then when the editor who was the Sunday editor ended up moving to the day shift . . . I got that." Then the sports department, her passion, called, this time with an assistant editor's position.

Critical Juncture

Assistant *Buffalo News* sports editor Wilson stood out. After all, most of the reporters were men. She worked to make her mark in this new group. Sullivan recalls, "She was very popular in the department, and popularity doesn't mean you're a good editor, but she was. She was well respected, well regarded, a good person."[25]

So, when the *Buffalo News* announced a wave of layoffs and buyouts in the spring of 2011, and the sports editor at the time decided to take the package, Sullivan, then managing editor, asked Wilson to take the job.[26] She was one of three assistant sports editors at the time and the least tenured. Nonetheless, Sullivan determined that Wilson was a logical choice: "Lisa was the obvious, obvious candidate, and of course it made me happy that she was a woman; it made me happy that she was a journalist of color; it made me even happier that she was a woman journalist of color, [but] it wasn't about those things."[27]

Despite this praise and confidence from Sullivan and the fact that Wilson would lead a staff at her "dream" paper, Wilson said she immediately started to feel resentment from a colleague, someone she had long considered a friend. Sullivan says she thinks that the colleague's resentment resulted not from Wilson's race or gender but rather his bitterness at not being offered the job.[28] Wilson agrees, but either way, she acknowledges that the situation caused tension and stress: "Our relationship changed after that. It [was] subtle. You know, nothing you could really write him up for, but I could tell the effort under me wasn't the same as it was under [the former] boss; and I think a lot of that was . . . not getting the job. The effort just wasn't the same; the attitude wasn't the same; the energy was different."[29]

Wilson and the colleague ultimately found time to talk through this situation, the first of many big moments Wilson would encounter now that she finally had the job she had longed for all those years. She was working in her hometown, leading a staff, and guiding coverage of her home teams, with her husband working under her. Wilson's professionalism apparently assuaged any fears of favoritism toward her husband, which otherwise might have been expected.

Soon after moving back to Buffalo, Wilson's husband was diagnosed with chronic myeloid leukemia, usually a treatable disease.[30] Allen saw the doctor every four months, but he was still able to travel and work. The Wilsons carried on. Lisa balanced caring for her family with her role as a deputy sports editor. Her daughter, Alissa, an amalgam of her parents' first names, was six months old at the time of Allen's diagnosis and grew up surrounded by extended family while her mother and father worked successfully together at the *News*.[31] But shortly after Wilson became sports editor, her husband's health deteriorated. The family initially thought Allen's brother could donate the bone marrow Allen needed, but it turned out the brother had the same disease. His sister was also a match but, by the time she cleared the testing process, Allen was in renal failure.

He died in December 2011, at age forty-nine, six months after checking into the hospital.

Wilson, however, instead of stepping away from journalism, followed her established pattern: she leaned on her family and continued to lead. Those experiences, and Wilson's decision to stay at the paper and invest more time in improving the newsroom culture for herself and her colleagues, helped cement her legacy at the *Buffalo News* and her reputation as a focused, driven leader.

Resolution

Wilson had a four-year-old child who needed her attention and a news staff grieving with her. She remembers distinctly Margaret Sullivan visiting her in the hospital and realizing that one need not lose a sense of compassion to be a leader. Here was her editor, in the hospital with her upon the death of her husband, supporting Wilson in her most vulnerable moment.[32] She had a leadership example she could follow. Wilson recalls what Sullivan's visit taught her: "You don't have to lose your compassion, your humanity; you can care about people and still be an effective leader. Because Margaret . . . promoted me and showed faith in me . . . I always wanted to do a good job. . . . To do everything I could to be the best sports editor I can be for her, and that taught me something. And maybe that's why people respect me and kind of like working for me. Because at times, if there's like something going on with family, and you have to get away, I tell them, 'Go ahead.'"[33] Wilson brought her full self to work, acknowledging her pain and letting her news staff grieve with her, but she also continued to do her job with a new awareness of the fragility of life.

Wilson's challenges at the time were gendered, not in the sense that familial care is women's work, but in the sense that, as the editor of the *Buffalo News* and one of the few women sports editors in the country, she was leading an all-men staff. Her decisions were already being watched under a microscope by the public. Wilson was representing more than herself in every decision that she made. Meanwhile, emotion, or the expression of emotion in the newsroom, has historically been used to discredit women, as if expressing emotion suggests that they're incapable of making rational decisions.[34] This assumption, however, is rooted in stereotypical understandings of gender, not reality. Wilson channeled her emotions in a way that enabled her to become an even more impressive leader. Sullivan said, "She just was really strong and graceful about it. She was devastated, and there was no doubt in anyone's mind that Allen was the love of her life . . . and this was the father of her only child, plus he was beloved in the sports department and at the paper, so she was dealing with a lot of other people's grief and 'upsetness' too."[35]

According to Sullivan, Wilson allowed herself to express her feelings in a way that enabled the staff to grieve with her, but she remained quietly strong and continued to lead in the newsroom with her same undeterred passion.[36] Her ability to balance her own emotions with the needs of her staff guided Wilson through two junctures—regrouping her staff after her promotion and leading through her grief. Wilson, however, still can't figure out how she kept herself so composed: "How did I navigate that? I still try to figure that out sometimes."[37]

Julia Boorstin, CNBC's senior media and tech correspondent, interviewed 120 women CEOs and leaders for her book *When Women Lead*.[38] Boorstin suggests that the most experienced, successful women business leaders often practice empathetic leadership—when a boss recognizes an employee's feelings and acknowledges their difficulties. Wilson embodied this principle. She was an important voice in the newsroom, someone who had been through a deep personal tragedy, but someone who could connect with others navigating hard times in a compassionate, fair manner. Wilson presented herself as a leader with drive and perseverance in the face of adversity, but she explains that this experience was far from simple given her identity in what Sullivan calls a "very white, very male" newsroom.[39] Speaking for herself, Wilson says, "I don't want to give the impression that it's always easy. I was the only Black person in the nation running the sports department [and] I've never considered leaving. I needed to stay in this so I can be someone for other Black journalists, other women of color. If it's truly what you wanted to do, you can do it at the highest level."[40]

Wilson would continue to be tested as a leader, including when she faced what is arguably every editor's greatest fear: a staff reporter who committed plagiarism. While Sullivan describes the situation as "maybe more sloppy than anything else," the newsroom was split on how to handle the problem.[41] Some thought the paper had a responsibility to make the incident public in the spirit of transparency and accountability. Others thought the editors were not sufficiently sympathetic to the reporter and his personal challenges. Wilson deliberated the case and considered all factors, including that the reporter was Black and someone Wilson had mentored as one part of her efforts to diversify her staff. Sullivan said that Wilson's compassionate conversations with the reporter stood out: "I definitely remember her making the case that he had some problems and some issues, and that ought to be taken into account, though she never made the case that it was OK."[42]

Wilson ultimately dismissed the reporter. Wilson listened to the reporter and advocated for mental health; but she was still the boss, a boss committed to the principles of journalism. Wilson's moral code has always stood out to Sullivan, who describes Wilson as someone who "doesn't preach, but she has a kind of solidity . . . that serves her well."[43]

An Ongoing Legacy of Leadership

During her tenure in Buffalo, Wilson's reputation as a reliable, dependable, and successful leader continued to grow and spread nationally. When Sullivan accepted a job at the *Washington Post* in 2016 as a media columnist, she tried to convince the *Post* to hire Wilson.[44] And Sullivan wasn't the only media leader interested in Wilson. Kevin Merida, then the editor in chief of *The Undefeated*, was also intrigued by the idea of hiring Wilson.[45] *The Undefeated*—ESPN's then embryonic vertical focused on the intersections of sports, race, and culture—intrigued Wilson too. She accepted Merida's request to apply for its sports editor position in 2017—just for options.[46] She was hired. Merida said he wanted someone with her editing expertise to help *The Undefeated* grow, and that he respected Wilson because of "her calm, her equilibrium, her sense of quiet confidence."

"Sometimes it's the quiet confidence," Merida says of Wilson, "that is the swagger."[47] He did have questions about her long (nearly fifteen years) tenure in Buffalo, noting that successful ambitious editors often rise up and move around the country; nevertheless, he said he admired Wilson's commitment to the *News* and the city of Buffalo.[48]

The Undefeated offered a new challenge for Wilson, though. It was not tasked with grinding out daily news on games and results but instead produced reflective pieces at the intersection of sports and society. Nor did it have a large staff with a lot of resources. Instead, it had a small staff with limited resources even as it was positioned inside a gargantuan international corporation. And it seemed not completely clear what it wanted to be or what it would ultimately look and sound like.[49] Merida said, "Coming out of the daily sports section is different than what we were trying to do. . . . So you have to have somebody like her . . . to want to lean into the idea of it, but also you need someone who really knows what they're doing and has enough confidence and is not going to be rattled by any of the challenges of starting something new."

The Undefeated gave Wilson something else she never had: a newsroom mostly of color and heavily staffed by women. Merida built a newsroom that, as he describes it, was run by Black women, creating a culture of shared experiences where women could embrace their individual personalities without needing to code switch: "You've got to realize how rare that experience is for people to come into a newsroom, to come into a place where pretty much everybody looks like you. I think that was very empowering for her."[50]

Wilson moved to Washington, D.C., as an editor with an upstart inside ESPN, a company that had attempted to hire her for years.[51] Wilson thrived at *The Undefeated*. Merida said her reporters respected her, and she brought a level of experience and confidence that elevated the website.[52]

Despite this, and despite the culture and the opportunity to grow *The Undefeated* in her vision, Washington was ultimately too foreign for Wilson. When she was approached at the 2017 Associated Press Sports Editors conference by *The Athletic* with the opportunity to lead its NFL coverage, which she could do from Buffalo, Wilson realized she was at another juncture: choose between her new role at ESPN, the flagship sports media company in the world, or a new opportunity at *The Athletic*. Wilson's former editors and her mentees respect her decision to return to her hometown, rejoining the community that reared her, to work for *The Athletic*.

Rana Cash, an executive editor at the *Charlotte Observer* whom Wilson has coached throughout her career, said, "She goes up to the mothership, you know, ESPN and *The Undefeated*, and decides that's not the best fit for her life, you know, not just professionally, but personally, it wasn't working for her life. A lot of people wouldn't have . . . the courage to do that because of perception, or how people might judge you or whatever, but she did what was best for her."[53]

Her leadership, however, was not just confined to her role as a national sports editor covering professional football, college basketball, and culture. Several editors approached her at that same APSE conference and encouraged her to run for a leadership position in APSE. She was initially hesitant—saying that she didn't know "what they saw in me."[54] But, as she had done many times before, she took the opportunity and ran with it. She moved up the three-year ladder from second vice president, to vice president, and to president in 2020, leading the group through the COVID-19 crisis.[55] This gave Wilson another "first" for her resume: she became the first Black woman president of the organization. Describing her career as a series of firsts, Wilson says, "It's awesome and wonderful to be the first, but at the same time you think: I know I can't be the only Black woman capable of leading a sports section."[56] She has become what Jayne Kennedy once was for her: a visible example for Black women that sports media is a space for them.

Conclusion

Friends and editors describe Wilson as thriving in leadership roles; she is unruffled and able to handle the newsroom's fast-paced pressure.[57] Mentors and mentees appreciate Wilson for her fairness, decisiveness, and kindness. She's trusted and respected for her work and her demeanor.[58]

Wilson is aware of her status as an influential figure in sports media, but she's hesitant to label herself a feminist: "Do I see myself as a feminist? You know, I don't get into titles. I know what a feminist is . . . I see myself as an advocate for women, for sure, in journalism. A feminist? I don't view myself like that. You can look at my career or my work and kind of decide if you think that is, but no, I see myself as more of an advocate for women in sports."

This tension over the label of "feminism" among journalists, even women journalists, is well documented by media scholars. In fact, scholar Louise North found that "feminism" can still be a "scare word," one that carries loaded stereotypes and prompts criticism from colleagues.[59] North also explains that "feminism is often understood as a subjective position—one not consonant with the objectivity supposedly required and deployed in news reporting."

Wilson does not reject the *principles* of feminism—given that she's proud to be an outspoken advocate for women—but her decision to not identify with the term itself may be a product of her newsroom environment as well as the era in which she rose through the ranks of her field. Her mentor, Margaret Sullivan, also reinforced Wilson's commitment to women's equality without outwardly calling her a feminist.[60] "If feminism means that women should be treated equally in the workplace and society, I know she believed in that," Sullivan said, adding that identifying with the label of "feminist" may be difficult if "you're leading a staff of macho guys."

Wilson's relationship to the term "feminism" may also be impacted by her experience as a Black woman in media. She's "proud to be a woman sports editor" but even more proud to be "the only Black woman" sports editor.[61] Her comments emphasize the intersectionality and duality of her identities.[62] Recognizing this relationship between race and gender for Black women, Alice Walker specifically contrasts "womanist" to "feminist" to encapsulate Black women's activism.[63] "Womanist" sees "gender as a structure of power that works with race," not independently from race, and values change that specifically benefits the Black community.[64] Scholar Patricia Hill Collins adds that "womanist" is "rooted in black women's concrete history in racial and gender oppression" and provides language for a worldview "accessible primarily and perhaps exclusively to black women."[65] Wilson's leadership cannot be reduced to a single term, but exploring her experiences through the lens of "womanism" offers a more holistic interpretation of her lived experience and leadership.

Wilson also acknowledges the community in Buffalo that built her into this thoughtful leader when she was simultaneously facing great personal tragedy. She leaned on the support of her family but also the graciousness of her editors. She admires and appreciates Sullivan in particular, the *News* editor who thrust her into leadership in her hometown paper and stood by her in her hardest moment.[66] In 2012 Sullivan left the *Buffalo News*, where she had been editor and vice president, to become the first woman public editor of the *New York Times*.[67] Sullivan has also written for the *Washington Post* and *The Guardian*. In 2023, Sullivan was named the executive director for the Craig Newmark Center for Journalism Ethics and Security at the Columbia Journalism School. When Sullivan reflects on her career, however, her decision to hire Wilson remains one of the moments that she's most proud of: "I hope Lisa never feels like I'm taking credit for her, but when I think back on my long career, promoting Lisa to sports editor at the *Buffalo News* is one of the things that, if I were making a top ten list, that would make it on to the top ten list, symbolically and professionally."[68]

It turned out to be a critical crossroads that impacted the dozens of reporters who subsequently went on to work for Wilson, and thus sports journalism.

Notes

1 Lisa Wilson, author interview, February 3, 2023; APSE, May 31, 2011, https://apsportseditors.com/on-the-move-wilson-named-buffalo-news-sports-editor/.

2 Margaret Sullivan, author interview, January 30, 2023.

3 Kennedi Landry, "Trailblazing Officer Takes Helm During APSE's Challenging Period," June 21, 2020, Sports Journalism Institute, www.sportsjournalisminstitute.org/latest-news/trailblazing-officer-takes-helm-during-apses-challenging-period; Paul Fichtenbaum, author interview, February 17, 2023; Paul Fichtenbaum, email correspondence, June 5, 2023.

4 Wilson, interview.

5 Alice Walker, *In Search of Our Mothers' Gardens: Womanist Prose* (Harcourt Brace Jovanovich, 1983).

6 Richard Lapchick, "The 2021 Sports Media Racial and Gender Report CardTM: Associated Press Sports Editors (APSE)," University of Central Florida, www.tidesport.org/_files/ugd/138a69_e1e67c118b784f4caba00a4536699300.pdf.
7 Kevin Hull, Denetra Walker, Miles Romney, and Kirstin Pellizzaro, "'Through Our Prism': Black Television Sports Journalists' Work Experiences and Interactions with Black Athletes," *Journalism Practice* 18, no. 3 (2022): 14, https://doi.org/10.1080/17512786.2022.2050468.
8 Wilson, interview.
9 Sullivan, interview; Kevin Merida, author interview, January 25, 2023.
10 Wilson, interview.
11 Erik Brady, "Lisa Bell Wilson," Association of Jesuit Colleges and Universities, www.ajcunet.edu/lisa-bell-wilson.
12 Wilson, interview.
13 Alan Pergament, "Media Watch/Lisa Wilson," *Buffalo Spree*, November 30, 2020, www.buffalospree.com/wny_life/media-watch-lisa-wilson/article_8c6e8c19-36fd-5296-849e-ba90971d63b3.html.
14 Wilson, interview.
15 Brady, "Lisa Bell Wilson."
16 Brady, "Lisa Bell Wilson."
17 Wilson, interview.
18 Wilson, interview.
19 Alan Pergament, "Media Watch/Lisa Wilson."
20 Wilson, interview.
21 Wilson, interview.
22 Wilson, interview.
23 Wilson, interview.
24 Wilson, interview.
25 Sullivan, interview.
26 Toby Carrig, "On the Move: Wilson Named *Buffalo News* Sports Editor," APSE, May 31, 2011, https://apsportseditors.com/on-the-move-wilson-named-buffalo-news-sports-editor/.
27 Sullivan, interview.
28 Sullivan, interview.
29 Wilson, interview.
30 Pergament, "Media Watch/Lisa Wilson."
31 Brady, "Lisa Bell Wilson."
32 Wilson, interview.
33 Wilson, interview.
34 Norman P. Lewis, "From Cheesecake to Chief: Newspaper Editors' Slow Acceptance of Women," *American Journalism* 25, no. 2 (2008): 33–55, https://doi.org/10.1080/08821127.2008.10678109.
35 Sullivan, interview.
36 Sullivan, interview.
37 Wilson, interview.

38 Julia Boorstin, *When Women Lead: What They Achieve, Why They Succeed, and How We Can Learn from Them* (Avid Reader Press/Simon & Schuster, 2022).
39 Sullivan, interview.
40 Wilson, interview.
41 Sullivan, interview.
42 Sullivan, interview.
43 Sullivan, interview.
44 Sullivan, interview.
45 Merida, interview.
46 Wilson, interview.
47 Wilson, interview.
48 Merida, interview.
49 Merida, interview.
50 Merida, interview.
51 Merida, interview.
52 Merida, interview.
53 Rana Cash, author interview, February 17, 2023.
54 Cash, interview.
55 Cash, interview.
56 Landry, "Trailblazing Officer Takes Helm."
57 Merida, interview; Wilson, interview; Cash, interview.
58 Wilson, interview; Sullivan, interview.
59 Louisa North, "Rejecting the 'F-word': How 'Feminism' and 'Feminists' Are Understood in the Newsroom," *Journalism* 10, no. 6 (2009): 740, 754, https://doi.org/10.1177/1464884909344479.
60 Sullivan, interview.
61 Wilson, interview.
62 Wilson, interview.
63 Walker, *In Search of Our Mothers' Gardens*.
64 Patricia Hill Collins, "What's in a Name? Womanism, Black Feminism and Beyond," *Black Scholar* 26, no. 1 (Winter 1996): 16.
65 Collins, "What's in a Name?"
66 Wilson, interview.
67 Steve Myers, "*Buffalo News* Editor Margaret M. Sullivan to Be Next *New York Times* Public Editor," Poynter, July 16, 2012, https://www.poynter.org/reporting-editing/2012/margaret-m-sullivan-to-be-next-new-york-times-public-editor/.
68 Sullivan, interview.

S. Mitra Kalita

Changing Newsrooms, One Story at a Time

Paromita Pain

Mitra Kalita is perhaps best known for her leadership as the senior vice president at CNN Digital (from 2018 to 2020). In that capacity she supervised breaking news and national news programming as well as the features and opinion teams; she managed nearly two hundred journalists, coordinated digital distribution on social media platforms, and set up efforts to diversify content. She was also in charge of the Live Story tool designed to help CNN audiences track news in real time. Her newsroom experiences include the *Los Angeles Times*, where she was the managing editor of the digital site; and the *Washington Post*, *Newsday*, and the Associated Press. At Quartz, an online news site covering business and the global economy that primarily serves business leaders, she served as the executive editor. Internationally, she supervised the launches of Quartz India and Quartz Africa. In a recent essay for the Aspen Institute, Kalita, who has been the president of the South Asian Journalists Association, explained, "I spent most of my career in mainstream media. I come from a background of moving from one local market to the next bigger market and on and on. I have truly worked everywhere."[1]

Each move helped to deepen her understanding of how the media worked in different landscapes, both nationally and internationally, and prepared her for new ventures. Today the veteran journalist is the cofounder and CEO of URL Media, a for-profit corporate network of Black and Brown community news outlets that share content and revenue with different mainstream newsrooms. In 2020,

Kalita became CEO/publisher of Kalita Mukul Creative Inc., which publishes three niche newsletters: *Epicenter*, *Unmuted*, and *Escape Home*. During the pandemic, she cofounded and published *Epicenter-NYC*, a newsletter designed to help New Yorkers navigate COVID-19, which was particularly devastating for New York City; for example, it helped more than five thousand people navigate the complexities of registering for vaccines. *Epicenter-NYC* works across a variety of platforms including flyers and podcasts. Artists, small businesses, culture, and civic life are highlighted by a team of reporters, known as ambassadors. And in 2024, the Mellon Foundation awarded *Epicenter-NYC* $250,000 to establish a multipurpose community hub in Queens, where it will serve as a space for video content creation, art exhibits and programming (including a podcast studio and studio space for artists), and civic engagement. In accepting the award Kalita said, "*Epicenter*'s model reframes newsgathering toward partnering with, rather than reporting on, people and places whose heritage and stories have not always been told on their own terms."[2]

The *Unmuted* newsletter focuses on schooling, originally, on schooling during the pandemic. The *Escape Home*, for homeowners, regularly shares content with MarketWatch, a subsidiary of Dow Jones & Company that is a financial website providing analysis, business news, and stock market data. Shifting from major mainstream newspapers to newsletters has not meant abandoning mainstream journalism. Rather, Kalita channels her years of experience as an entrepreneur and business journalist as a weekly columnist for *Fortune* and *Time* magazine.

This case study of Kalita's leadership uses an interview with her as well as what she has written or said in essays and public presentations to explain how she navigates complexities in her own community while serving varied audiences and enhancing diversity in the newsroom. Rather than focusing on a particular crisis or juncture, it centers on how a woman of color raised by immigrant parents created her own opportunities to innovate digital storytelling and improve newsroom management and diversity. In so doing she managed to augment opportunity and innovation in U.S. media. During an interview with *Ms.* magazine, she emphasized that the push to diversify journalism was an important reason for her to get into the profession. She "intentionally" applies this to her career and sees her role as a change agent, "to change journalism as we know it."[3]

Kalita's concept of leadership offers important lessons about how journalists need and respond to management, and how management involves understanding and responding to these needs; for her, management does not involve traditional notions of power centered on prestige and being an all-commanding presence. That said, she is not convinced leadership can be taught: "I've been in leadership roles at this point, for more of my career than not, and I don't really know that anything adequately prepares you for it. You know, certainly, people talk about coaching and like leadership academies, executive education, but the reality of management is that you kind of have to just do it to see what everybody's talking about."[4]

Described as "wonderfully blunt" by CNN anchor Brian Stelter, Kalita seeks to change journalists' attitude about engagement.[5] In a lecture at the University of Missouri School of Journalism, she acknowledged the difficulty of getting newsrooms "to think about engagement . . . but we must see this as core to everyone's job and not as a separate function."[6] Kalita emphasizes that while the Internet expects interaction, going out to meet newspaper readers is essential since journalists are members of the community as well.

Background

Kalita (whose legal name is Sangha Mitra) was born in Brooklyn; her family moved to Long Island when she was two. Her kindergarten teachers called her Mitra and the name stuck. Her family moved to Puerto Rico when she was eight years old. When she was twelve she moved to central New Jersey, where she finished middle and high school. Wherever the family was, every few years her parents would take her to Assam, their home state in India. She says, "It was quite idyllic in terms of being very remote, with lots of cousins, dozens of cousins. So, it was a really fun experience. But then we would come back to the U.S., which was, really just my immediate family." She majored in history and journalism with a minor in

Spanish at Rutgers University. After graduating in 1998, she earned an MS in new media at the Columbia University Graduate School of Journalism.

Her earliest memory of "media" exemplifies, she says, nontraditional media and communication: as a child, she helped record cassette tapes that went back and forth among the extended family in India. "We might record our voices there and leave it, and they would listen to us. Or we would all gather and sing songs, or my grandfather would say a few words, and then we would have these cassettes, and we would listen to them back in the U.S.," she says. Kalita's first journalism experience was creating a newspaper called the *Kalita Times* to protest the move from Puerto Rico to New Jersey. She says of this, "I think in that way, media chose me, because I clearly saw putting things in the format of a newspaper and equated that to them having to listen to me."

After internships at the *Wall Street Journal*, *Baltimore Sun*, *Patriot Ledger*, and the WSJ Classroom Edition, Kalita worked for the Associated Press in Trenton, New Jersey. She has also worked at *Newsday*, in New York, and at the *Washington Post* as a business reporter. She joined the *Wall Street Journal* in 2010. There she led the coverage of the Great Recession, oversaw the launch of a local news section for New York City, and contributed in-depth reporting on the housing crisis. As the ideas editor at Quartz, Kalita contributed to its most popular sites and wrote viral stories on a wide variety of topics, from baby blankets to monetary policies. She was a member of the senior leadership determining content and direction for *Mint*, a startup business-oriented publication of the *Hindustan Times* and the *Wall Street Journal* in New Delhi. From May 2015 to June 2016, as managing editor for the *Los Angeles Times*, her leadership with new forms of digital storytelling and audience engagement saw latimes.com traffic touch nearly sixty million unique visitors monthly.[7]

Meanwhile, she helped the *Times* to connect to new communities and enhance its community outreach by establishing new beats and partnerships. She formed new partnerships with Apple News and Google, revitalized headlines and the framing of news stories, and formulated a new audience strategy, including translating general stories and videos into Spanish. During her tenure, the number of journalists of color at the *Times* grew from 23 percent to 35 percent. She ensured more constructive partnerships with advertisers and sales teams to promote content. Under her leadership, the general graphics department developed a data visualization team that produced interactives, 360 videos, and virtual reality content about space, including the planet Mars. The *LA Times* found a robust presence on Snapchat, Medium, and Tumblr, and its brand got new life through strategies like Reddit's "Ask Me Anything" (AMA).

Kalita is a board member and visiting faculty at the Poynter Institute for Media Studies, teaching in its women's academy, program for journalists of color, and a seminar for new managers; she also teaches in the accelerator program of the Online News Association. She has taught as an adjunct at Columbia Journalism School, St. John's University, CUNY Journalism School, and UMass Amherst, and was a visiting fellow at Harvard University. Besides being a board member of the *Philadelphia Inquirer*, Mitra extensively consults and speaks on newsroom management and diversity, equity, and inclusion.

Innovating new, deeply audience-centered forms of storytelling that are designed to help the public understand issues, follow news, and develop a nuanced understanding of issues is key. For example, many newsrooms across the United States follow Kalita's theory highlighting the "arc of a story": each new experiment has stemmed from the awareness that "we need to do news better."[8] This was brought home forcefully when, during her time at CNN, the George Floyd murder and the global pandemic saw audiences raise important questions about the purpose, service notion, and objectivity of news organizations.[9]

In a recent essay for the Aspen Institute, Kalita showed how her understanding of participation is informed by a serious critique of the journalism profession and education: "Many journalists come from a trajectory that has you starting out covering the school board or city council and steadily progressing with the end goal being covering Congress or the White House. Meanwhile, the trajectory of life has most of us articulating a foreign policy in college and only learning to care about schools, garbage pick-up and other day-in-day-out local issues in our 30s and 40s. These two trajectories of journalism talent and the lives of our communities are at odds with each other."[10]

Meeting journalists where they come from and then helping them explore and understand different contexts is an extension of her many attempts to encourage greater diversity in newsrooms and news narratives, even when this wasn't part of her official title or responsibility. "There's a diversity theme that runs through my career. It's not a strategy. It's not just a thing I talk about at conferences, but it really is how I live my life and how I commit journalism."[11]

Her first management role was in India, having moved there in 2006 to launch a paper called *Mint*. She went from supervising three people to supervising twelve. Starting with a small team proved to be an important advantage. But little prepared her for how needy journalists can be. She also realized that the best journalists actually need more management, not less. Later she looked back on her career and herself as an individual and came to understand that everybody needs management. Being global and going global were critical in the various strands of her career. She has often been immersed in new situations, which forced her to see multiple perspectives and taught her how to lead people who are older than her, from different cultures, and/or who are skeptical. Indeed, Kalita says if one can work in India, given the inevitable uncertainties of everyday life there, one can work anywhere in the world.

In 2016 she became CNN Digital's senior vice president for news, opinion and programming. In introducing Kalita before she spoke at the opening session of the 2017 conference of the Online News Association, the ONA Executive Director Irving Washington described her leadership style at CNN as "very inclusive"; moreover, she has "the knowledge to think in a different way and the way she thinks is like a breath of fresh air."[12] He commended Kalita for bringing an international outlook to global issues and that she is "a great listener even if it doesn't fit with her point of view."[13] Kalita has often reflected on the advantages of shared leadership since that can provide "more opportunity for a company to infuse its top ranks with diversity in all aspects, including age, race, gender, and skillset, as well as more experience with management, communications, and digital prowess."[14] That is, diversity is key to newsroom modernization.

Team-Centric Management

In her 2017 keynote for the Online News Association, Kalita emphasized that newsroom change and innovation occur one story at a time; she takes solace in small victories: "I think at conferences we focus on such vast change . . . and it's just so big, it feels like I can't take that on. . . . You can't start writing a book until you write one word on a page. And then one word becomes one paragraph, and then one paragraph becomes one page. And then you have a chapter. And, again, that sounds so basic, but in many ways change in a newsroom is really similar. It's one story at a time. . . . There is of course a broader strategy but in the short term, there's what can I do today, and sometimes I actually find that liberating because the best I can do is with the story I'm trying to tell right now."[15]

Kalita explicitly acknowledges that mistakes are inevitable. She believes in being upfront and transparent about vulnerabilities and insecurities: "Right now, for example, I'm really grappling with bandwidth. I don't have enough time to manage the teams that we've built. And I think my teams, if you were to ask them, 'what's her number one issue or concern right now,' they would be able to identify that. So really being transparent about your shortcomings feels an important part of this." This transparency also helps Kalita be clear about her mission and make that clear to people around her. She keeps a document listing what attracted her to the job in the first place and refers to it when she needs a refresher to keep her optimism and idealism alive.

Kalita is committed to creating and maintaining connections with her team through lots of team and individual meetings and random phone calls—just to get a pulse. She remembers details about their lives and needs, knowing how these things matter to people. She sends people food. One time, a political reporter who had to work through Easter weekend told her that she really missed her mother's Easter baskets. So, Kalita sent her an Easter basket.

Even during a crisis, having committed herself to a "career of crisis," Kalita rarely forgets the importance of focusing on her team. She has learned to assess the crisis, figure out a response, and then go into execution mode. She describes several aggressive mergers and acquisitions as particularly challenging: she has been through five or six major changes of corporate media ownership and management. She believes that being honest with teams about changes and challenges gets her much further and helps minimize backlash. "A line that I turn to a lot is that nobody buys you to leave you alone," she says. "And it sort of preps teams for the reality of what's to come. I think a lot of leaders will say, 'We're just going to act like everything's normal, we'll just keep going, when it's literally impossible to do that during such times of change.'"

Writing two acclaimed books taught her valuable lessons that inform her leadership. Writing her 2003 book *Suburban Sahibs: Three Immigrant Families and Their Passage from India to America*, about how immigrants redefined New Jersey, was transformative. As she says, "When you're trained as a journalist, you're just listening for like a good quote. You're not really going underneath the story. And so, writing a book helped me go underneath a story; I had to get details." She needed to understand the context and consistently consider what was happening around people and their lives rather than merely noting what people said explicitly. This has also proven to be an effective management tactic: "We manage teams; they'll often respond to things with emotion or outrage or . . . feeling a certain way; but so many times that emotion or that reaction is more a function of the stuff around them, versus you."

Kalita's 2010 book *My Two Indias* tells the story of how her exasperation at India's inefficiency turns to appreciation of Indians' hustle and innovation, lessons that became woven into daily professional decisions. More recently, she described a media atmosphere rife with misinformation: "If we keep saying this information is the problem, we get to blame other people instead of asking the fundamental question, which is, Why am I not trusted? Why am I not turned to? And why am I not the solution, the provider of news and information? . . . Information is the ultimate power in our ability to uplift people . . . but . . . we know that the essence of providing that information equals power."[16]

Thus, Kalita's concept of community and what constitutes the local is equally broad: "But how do we define local? It's a word that is bordered and closed off, defined by geography or zip code. Of course, most people do not live, work, or worship all in the same place. How do we capture families like mine that spent every weekend driving hours and hours across state lines to create community with people from a remote region with a distinct language—what place does local news make for these overlapping communities?"[17]

Several of her career decisions and professional arrangements were agonizing. In any event, strong mentorship keeps her motivated, she says. Kalita's much-trusted mentors, many from outside the organizations she is a part of, have been extremely helpful. They have made her feel like she has a kitchen cabinet looking out for her. She can consult with her mentors about mistakes or professional issues that have not quite worked out the way they were meant to.

Addressing Ethical Questions

Kalita often faces difficult choices around the ethical collisions between public service, professionalism, personal ethics, and commercial orientations. Tensions over the roles and responsibilities of news media have arisen most prominently because of ownership issues, such as when Rupert Murdoch took over the *Wall Street Journal*, and at the *LA Times*, when Michael Ferro came in as a new investor. Kalita always tries to find the middle ground and maintains that she has never needed to make major sacrifices to achieve this.

But sometimes, she sticks to her guns. This general tendency to try to make the best of situations but also be able to hold one's own has been very helpful in her current work at *Epicenter-NYC*, the newsletter originally intended to help New Yorkers get through the pandemic and an inaugural member of her URL Media network. Kalita is the publisher, but she wears all hats at *Epicenter*: she sells advertisements and creates and edits content. It requires her to be out in the community, address questions as they arise, and deal with ethical issues. Many people questioned why *Epicenter* was helping people register for vaccines; critics apparently said this is not within the purview of a media organization. Kalita told a *Vice* interviewer that she launched *Epicenter* given the problems of the vaccine rollout: "The folks who should be at the front of the line, elderly, and essential workers, don't have the tools or digital savvy to play. The state needs to talk to people in terms that are concrete and accessible—there's so much confusion within the categories. Again, to circumvent the system, you must know the system."[18] Kalita does know the system well, whether related to vaccines or the media.

Understanding the importance of strengthening media produced by and for traditionally marginalized voices, Kalita and another media executive and entrepreneur, Sara Lomax-Reese, cofounded URL Media as a network for sharing resources—money and power—with Black- and Brown-owned media outlets. Lomax-Reese is the president and CEO of WURD Radio, an African American–owned talk radio station. Funding for this project initially came from advertising, partnerships, sponsorships, and grants, including the Archewell Foundation, the nonprofit of the former Duke (Prince Harry) and Duchess of Sussex. Here, too, Kalita emphasizes serving otherwise underserved communities. Kalita told the president of the News Media Alliance, "From a mission perspective, we did not want Black and Brown audiences to be only charitable endeavors. We see our people as a very important, vital, necessary market."[19]

Kalita emphasizes the importance of ethics in terms of how and why media organizations make money. She appreciates advertising being a part of *Epicenter*'s journalistic strategy, for example. Unlike the so-called Chinese wall between editorial and advertising at traditional media, she says, "For me, uplifting these businesses is as important as uplifting our communities because they are a part of the community." Dealing with such ethical landmines has helped her navigate this world where the media must redefine themselves to find relevance to audiences and build trust in communities. She is convinced that media need to be community focused and to tell stories from the point of view of communities.

Resolution: Moving Beyond Ideal Notions of Feminism

Maintaining a balance also extends to life beyond the professional sphere. Kalita describes herself: "I am a journalist, but I'm also . . . a mother, daughter, wife, neighbor, friend, Assamese, Indian, South Asian, Asian, American."[20] Her immigrant roots are reflected deeply in the Indian and Assamese aspects of her identity, but clearly they extend into the community where being an integral part of her locality as a neighbor and friend is also important. Kalita is very proud of being a mother and having "been there" for her two children, often going to great lengths to make it to their functions so that her children realize she is still a part of their lives. Much of her career has been shaped by her children. One of the best tips a mentor gave her was to be as involved as possible in their lives—because then things could happen on her schedule. Her home is always open to her children and their friends, and teenagers enjoy gathering there. She has had two long-term nannies for her children and considers both "extremely important parts of our life." Every time she got promoted or something good happened personally or professionally, her mother would remind her to raise their wages as hers were increasing. Kalita sees this as a way to balance work and family life and ensure that her children and the nannies see her success as their success and vice versa.

Feminism in the South Asian context doesn't always fit a singular or defined framework;[21] as the daughter of Indian immigrants raised in Puerto Rico, Kalita's version of feminism is highly flexible, pragmatic, and inclusive, such that practices expected of Indian women also find space. Kalita's mother-in-law used to fast once a year on the holiday Karwa Chauth, celebrated in northern and western India for the well-being and health of one's husband. Kalita acknowledges that this holiday would not be seen as exemplifying feminist ideals. However, it was important to her mother-in-law. Moreover, she needed to have her mother and her mother-in-law basically ready to come in and watch her children if she needed to go on a business trip or work late or got particularly busy. Therefore, Kalita would also observe the Karwa Chauth fast. Her feminism is based on deeply thought-out aspects of what it takes for women to raise children and maintain family well-being, along with achieving career success.

Kalita acknowledges that the challenges of maintaining the fragile work-life balance are largely gendered. Nevertheless, she does not always see the world through a gendered lens, nor does she embrace or resist some particular version of feminism. She underscores that she does not define herself in the same ways that men do, but she acknowledges that she had to learn how to be more "masculine" in order to ascend the career ladder. Indeed, she asks rhetorically, "Why don't men have to be more like women in order to ascend in their career?" She elaborates on what it means to be "like women": "It's the ability to multitask, the ability to show compassion in management and leadership, the ability to have a holistic view on how information lands, and then importantly, the ability to not be so single-minded and think about community. And this idea of, you know, 'my success is your success; your success is my success,' and to not be so individualistic."

Put more broadly, part of Kalita's feminism is a matter of recognizing that her success depends on help from her mother, mother-in-law, and nanny. Again, keeping her mother-in-law happy enables her to embrace feminist ideals and achieve other life and work goals, such as becoming a corporate senior vice president. She says this support has proved to be a strong propeller: "Rarely do we focus on the complexity of what it really takes for women to get to where they are and the kind of sacrifices made along the way." Kalita insists that feminism should not require her to sacrifice her individuality. Meanwhile, she emphasizes her commitment to providing ongoing support and assistance to the women around her, both at home and at work.

Her accomplishments and recognition have established her as a major thinker regarding news innovation. Part of her leadership has been the conceptualization of modernization as requiring inclusivity and diversity, with communities at the center. As the Rockefeller Foundation Global Strategy group concluded, "The only way to address and overcome preconceptions and barriers is to have more women in positions of leadership; providing the support and role models women desperately need to advance in their careers and bringing about much-needed changes in the workplace benefitting both genders."[22] Kalita's leadership, centered on service to her community, indicates precisely that inclusive way forward.

Notes

1 S. Mitra Kalita, *Designing for Community*, Aspen Institute, 2020, www.aspeninstitute.org/longform/designing-for-community/.

2 During that same interview, Kalita emphasized how important it was to her to ensure that collaboration and community were valued for enhancing traditionally marginalized voices. Carolina V. Valencia, "*Epicenter-NYC* Secures $250,000 Mellon Foundation Grant to Establish Community Hub in Queens," *Epicenter-NYC*, January 30, 2024, www.editorandpublisher.com/stories/epicenter-nyc-secures-250000-mellon-foundation-grant-to-establish-community-hub-in-queens,247923.

3 International Women's Media Foundation, "The Story Behind Her: For Journalist S. Mitra Kalita, Community Is Everything," *Ms.*, March 18, 2021, https://msmagazine.com/2021/03/18/the-story-behind-her-journalist-s-mitra-kalita/. During that interview for Women's History Month, she emphasized the importance of the Kerner Commission Report and the civil rights movement.

4 All direct quotes attributed to S. Mitra Kalita, unless stated otherwise, are from interview responses she provided specifically for this chapter.

5 Skoll Foundation, *Closing the Gap between Fact & Fake: Disinformation Solutions*, Skoll, 2021, https://skoll.org/session/skoll-world-forum-2021/closing-the-gap-between-fact-fake-solutions-to-disinformation/.

6 Reynolds Journalism, *S. Mitra Kalita, Quartz—How to Integrate Audience into Every Workflow*, YouTube, April 3, 2015, www.youtube.com/watch?v=gneg3aZTMDg.

7 Deirdre Edgar, "L.A. Times Expands Leadership, Adds Mitra Kalita as M.E.," *Los Angeles Times*. March 18, 2015, https://www.latimes.com/local/readers-rep/la-rr-times-leadership-reorg-mitra-kalita-20150318-story.html.

8 S. Mitra Kalita, "The Arc of News and Audience," Nieman Lab, December 2017, www.niemanlab.org/2017/12/the-arc-of-news-and-audience/.

9 Arnelle Pierre-Louis, "Catalyst for Change: A Conversation with S. Mitra Kalita," Managing Editor, December 1, 2021, https://managingeditor.com/catalyst-for-change-a-conversation-with-s-mitra-kalita/.

10 Kalita, *Designing for Community*.

11 S. Mitra Kalita, *Managing for Innovation and Culture Change in News* [keynote speech], Online News Association, May 19, 2017, https://journalists.org/resources/opening-keynote-managing-for-innovation-and-culture-change-in-news/.

12 Irving Washington, "Introduction," Opening Keynote: Managing for Innovation and Culture Change in News, Online News Association, May 19, 2017, https://journalists.org/resources/opening-keynote-managing-for-innovation-and-culture-change-in-news/.

13 Washington, "Introduction."
14 David Chavern, *News Take: Encouraging and Sustaining Diversity in News Media*, News/Media Alliance, September 13, 2022, www.newsmediaalliance.org/news-take-episode-104-encouraging-and-sustaining-diversity-in-news-media/.
15 Kalita, *Managing for Innovation.*
16 S. Mitra Kalita, *Information Is the Ultimate Power in Our Ability to Uplift People*, Skoll, April 15, 2021, www.youtube.com/watch?v=BV1HBxYg9uo.
17 Kalita, *Designing for Community.*
18 Gita Jackson, "The Unofficial Guide to Getting a COVID Vaccine," *Vice*, March 12, 2021, www.vice.com/en/article/k7av4a/the-unofficial-guide-to-getting-a-covid-vaccine.
19 Chavern, *News Take.*
20 International Women's Media Foundation, "Story Behind."
21 Kathryn Robinson and Kuntala Lahiri-Dutt, "'Period Problems' at the Coalface," *Feminist Review* 89, no. 1 (2008): 102–121.
22 Rockefeller Foundation, *Women in Leadership: Why It Matters*, May 16, 2016, www.rockefellerfoundation.org/wp-content/uploads/Women-in-Leadership-Why-It-Matters.pdf.

Iman Zawahry

A Muslim Hijabi Filmmaker Using Humor to Shatter Stereotypes

Nahed Eltantawy and Chloe Terani

A pioneer for women and the Muslim community, Iman Zawahry has broken down boundaries in the entertainment industry as a Muslim hijabi filmmaker, presenting narratives of Muslim women that have never been seen before. Her films have screened in venues across the globe and have earned significant recognition; her honors include being selected as a Sundance Momentum Fellow, an Emmy Award winner, a Lincoln Center Artist Academy Fellow, and a Princess Grace Award recipient.

While Zawahry does not publicly identify herself as a leader in Hollywood filmmaking, she clearly recognizes that she is one of the few to be doing the work that she does: "I am one of two or three first Muslim hijabi female filmmakers in the nation."[1] Hoping to humanize this otherwise marginalized community through comedy that resonates with audiences, Zawahry rejects the negative representations and pushes past the recycled portrayals of Muslims in Western media. Scholars have shown that Muslim women are far too often portrayed only in four ways: as oppressed, hypersexualized, victimized, or generally associated with violence.[2] Zawahry agrees. Western audiences, she said, "just want to see Muslim women being tortured . . . [and] trauma porn. . . . We just want to see Muslim women with joy."[3]

As a leading Muslim filmmaker, Zawahry has launched initiatives to create further change in the industry through youth empowerment. Working with the Islamic Scholarship Fund, Zawahry played a key role in establishing the first film grant to aid American Muslim filmmakers.[4] The goal of the ISF's annual grant of $220,0000 is to increase Muslim representation on screen and in government to help reduce stereotypes and marginalization.[5] Meanwhile, as a senior lecturer at the University of Florida's Department of Media Production, Management, and Technology, she created several narrative-focused classes in its Digital Film and Television Production program.[6] UF's College of Journalism and Communications named her one of UF's "Most Inspirational Women."[7]

Background

Zawahry grew up in Panama City, Florida. She found the lack of diversity in that predominantly white small town extremely isolating. More to the point, as one of the town's few Muslims "or, at the time, Brown people," she faced "extreme racism."[8] A total of five "Brown Muslim" girls, as she puts it, lived in Panama City: they were all family friends, as their parents were local physicians. "We did come from a privileged, affluent life, but it was really juxtaposed by this minority status. And people never saw us as anything but Brown or Muslim, like worshiping the moon God or whatnot."[9]

Popular culture was a considerable influence on Zawahry and her Muslim friends as children; they constantly watched American movies and television. Yet, Zawahry and her friends were keenly aware of a lack of representation in these television shows at the time.[10] Meanwhile, rather than denying or hiding their Muslim identity, Zawahry and her childhood friends stayed true to their identities and dealt with these challenges through humor and creativity. As she puts it, "We never denied who we are." Instead, they began to create commercials, skits, and mock talk shows with personal twists reflecting their own Muslim identity.[11] They created for themselves the representation they lacked and desired on screen. "Instead of the Arsenio Hall show, we had the Iman Hall show where I was the host. Also instead of a Mrs. USA pageant, we created a Ms. Arab pageant and played contestants with funny talents and dances," Zawahry explains.[12] "Using comedy to tell stories and to deal with the 'trauma' that I grew up with in the South was the best way for me to dismantle what was happening in our lives and to educate myself and others through a way that really connects and relates to people."[13]

As a sixth grader, Zawahry decided it was her mission to take a stand and educate others about Islam and Muslims.[14] She was determined to use storytelling and comedy to change negative perceptions of Muslims in the global West: "My favorite quote of all time is, 'Laughter is the shortest distance between two people.' And that's what I live my life by. If we can laugh together, we can communicate, we can connect, we can create peace, and we can create understanding."[15]

Resolve and Decision-Making

Zawahry's rise to leadership sped up as an undergraduate at the University of Florida: she took it upon herself to act as a spokeswoman for other Muslim women. "I was like, I'm going to change everybody's opinions on Muslim women being oppressed and hypersexualized."[16] As a sophomore, she bravely decided to adopt the hijab, not only for reasons of religion and spirituality, but also to humanize Muslims and further dispel stereotypes around them.[17] Yet, making choices based on what she believes is right comes with its challenges. "I put this huge burden on myself," Zawahry explains, referring to the public criticism and even oppression that she and many other Muslim hijabi women face in Western societies when adopting Islamic clothing.[18]

To add more challenges to the equation, when Zawahry was a college junior, 9/11 occurred. She recalls waking up on the morning of 9/11 to a flood of phone calls, and journalists requesting a reaction from her as president of the Muslim Student Association at the University of Florida. Immediately, as part of her leadership efforts, Zawahry was forced to defend herself and the Muslim community and to protect the reputation and image of Muslim students. She needed to do this at the same time that she—like everyone else—was mourning for her country. She rallied the MSA, which put out a statement, and went to the student newspaper. "I came back on the defensive again, having to show that we're great people; we're not terrorists."[19] As a result, the need to eliminate Muslim stereotypes never felt greater.

Critical Juncture

Like many children of immigrant families, Zawahry was expected to pursue a career in medicine or engineering. "Particularly being Muslim and being Brown, all of my family members—my dad is the eldest of seventeen siblings—they are all physicians."[20] However, knowing that this path was not for her, Zawahry took the risk of deviating from her family's expectations and majored in Near Eastern languages, cultures, and religion. She initially planned to pursue a PhD in Islamic studies in behalf of her hope to advocate for her community. "But I realized that you couldn't reach out to Billy Bob in the Midwest by being a professor because everybody who comes to school is educated."[21]

Her career plans changed dramatically when she encountered an Arab friend who was a film student at Florida State University's College of Motion Picture Arts, one of the top film schools in the United States. At that moment, Zawahry realized that pursuing her former academic goals would not allow her to "address the masses."[22] Defying cultural norms and expectations, she decided to apply to film school in addition to PhD programs in Islamic studies. Zawahry's parents, who had moved to the United States from Egypt in 1973 and divorced during her childhood, did not back her artistic pursuits. "I always had a love for film, but I never thought . . . growing up as who we are . . . that that would be an avenue for me."[23] Coming from a family of medical doctors who expected her to follow in their footsteps, Zawahry initially kept her application to film school a secret. Her decision marked a significant step toward creating change in both Hollywood and society at large.

During the interview portion of her application to film school, Zawahry needed to pitch a story. This turned out to be one of her earliest storytelling attempts aimed at humanizing Muslim families: for her application, she pitched a comedy based on her own life, where she sat at a rather chaotic family dinner table. These dinners typically involved inviting a large crowd of people and "a lot of loudness." Zawahry was accepted to Florida State's film MFA program and thus began her journey to change Western perceptions of Muslims. "Getting into film school provided me with an avenue to try to educate others and to show people that we're human like everyone else. . . . I didn't realize at the time that I was one of the first and only [filmmakers] . . . doing it."[24] Zawahry made it her mission to change Western negative perceptions about Muslims in general and Muslim women in specific. "I put this huge responsibility on myself to tell these stories, specifically Muslim women's stories."[25]

Soon after graduating college, Zawahry got married and, at age twenty-three, became pregnant. Her mother had opposed the idea of her getting married, emphasizing the importance of self-sufficiency. "She wanted me to be independent and not to rely on anybody," Zawahry explained.[26] Nevertheless, with support from her husband, then in law school and preparing to take his bar exams, as well as support from both their mothers, she managed to gain the film studies education she desired. Her strength, persistence, and determination to resist her family's education preference to pursue her filmmaking dream, enabled her to launch a successful career as a Muslim hijabi filmmaker. Looking back, she admits that her family was "definitely" apprehensive, but they did not stop her: "They let me do what I needed to do . . . but they wanted me to find stability."[27]

As a religion major at the University of Florida, Zawahry created four student-Emmy-Award–winning short films, "Neighbors of Mass Destruction," "The Cape," "Undercover," and "Tough Crowd." She reached the finalist level when pitching a sitcom to NBC. Her student film and sitcom projects, which she describes as broad comedies that incorporate characters who are Muslim women, have been screened during one hundred film festivals across the globe. Zawahry says, "But they were seen and received so well because people have never seen it before, and that was something that really stuck with me."[28]

Nevertheless, Zawahry's path to a successful career in filmmaking was difficult given the challenges of trying to make it in

Hollywood as a Muslim and as a woman: "The Hollywood community is supporting the Muslim male . . . so we're still trying to find the Muslim female space."[29] Zawahry took extreme initiative to find the necessary funding and backing for her film projects, especially from other American Muslim women who created their own little community. Zawahry says she and other Muslim women "support each other and uplift each other."

For the most part, the only way Zawahry has been able to make her films has been by creating her own opportunities and being proactive in raising the necessary money. "That's the only way that it's been happening."[30] With independent films costing anywhere between $25,000 and $5 million to produce, Zawahry and her team had to work hard to raise large sums of money to fund her films, and always privately. "The way that I have raised it has all been through personal financing and pitching to non–film-business individuals," says Zawahry. "We had made it the goal to only reach out to American or UK Muslim investors, and we flew all around the country pitching the film."[31]

The initial attempts to raise money failed. Then they realized that they were pitching to men. They decided to change their strategy and focus more on women investors. "We ended up receiving the majority of our funds from friends and family who followed our journey, and 90 percent of them were women," says Zawahry. She is convinced that the fact that they were women explained why men were generally unwilling to invest in these projects. "We were seeing men, younger and less qualified than us, receiving funding from the same people we pitched to," Zawahry adds. Now that she has a successful film out, she hopes the same people can and will support her future projects. "However, it is always difficult to make the next thing, even if it's successful in funding films independently."[32] She adds, "In terms of audiences, I make what is meaningful to me, and the more specific you are, the more it will resonate with others, we have found."[33]

It took Zawahry several years after graduation to complete her first feature film. "I longed for the nostalgic touch of a feel-good movie but with hijabi Muslim women featured as leads."[34] Yet, Zawahry saw that Hollywood was not ready for such Muslim-focused films. This changed in 2017, after Donald Trump, soon after assuming his first term as president, imposed a so-called Muslim ban, which prohibited travel to the United States for ninety days from seven Muslim-majority countries.[35] Trump's executive order sparked mass protests across the United States and led to significant strides in the representation of Muslim men in television and film. A flood of shows at the time featured Muslim characters, including *The Bold Type*, *Quantico*, *Patriot Act*, *Ramy*, and *Transplant*. Despite these significant advances, however, Muslim women remained absent in film and television. A 2021 USC Annenberg report found that the ratio of Muslim men characters to Muslim women characters across a survey of 200 films is 175 to 1.[36] When featured, Muslim women were largely portrayed as family members or romantic partners. This clear lack of representation of Muslim women in film and television prompted Zawahry to take the initiative on behalf of change: "The importance of being the agents of our story cannot be understated."[37]

Resolution

Americanish, Zawahry's first feature film, aimed to challenge the traditional Western media portrayals of Muslim women. Zawahry regards comedy as an often-overlooked tool for educating the public and transforming opinion, especially when it comes to politics and religion. This romantic comedy takes place in an immigrant neighborhood in Queens, New York. Yet, unlike many rom-coms, the three leads are complex, striving Pakistani young women trying to balance careers and love while living in Trump's America. *Americanish* screened in various film festivals, including Riverrun, the Women and Film Festival, CAAMFest, and the Asian World Film Festival. The film scored twenty-five prestigious national and international awards, including Best Narrative Feature (Beloit International Film Festival), Best Comedy Narrative (Sedona Film Festival), Women's Voices Award (Portland Film Festival), and Best Feature Director (LaFemme International Film Festival).[38] In January 2023, Sony Pictures International Productions acquired global rights to *Americanish*.[39]

As a self-proclaimed feminist, Zawahry has strived to use her work to uplift Muslim women. She observes that mainstream media often overlook the version of feminism that encompasses women of color and that Muslim women are rarely included in the conversation. According to her, feminism requires speaking out for women and women's choices. "No matter what they want . . . this is a part of what we do . . . as feminists. We support the women and we uplift them."[40] Zawahry also notes that Islam was one of the first religions to embrace feminism. According to Zawahry, *Americanish* sends a significant message to viewers and Muslim women:

> The film . . . highlights different layers of feminism as it intersects with religion, culture, immigration and the current sociopolitical climate. We have to champion and commandeer these efforts to make American Muslim women uniformly represented in the portrayal of the American narrative. I made a film in an accessible genre that I feel has a globally relatable story with the potential to reach audiences from intersectional experiences. It's particularly meaningful to our cast and crew, as many of us are women, women of color, and/or Muslim women. . . . I hope that when audiences watch authentic portrayals of American Muslim women, they can begin to understand that there is more unifying us than separating us.[41]

Zawahry recently directed two episodes of CBC Gem's *Zarqa*, a sitcom about a divorced Canadian Muslim hijabi who signs up online for a date with a white brain surgeon to bring along to her ex's wedding. The show stars and is produced by Zarqa Nawaz, known for creating *Little Mosque on the Prairie* in 2007, one of the first Muslim sitcoms to portray Muslims as normal men and women, free from dominant stereotypes.[42] Zawahry hopes to normalize this idea of films that portray "real" Muslim Americans fairly and realistically.

She is currently working to raise money to fund three separate film projects. Now that *Americanish* is owned by Sony, Zawahry can devote herself to developing one of these projects. She is especially passionate about one project—based on her own teenage experience—about three Muslim Arab girls who skipped school to go to MTV's *The Grind*. "It's what happened to me. It deals with a lot of racism. It's a female version of *Superbad*," Zawahry explains, referring to the 2007 teen comedy about two high school boys planning a booze-soaked party."[43]

Teaching Film with a Muslim Flair

While studying in film school, Zawahry also dreamed of teaching filmmaking, especially because she lacked mentorship in her own personal journey to become a filmmaker: "I didn't have a mentor and I didn't have anybody I could look up to. So, I put it on myself to mentor others and to support others. . . . My goal had always been to teach and to make films. It was never just one or the other."[44] Her opportunity came soon after completing film school, while she was working with Adele Romanski, an independent producer with a large body of work, including the 2016 movie *Moonlight*, which was nominated for eight Oscars.[45] Romanski, who is an alumnus of Florida State University's film school, made a call looking for FSU alumni producers to help with her film *Paperback*. Zawahry, who was living in Gainesville at the time and was filming there, reached out to Romanski; she ended up being the producer for this microbudget film, with Romanski as the executive producer.[46] While working on *Paperback*, Adam Bowers, the director and another FSU alumnus, asked Zawahry to contact Houston Wells, a lecturer at the University of Florida's Department of Media Production, Management and Technology, about finding student volunteers to work on the set.[47] That connection with Wells opened the door for Zawahry's teaching career: Zawahry became the lab instructor for his film production class taught by Wells.[48] Over the course of teaching a variety of film production classes, Zawahry fell in love with teaching, creating, and connecting with students, and her career as an educator (first as an adjunct and promoted in 2024 to senior lecturer) took off at the University of Florida.

Zawahry eventually created an Islam, Media, and Pop Culture class that explores the complex ways in which various media forms portray Muslims. Zawahry explains, "I really wanted to create a way for students to learn how to tell a story that's not their own. . . . It's not just about being Muslim, but in general interacting with people who have a different ethnicity or culture than your own and that you're able to open up to it. . . . And then also tell the historical perspective of how our country has portrayed and told stories about Muslims and other minorities, so that we can be informed on how to really tell those stories."[49] Zawahry and her University of Florida students were, she says, "changing the world" through creating public service announcements, comedies, and shorts with Muslim narratives and perspectives. Those student films have won awards from festivals across the nation, including a Student Regional Emmy Award.

Working with ISF to Prepare Future Muslim Filmmakers

Zawahry is also striving to fund young Muslim filmmakers, who often lack the necessary support and backing for their creativity. In partnership with the Islamic Scholarship Fund, in 2014 they cocreated a film grant, the first American Muslim Film Fund. "The grant specifically aims to support emerging Muslim filmmakers, who are creating artistic, engaging, and positive stories about their community,"[50] says Zawahry, who is the ISF director of film programs. The idea for the grant reflects Zawahry's own experience with funding. In 2009, the ISF offered her its very first grant to fund Muslims in nonscience majors; she used the money for her thesis film. At the time, the ISF asked for Zawahry's help in determining what else the organization could do to support Muslim filmmakers. She was just then seeking funds for her own film, and "there was no one to support me. So, I suggested that they create a film grant."[51] Over a period of nine years, the IFS has financially supported over one hundred Muslim filmmakers.

The ISF offers six grants a year for narrative and documentary films (between $5,000 and $15,000 each) and two $5,000 distribution grants.[52] The ISF also offers other forms of support, including a writer's lab, alumni support, as well as mentorship. "I always say I'm a filmmaker first, and my films are really incredibly important [to me], but I want to give way to others so they can kind of pay it forward to build bigger," Zawahry explains. "Because if we think on a small scale, if it's just about my one film, or this person's one film, it's just going to stay there. It has to be bigger. We have to think from a bigger community organization standpoint."[53] Zawahry's ultimate goal is to create a strong Muslim filmmaking network within the United States, with an emphasis on the American Muslim identity: "Because there is a perception that if you're Muslim, that equals foreign, and that's not the case. We are American, we are Muslim, and they're not mutually exclusive."[54]

Conclusion

Zawhary has accomplished a lot in a short time—creating nationally acclaimed films, helping educate future filmmakers, and mentoring and funding existing Muslim filmmakers. It wasn't always easy and she acknowledges making mistakes along the way. "My biggest mistake was switching hats and maintaining professionalism" while working on *Americanish*, Zawahry admits. She and her producing partner Azzizah Fatima, who was also lead actress, were constantly needing to take on producing responsibilities that no one else could manage to do: "We both needed to switch our roles, me from director and her to actor." This was challenging for Zawahry, especially since she feels she didn't provide Fatima with enough direction and coaching. "That made it harder for her to perform as an actor, and I should have done a better job being a director with her."[55]

Being a leader in the competitive film industry also brings challenges. For Zawahry, work-life balance was a challenge. "Holding boundaries for family time and work time" is something she struggled with tremendously.[56] She also found it difficult at times to offer feedback to her mentees without being, or being judged as, a harsh critic. "As a mentor, I tend to give very direct feedback, which sometimes doesn't go over well, and I have learned to be more diplomatic with my criticism or help with my mentees."[57]

Zawahry did not start out with the intention to be a leader. But she recognizes that she became just that by identifying a need for more equal representations of Muslims in film and the need to assist Muslim women who seek film-industry careers. "I never saw myself as a leader. I just did the work particularly where I saw we were not being seen," Zawahry explains. "So, no films about us. No Muslims in film school. I am going to film school and making films about Muslim women. No one to support Muslim filmmakers. I'm going to help create a grant for Muslim filmmakers. No mentors for Muslim filmmakers. I will find some and be one myself."[58]

Zawahry emphasizes her hope to leave a legacy of strong support and encouragement to other Muslim filmmakers: "I want to put it on my tombstone . . . the work that I do with ISF, creating the film programs, [and] creating the grant. What I want my legacy to be is to uplift and support other Muslim filmmakers."[59] Mentoring others is her way of enabling other Muslim filmmakers to make it in the industry and to give back and pay it forward by helping future Muslim filmmakers. Meanwhile, Zawahry strives to do more and intends to continue with her passion: directing films and television comedies that build understanding and create connections among people and that promote social justice. "If we can laugh together, we can communicate, we can connect, we can create peace, and we can create understanding."[60]

Notes

1 "We Are CJC—Iman Zawahry," UF #WeAreCJC, YouTube, March 2021, www.youtube.com/watch?v=7K7DoFQq22g.

2 A large body of literature discusses Western media representations of Muslims in general and Muslim women in particular. See Saifuddin Ahmed and Jörg Matthes, "Media Representation of Muslims and Islam from 2000 to 2015: A Meta-Analysis," *International Communication Gazette* 79, no. 3 (2017): 219–244; Nahed Eltantawy, "Above the Fold and Beyond the Veil: Islamophobia in Western Media," in *The Routledge Companion to Media & Gender*, ed. Cynthia Carter, Linda Steiner, and Lisa McLaughlin (Routledge, 2013), 402–412; Myra Macdonald, "Muslim Women and the Veil: Problems of Image and Voice in Media Representations," *Feminist Media Studies* 6, no. 1 (2006): 7–23; and Amir Saeed, "Media, Racism and Islamophobia: The Representation of Islam and Muslims in the Media," *Sociology Compass* 1, no. 2 (2007): 443–462.

3 Iman Zawahry, author interview, December 8, 2022.

4 "Advocacy," Imanzawahry.com/advocacy/#industry.

5 "Our Mission," islamicscholarshipfund.org/about/#mission.

6 "We Are CJC."

7 "Iman Zawahry: Telling Meaningful Stories," *Knight Talks PBS*, accessed January 23, 2023, www.pbs.org/video/iman-zawahry-telling-meaningful-stories-rgj9hb.

8 "We Are CJC."
9 "Iman Zawahry Discusses Filmmaking, Mentoring Young Muslim Artists, and Comedy for Social Change," *Medium*, March 3, 2021, https://medium.com/university-of-florida-college-of-journalism-and/iman-zawahry-discusses-filmmaking-mentoring-young-muslim-artists-and-comedy-for-social-change-9132ae6307a5.
10 "We Are CJC."
11 "We Are CJC."
12 Iman Zawahry, author interview, June 7, 2023.
13 "Iman Zawahry Discusses Filmmaking."
14 "We Are CJC."
15 "Iman Zawahry Discusses Filmmaking."
16 Zawahry, interview, 2022.
17 Zawahry, interview, 2022.
18 "Iman Zawahry Discusses Filmmaking."
19 "Iman Zawahry Discusses Filmmaking."
20 "Iman Zawahry: Telling Meaningful Stories."
21 Julia Mitchem, "Meet Filmmaker Iman Zawahry, One of UF's Inspirational Women," Her Campus, March 26, 2019, www.hercampus.com/school/ufl/meet-filmmaker-iman-zawahry-one-uf-s-inspirational-women/.
22 Zawahry, interview, 2022.
23 Zawahry, interview, 2022.
24 "Iman Zawahry Discusses Filmmaking."
25 Mitchem, "Meet Filmmaker Iman Zawahry."
26 Corinne Lestch, "This Muslim Director Is Flipping the Rom-Com Genre with Her New Film *Americanish*," The Story Exchange, March 15, 2022, https://thestoryexchange.org/muslim-filmmaker-iman-zawahry-flips-rom-com-genre-americanish/.
27 "We Are CJC."
28 Mitchem, "Meet Filmmaker Iman Zawahry."
29 Zawahry, interview, 2022.
30 Zawahry, interview, 2022.
31 Zawahry, interview, 2023.
32 Zawahry, interview, 2023.
33 Zawahry, interview, 2023.
34 Iman Zawahry, "Is Hollywood Ready for Muslim Women Leads?," The Wrap Guest Blog, November 20, 2020, www.thewrap.com/is-hollywood-ready-for-muslim-women-leads-iman-zawahry/.
35 "Muslim Travel Ban," *Immigration History*, 2019, https://immigrationhistory.org/item/muslim-travel-ban/.
36 Al-Baab Khan, Katherine Pieper, Stacey L. Smith, Marc Choueiti, Kevin Yao, and Artur Tofan, *Missing & Maligned: The Reality of Muslims in Popular Global Movies*, USC Annenberg Inclusion Initiative, June 2021, https://assets.uscannenberg.org/docs/aii-muslim-rep-global-film-2021-06-09.pdf.
37 Zawahry, "Is Hollywood Ready?"

38 Iman Zawahry website (n.d.), www.imanzawahry.com.
39 Matt Grobar, "Sony Pictures International Productions Picks up Iman Zawahry Comedy *Americanish*," Deadline, January 11, 2023, https://deadline.com/2023/01/americanish-comedy-from-iman-zawahry-acquired-by-sony-international-1235218676/.
40 Zawahry, interview, 2022.
41 Zawahry, "Is Hollywood Ready?"
42 Vanessa Conley, "Zarqa Tells the Story of a Muslim Divorcee Looking for Revenge," CBC, May 13, 2022, www.cbc.ca/news/entertainment/zarqa-cbc-gem-1.6450611.
43 Zawahry, interview, 2022.
44 "Iman Zawahry Discusses Filmmaking."
45 For information on Romanski, see "Adele Romanski," Wikipedia, https://en.wikipedia.org/wiki/Adele_Romanski.
46 Zawahry, interview, 2023.
47 Houston Wells is currently a senior lecturer; see "College Directory: Houston Wells," UF College of Journalism and Communications, www.jou.ufl.edu/staff/houston-wells/.
48 "College Directory: Houston Wells."
49 "Iman Zawahry Discusses Filmmaking."
50 Islamic Scholarship Fund, 2021.
51 "Iman Zawahry Discusses Filmmaking."
52 Zawahry, interview, 2023.
53 Zawahry, interview, 2022.
54 "Iman Zawahry Discusses Filmmaking."
55 Zawahry, interview, 2023.
56 Zawahry, interview, 2023.
57 Zawahry, interview, 2023.
58 Zawahry, interview, 2023.
59 Zawahry, interview, 2022.
60 Zawahry, interview, 2022.

Acknowledgments

A lifetime—or at least a career's worth—of mentors, teachers, colleagues, and supportive friends provided me with the grounding for this book. Too many to acknowledge here. For her sane and sanity-producing feedback, I do want to thank Mary Trigg of the Institute for Women's Leadership at Rutgers University. Gratitude also goes to Kimberly Guinta, the (now former) editorial director at Rutgers University Press, and Michelle Scott, of Westchester Publishing Services.

Finally, I express the deepest appreciation for the sage counsel and support of Sarah Salomon, my amazingly wise daughter.

Contributors

KEVIN BLACKISTONE is professor of practice in the Philip Merrill College of Journalism at the University of Maryland, as well as a regular panelist for ESPN's Around the Horn. He critiques society and sports as a *Washington Post* columnist and a National Public Radio commentator. He recently cohosted and codeveloped a ten-part podcast, *Our New South*, and coproduced and cowrote the award-winning documentary *Imagining the Indian: The Fight Against Native American Mascoting*.

SADIE COUTURE is a PhD student in the Department of Art History and Communication Studies at McGill University in Montreal, Quebec, Canada. Her work lies at the intersection of radio history, science and technology studies, and community-engaged art. She coauthored *On this Patch of Grass: City Parks on Occupied Land*. Recent projects include podcasts and the digital storytelling project *Mayne Island Sound Map*; she is the audio production mentor at Solid State Community Industries.

MICHELLE DUSTER is an educator and activist located in Chicago, Illinois, whose advocacy has led to street names, monuments, historical markers, murals, and other public history projects. She is the author of several books, including *Ida B. the Queen: The Extraordinary Life and Legacy of Ida B. Wells* and *Ida B. Wells, Voice of Truth*, which are about her paternal great-grandmother. She has written several book chapters and dozens of articles for, among others, *CNN Opinion*, *People*, *Teen Vogue*, *Daily Beast*, *Essence*, *Time*, the *Washington Post*, *Glamour*, and *Ms.* magazine. She is a columnist and cultural education editor for *Rebellious Magazine for Women*.

STINE ECKERT is associate professor at Wayne State University in Detroit, Michigan. She is coeditor of *Journalism Research/Journalistik*. She is coeditor of *Reflections on Feminist Communication and Media Scholarship: Theory, Method, Impact* and *Feminist Manifestos for Media and Communication*, as well as multiple book chapters and journal articles. She has been a co-PI on several projects, including for the World Health Organization, the U.S. Agency for International Development, and the U.S. National Science Foundation ADVANCE grant Gender Equity Advances Retention in STEM, addressing Wayne State University campus equity issues.

NAHED ELTANTAWY is the interim dean and associate professor of journalism in the Nido R. Qubein School of Communication at High Point University in North Carolina, where she teaches and/or studies convergent journalism, media representation, social media activism, and women and gender studies. She is the editor of *Women and Media in the Middle East: From Veiling to Blogging* and has published book chapters and journal articles. She worked as a Reuters correspondent in Egypt before moving to the United States.

TRACY EVERBACH is professor of journalism in the Mayborn School of Journalism at the University of North Texas, where she has chaired the Women and Gender Equity Network. She is coeditor of *Mediating Misogyny: Gender, Technology & Harassment*, *Testing Tolerance: Addressing Controversy in the Journalism and Mass Communication Classroom*, and *Not Playing Around: Intersectional Identities, Media Representation, and the Power of Sport*. Her scholarship appears in journals such as *Journalism & Mass Communication Quarterly* and *Newspaper Research Journal*. Everbach spent twelve years on the city desk at the *Dallas Morning News*.

CONSTANCE MITCHELL FORD served a number of senior roles at the *Wall Street Journal*, including as the global real estate and property bureau chief and, previously, economics editor. She now is a lecturer in the Philip Merrill College of Journalism at the University of Maryland. Ford's stories about the subprime mortgage crisis won a Scripps

Howard National Journalism Award for business and economics reporting. She has been an invited speaker at national and international events, including the World Economic Forum in Davos, Switzerland.

AMY JORDAN is professor and chair of the Department of Journalism and Media Studies at Rutgers University-New Brunswick in New Jersey. Her focus is the role of media in the lives of children and adolescents, and she has also created and tested culturally sensitive health-related media content. Recent books include *Media and the Well-Being of Children and Adolescents* and *Children, Adolescents, and Media: The Future of Research and Action.* She has published in a wide range of journals, including *Journal of Communication, Pediatrics, Communication Research, Journal of Family Communication, and Media Psychology.* Jordan was coeditor of the *Journal of Children and Media.* She serves on the Board of Trustees of Sesame Workshop.

PAROMITA PAIN is assistant professor of global media studies at the Reynolds School of Journalism at the University of Nevada, Reno. Her research focuses on alternate media and global journalism practices from feminist perspectives. She has written for the *Hindu Newspaper, The Guardian,* and *Al Jazeera.* Her research has appeared in *Journalism and Mass Communication Educator, Journalism Studies, Journalism Practice, Media Asia,* and *Feminist Media Theory.*

SHANNON SCOVEL is an assistant professor of sports communication at the University of Tennessee-Knoxville. A former competitive swimmer, her main research interests are sports media and athlete branding, especially the gender implications of name, image, and likeness (NIL). For her freelance reporting for NCAA.com on NCAA wrestling, the National Wrestling Media Association named her the 2022–2023 Journalist of the Year. She has also written for *Sports Illustrated*, Yahoo Sports, and *USA Today.*

LINDA STEINER is professor of journalism and associate dean for faculty affairs in the University of Maryland's Phillip Merrill College of Journalism. She was the director of the ADVANCE program in the UMD Office of Faculty Affairs. She is editor of *Journalism & Communication Monographs* and, besides some one hundred book chapters and journal articles, has published nine coauthored or coedited books, most recently, the coedited books *Newswork and Precarity, Front Pages, Front Lines: Media and the Fight for Women's Suffrage* and *Journalism, Gender and Power.* She worked for a weekly newspaper in upstate New York.

CHLOE TERANI is an undergraduate student at the University of California San Diego, interested in political science and sociology. She has researched the Middle East and women's issues and has based personal memoir and short films on that research. She currently works at The Representation Project.

ELIZABETH L. TOTH is professor emerita in the Department of Communication at the University of Maryland, where she was department chair. Toth was editor of the *Journal of Public Relations Research.* She recently coauthored *The Future of Feminism in Public Relations and Strategic Communication: A Socio-Ecological Model of Influence* and is coauthor, editor, or coeditor of eight other books including *Women and Public Relations: How Gender Influences Practice, Rhetorical and Critical Approaches to Public Relations II,* and *The Velvet Ghetto.* She worked in public relations and won major awards for her PR leadership.

Index